THE
AMERICAN IMAGE
OF
THE OLD WORLD

THE
AMERICAN IMAGE
OF
THE OLD WORLD

Cushing Strout

HARPER & ROW, PUBLISHERS

NEW YORK, EVANSTON, AND LONDON

For Jean

CONTENTS

PREFACE

This book is a narrative and critical history of the American image of Europe as it has shaped and expressed national politics and culture.* It is the story of the rise, development, and decline of a powerful tradition of looking across the Atlantic at an alien "Old World" whose characteristics (whether condemned or admired) have usually been understood to be the very opposite of the "New World." Many Americans have comfortably rested in this vision of their relation to Europe while the ground has shifted under their feet and the horizons have been transformed. Ambivalence and ambiguity, as the most perceptive American writers have always told us, have mingled with myth and legend to complicate the relationship. It has been as hard for the American to see Europe realistically as it has been for him to see clearly his own country, because he has almost always understood himself only in relation to Europe.

* An image is not a neutral description but a mental picture, true or false in various degrees, which is implicated in ideas, values, feelings, and prejudices.

Americans are currently anxious about their image in the eyes of other peoples in the world. We believe that we are better, more worthy of respect—for all our faults—than the image which even our closest allies hold of us. We may be right, but we shall not gain any self-knowledge merely from being convinced that others are wrong about us. If we want to learn something important about both ourselves and them, we would do better to look critically at the record of our images of them. What purposes have they served? What distortions have they entailed? What changes have they suffered? These are the questions which are especially appropriate to ask about our historical conceptions of Europe, for Europe has been to us stern father and kind mother, formidable enemy and brave ally, helpful teacher and reluctant pupil, perpetual stimulus, perpetual irritant.

Perhaps a European could tell this story much better than any American could. But as Americans we would not be readily inclined to believe him, suspecting (probably correctly) that he had an ax to grind, as we do ourselves when we set out to put the Europeans straight about us, to have them accept us in our role as a primary power in the Cold War. An American historian knows from experience how the insiders have looked at the outsiders. He will suffer the risk of failing to transcend his own people's prejudices, but the historian is professionally bound to be as critical as he can, to tell the truth, no doubt not the whole truth, but hopefully nothing but the truth.

Inevitably, he will be himself a part of the process which he passionately and humbly seeks to describe and understand. I grew up during the struggle over American policy with respect to intervention in the Second World War when the "isolationist" prejudices against Europe were still powerful, and I was weaned in college on the literature written by American "expatriates" in the Europe of the 1920s. I first experienced "History" as an enlisted infantryman in the U.S. Third Army in Europe. I have lived through a revolution which has made both isolationism and expatriation obsolete. From this vantage point I have looked back to understand the complex story of American response to a Europe both feared and loved in a peculiarly American way.

History may provide an opportunity for national self-knowledge. Current fashions of popular history see in the past only a reassuring link with venerable ancestors, a stimulus to patriotic pride in America, or an escape from a troubling present into the romantic glory of epic events. These uses of the past have their place, but the sense of history, at its best, is for the sense *in* history. It appeals to our capacity and willingness to see what time and change can teach us about ourselves and our world. The recent past, especially, is vulnerable to political passions; and simple minds and mean motives have collaborated in these postwar years to make political profit out of conspiratorial explanations of history, which dangerously serve to confirm many Americans in their most cherished illusions. Without having the animus of the "debunker" (who thinks reality is always worse than our myths about it), I have tried to tell a story in which the truth (relating myth and reality) emerges as being much more fascinating than any distortion of it.

Historical emphasis on the conflicts between liberals and conservatives, agrarian and industrial forces, or on sectional differences or expansion westward have intrigued earlier writers of serious history. These themes have recently been abandoned by historians who have rightly protested against an overemphasis on insular perspectives and Manichaean categories. These new historians (Hartz, Hofstadter, Potter, Boorstin) have turned their attention instead of the underlying factors unifying American society, whether ideological, institutional, economic, or psychological. The new school has redressed the balance at the price of causing some alarm about the blotting out of conflict.

One of the advantages of the point of view I have taken here is that it cuts through American history both vertically and horizontally, without isolating it from the rest of the world, and without sacrificing conflict to unity, or consensus to division. It is only a way of looking at one dimension of American history, but it may provide a room with a view on aspects of the scene which conventional or current approaches ignore or obscure. Because Europe has meant so much to Americans as a homeland, an enemy, a teacher, and, recently, an ally, the history of American response to it must in some ways go to the very center of national life.

Writing history is a perpetual exercise in judgment. I have

shifted my focus back and forth from groups to individuals, from leaders to the public, and from politics to literature depending upon my assessment of their relative importance in illuminating my subject. Some individuals have a representative character; others are quite untypical, but significant for their insight. A literary artist, however untypical of average Americans, does not live in a cultural vacuum; he may, in fact, be especially sensitive to cultural currents, even if he has no "influence" on the reading public. His productions may not be read as documentary descriptions, but they may be symptomatic or express an insight into actual affairs deeper than any illusion of literal realism.

Attitudes are, of course, different from events, but the evidence for them is found not only in documents; it is implied in the actions themselves which produce the events. Men make history in the light of their ideas, values, opinions, and prejudices, and when they learn from their experiences they reassess their attitudes. Thought and action focus each other in history. I have concentrated on the mental side of this doubleness in an effort at writing a kind of "intellectual history" which is not confined to intellectuals. I hope it may serve to break down the self-contained isolation in which literary and diplomatic history are often studied, yet without confusing the standards of judgment appropriate to each.

"Europe" for Americans has meant not so much a specific geographical place as it has a projected contrast in ideas, values, and institutions to their own "New World." It has often included England, despite an Englishman's quite different sense of Europe, and Russia, though it may be more Asiatic than European. What is now called "Western Europe" has usually been at the core of the American sense of the "Old World." The history of an idea, dynamically related to actuality, cannot be treated as a fact one might find in an atlas.

My work has gratefully and necessarily depended upon exploiting the work of many other scholars who have usually had quite different interests and questions. I have used them freely for information on biographical and historical events, indicating in text or footnotes where I have profited from their perspectives. For my central subject—thoughts and feelings—I have explored at first hand the letters, journals, speeches, articles, and stories of my cast of characters, and I have used voting records and opinion polls for essential clues to group action and outlook. I hope I have nowhere indulged in that old-fashioned, deliberate ignorance of insights and data produced by other disciplines—a prejudice sometimes practiced by historians, literary critics, and sociologists. Like war, history is too important to be left to the specialists. What the public does not know may hurt it badly in a world which puts a high price on the consequences of action based on ignorance or misconception. The United States is now deeply engaged in a common task with European allies to preserve the best elements of Western Civilization without plunging the world into the meaningless horrors of nuclear warfare. For such an occasion the history of the American image of the Old World may prepare the mind and will through knowledge and understanding.

Europeans and Americans alike have often been obsessed with the idea of America as an anti-European New World. Whenever "the emergent mythology of the new world has been recognized and exploited as a stable resource," Prof. R. W. B. Lewis has written in his penetrating *The American Adam*, "the writer has found means, at hand and at home, for a fresh definition of experience and a fresh contribution to the culture."* America, he suggests, has come of age in these moments of recognition. I would prefer to say (even on the basis of his own literary evidence) that Americans come of age when they perceive the tension between the myth and history—and so learn to revise their outlook. I am convinced that the best Americans have been critically open to the Old World and more effective for their complicated relationship to it.

Americans are freer now than they ever have been to be themselves without being resentful, servile, or ambivalent to the European they harbor in themselves. Now each has to live with the other in common cause—the best grounds for finding their own identities without exaggerating their differences.

---

* *The American Adam: Innocence, Tragedy, and Tradition in the Nineteenth Century* (Chicago: University of Chicago Press, 1955), p. 129.

ACKNOWLEDGMENTS

In 1952 at Yale University I worked out a seminar in American attitudes toward Europe and taught it in the undergraduate American Studies program for several years. I want to thank my students for being "guinea pigs" for this book. I owe debts to Philip Rahv for the stimulation of his anthology about Americans abroad, *The Discovery of Europe,* and to Henry Nash Smith for the analogous model of his pioneering "image" study, *Virgin Land: The American West as Symbol and Myth.* I was greatly helped by receiving a Morse Fellowship at Yale in 1956–1957 to begin my writing on this book and by a grant from the Johnson Fund of the American Philosophical Society in 1961 to finish it. Without these influxes of grace my limbs would have grown cold, the project perished.

For various courtesies connected with this book (which they have not seen) I want to thank John Higham, Perry Miller, David M. Potter, Norman Holmes Pearson, Daniel J. Boorstin, Charles Newman, David Riesman, Warren I. Susman, George F. Kennan, David Smith, Russel Bastert, Mark Curtis, George MacMinn, and Winston V. Morrow. The California Institute of Technology has helpfully given me a quarter's freedom from classes so that I might roll my rock up and over the hill. Mrs. Lucille Lozoya has admirably performed the unsung role of typist. Librarians Doris Logan and William Stanley have made my work an easier pleasure. My wife, with the care of three other children, has suffered and improved this one immeasurably.

C. S.

THE
AMERICAN IMAGE
OF
THE OLD WORLD

An American is the born enemy of all the people of Europe.
P. A. ADET, FRENCH DIPLOMAT

America looks toward the Old World; all its slopes and its long plains slant toward the Atlantic, toward Europe.
ARNOLD GUYOT, SWISS SCIENTIST

It's a complex fate, being an American, and one of the responsibilities it entails is fighting against a superstitious valuation of Europe.
HENRY JAMES

1

OF PURER ENGLISH BLOOD

FOR MUCH OF THEIR HISTORY Americans have defined themselves through a deeply felt sense of conflict with Europe. In the American imagination the New World has stood in symbolic antithesis to the Old. Whether they condemned Europe's vices or yearned for its virtues, Americans agreed that it was a polar opposite of the New World. They have usually forgotten that this view of the relation between America and Europe emerged only gradually as the final result of one hundred and fifty years of colonial history. During most of that time the colonists would have been astounded to think of themselves as being inherently non-European.

In popular tradition the early emigrants to America are trans-figured by the glory of heroic flight to freedom. Condemned by Europeans for heresy, sedition, poverty, or crime, they fled to a land of religious liberty, political freedom, economic opportunity, and brotherly love. It is a noble legend, and like most legends not

1

without some foundation in historical fact. Its persistence, however, has had more to do with pride than with history. For Europeans it pictured America as a land contaminated by the dregs of the Old World; for Americans it dramatized Europe as a land of despotism. Yet most of the leading citizens of the New World during the greater part of the colonial period would not have recognized themselves as the protagonists of such an endearing and melodramatic epic. For them preservation of their links with Europe was not so much a duty as a necessity: they did not think of themselves as American, anti-European by definition. They merely manned the outposts of European civilization planted across the sea. In the two oldest colonies, Virginia and Massachusetts, which later provided much of the leadership for the American Revolution, this piety toward Europe was a deep vein in the Republicanism and Puritanism that eventually nourished "the spirit of '76."

The self-made gentleman of Virginia, his pretensions supported by the success of his shrewdness in calculating the value of tobacco, slaves, and the marriageable daughters of the well-to-do, was "proud to have it thought that his mind as well as his house was furnished after the best English fashion."[1] Like William Fitzhugh, for example, who came to America in 1670 as the son of a woolen draper of Bedford, England, he dreamed of having an estate in England, collected silver plate emblazoned with the family crest, sent his son to Oxford, Cambridge, or Edinburgh, named his manor after his English birthplace, lived by the gentleman's code as defined by Henry Peachem, and boasted of his loyalty to English monarchy. When King Charles the Second was restored to the throne, the people of Virginia, who had accepted the rule of the Puritan Commonwealth only because of economic coercion and the threatening presence of an English war fleet off the coast of Jamestown, gladly returned to their monarchial loyalty. For

[1] Carl L. Becker, *Beginnings of the American People*, William E. Dodd, ed., Riverside History of the United States, vol. 1 (Boston, Houghton Mifflin, 1915), p. 170. See also Philip Alexander Bruce, *Institutional History of Virginia in the Seventeenth Century*, 2 vols. (New York, Putnam's, 1910) and Louis B. Wright, *The First Gentlemen of Virginia* (San Marino, Huntington Library, 1940), pp. 1–63, 155–186.

the colony's enforced lapse of faith the Virginia Assembly apologized by declaring the anniversary of the death of King Charles I a day of fasting and prayer to expiate their guilt. In the eyes of most Virginian men of substance, disobedience to the Crown and Church of England was the repellent vice of New Englanders.[2]

Men of standing in colonial New England would have repudiated the slander and lamented the sad prejudice of their fellow-colonists in the South. Sober Puritans might well be shocked that a Virginian gentleman like William Byrd II should, when in London, attend masquerade balls, enjoy gambling parties, patronize the theaters, and keep several mistresses; but even Samuel Sewall, presiding judge at the Salem witchcraft trial in 1692, was pleased to taste the pleasures of London by hearing a concert at Covent Garden, drinking wine, playing ninepins at the Dog and Partridge, attending Green Goose Fair, and taking a swim in the Thames.[3] Planters in the Southern colonies had economic ties with the English tobacco market; merchants in New England had equally important commercial connections there. If the graduates of the College of William and Mary went to England for their Anglican orders, the graduates of Harvard College were often tempted to seek their fortune abroad. If the dashing William Byrd had time, amidst the social whirl of London, for the scientific meetings of the Royal Society, John Winthrop, Jr., made an early fellow of the Royal Society, burnished the intellectual luster of the Yankee culture by his extensive correspondence with European scientists.

To the English, the New England Puritans soon became a stiff-necked, potentially subversive minority group, constantly wooing heresy and sedition. To themselves they were only good Englishmen, somewhat better than those left behind, blessed with the opportunity of putting into practice in the convenient isolation of the New World a purified religious society which in God's own time would eventually illuminate the temporary darkness of the English church, grievously lost in the shades of popish tend-

[2] See Bruce, *op. cit.*, II, 274–286.
[3] For Byrd and Sewall see William L. Sachse, *The Colonial American in Britain* (Madison, University of Wisconsin Press, 1956), pp. 27, 147.

encies. In a document signed on board the *Arbella* on April 9, 1630, before the Puritan Armada of eleven ships set sail for Massachusetts Bay, the emigrants begged forgiveness for any regrettable "disaffections" between themselves and "our deare Mother," the English national church, humbly referred to themselves as "loyall Subjects," and confessed their disposition to be sad and tearful at leaving behind their native country. This pious petition, signed at the request of the promoter of the Massachusetts Bay Company, was designed to allay fears that the heresy of separatism was once again being carried across the ocean, as the Pilgrims had taken it to Plymouth. For all the intricacies of their Covenant theology, the Bay Colony Puritans never acknowledged any rupture with the theological faith of the Thirty-Nine Articles of Anglicanism. New England had a profound nostalgia for solidarity with the mother church; "never, by any act of its own," as Perry Miller has said, "had it severed itself from the national communion."[4] By the end of the century, the writer of an "attestation" to Cotton Mather's celebratory history of the Puritan experiment, the famous *Magnalia Christi Americana*, could still crave the "*blessing* and favour" of "Mother *England*" and speak of New England as a "little daughter" that had been forced to make "a *local secession*, yet not a *separation*," from the English church to an "undesired local distance from her dear *England*" in "a *remote wilderness*" from which place she promised "all that reverence and obedience which is due to her good *mother*, by virtue of the *fifth* commandment."[5]

"Dear mother" had some reason to question the filial tenderness of her "little daughter." When Charles I sent for the Bay Colony's charter of 1634, Governor John Winthrop hurried to have a beacon erected on the hill to rouse the country in case of an enemy invasion. When victims of Puritan intolerance appealed to the

[4] Perry Miller, *The New England Mind: From Colony to Province* (Cambridge, Harvard University Press, 1953), p. 464. For the pious petition signed on the *Arbella* see Samuel E. Morison, *Builders of the Bay Colony* (Boston, Houghton, Mifflin, 1930), p. 47.

[5] Quoted by Thomas Goddard Wright, *Literary Culture in Early New England 1620–1730* (New Haven, Yale University Press, 1920), p. 155.

rights of Englishmen under the law, they were told, as was the Presbyterian Robert Child in 1647: "Our allegiance binds us not to the laws of England any longer than while we live in England, for the laws of the parliament of England reach no further, nor do the king's writs under the great seal."[6] New England Puritanism was inspired with a messianic conviction of righteousness and a fanatical sense of historical mission that inevitably engendered a fiercely independent spirit. "Other plantations," wrote the proud Winthrop in a message to be given the English authorities as an explanation of Puritan conduct,

have been undertaken at the charge of others in England; and the planters have their dependence upon the companies there, and those planters go and come chiefly for matter of profit; but we came to abide here, and to plant the gospel, and people the country, and herein God hath marvellously blessed us.[7]

Full particulars as to doctrine, church government, and civil polity had all been found in the Bible by English Congregational theorists like William Ames. It was unhappily impossible to put the truth into practice anywhere in Europe, so powerful was the sway of popish tendencies; but in the New World there was providential opportunity to do so, and woe to those whose spiritual errors blinded them to New England's opportunities!

For all their pious respect for mother England, the loyalty of the colonists was qualified by their common conviction, as William Stoughton expressed it in 1670, that New Englanders, being "Covenant-born unto God," were especially singled out above all other peoples by unique advantages and privileges with "a wall of fire round about us": "God sifted a whole Nation that he might send choice Grain over into this Wilderness."[8] For later descendants, who inherited some of this Puritan tenacity to hold fast to that which is good, the image of a Europe lost in formal-

[6] Quoted by Morison, *op. cit.*, p. 255.

[7] John Winthrop, *Winthrop's Journal "History of New England," 1630–1649*, James K. Hosmer, ed., Original Narratives Series (New York, Scribner's, 1908), II, p. 315.

[8] William Stoughton, "New-England's True Interest," in Perry Miller and Thomas H. Johnson, eds., *The Puritans* (New York, American Book, 1938), p. 246.

ism and standing in need of redemption by the purity of the American example was barely submerged beneath the surface of their minds, ready to rise whenever they faced the challenge of the Old World.

Winthrop's blazing conviction that New England was "as a city upon a hill" with "the eyes of all people" upon it guided the destinies of the Puritan experiment during the passionate purity of its early years until the beacon was gradually dimmed by a growing secular spirit of accommodation, a worldly concern for business, and a jealous distrust of clerical power.[9] The defenders of this changing ethic were then accustomed to resort to the strategy of challenging Puritan theocracy by an appeal to "the rights of Englishmen." Despite the authoritarianism of the brief Cromwellian Protectorate, in which many New Englanders actively participated, the practical compromises and loosened restraints of a time of turbulence had left England more tolerant of diversity than New England ever had been. After the Restoration in 1660 an influx to the colonies of English merchants—Royalist, Anglican, and commercially imperialist—increased the number of those who strained at the restrictive and isolationist rule of the Puritans. New England merchants increasingly discovered that the path to political preferment and economic privilege "stretched across the Atlantic and wound through the maze of English government and London society."[10] When the "Glorious Revolution" of 1688 brought William and Mary to the throne and solidified the power of Parliament, New Englanders could rejoice at home in their own overthrow of the brief repressive regime of Sir Edmund Andros's Dominion. It was now easier for New Englanders to feel a sense of continuity with the mother country. They clung to it for a century—and, despite growing friction, even after 1763—until in April, 1775, the last bridge—that "rude bridge that arched the flood" at Concord—had been burned behind them.

In the popular imagination "the spirit of '76" is a perpetually

[9] *Ibid.*, "A Modell of Christian Charity," p. 199.
[10] Bernard Bailyn, *The New England Merchants in the Seventeenth Century* (Cambridge, Harvard University Press, 1955), p. 126.

tonic reminder of a real Americanism which first gave the notoriously perfidious British a much needed comeuppance. What has impressed modern historians, however, is the reluctance with which the colonists set their faces against their mother country. Most colonial Americans shared Francis Hopkinson's sentiments when, ten years before the Revolution, he declared: "We in America are in all respects Englishmen, notwithstanding that the Atlantic rolls her waves between us and the throne to which we all owe our allegiance." On that throne, for example, after the colonial troubles with England had well begun, Dr. Benjamin Rush, while visiting the "sacred Ground" of the House of Lords, not then in session, was pleased to sit for some time, enjoying, no doubt, those sensations of awe and wonder proper to a colonial son, who had no inkling that in a few years he would be scrawling his name to the Declaration of Independence.[11]

When the colonists began to protest after 1763 against the new imperial policy of compelling them to fulfill their economic obligations to hard-pressed England, they were complacently confident that a flourish of colonial charters and a pious invocation of "the rights of Englishmen," would soon bring the British government to its senses. Educated like enlightened gentlemen to a reverence for the classical republicanism of Greece and Rome, nurtured to a veneration for the glorious heroes of the English civil wars, and trained to hard-headed shrewdness by the practice of the law, the voluble leaders of the colonial cause met their opponents on their own ground with arguments insidiously difficult to resist. In John Adams, for example, a piety towards his idealized Puritan past combined with a decent respect for classical antiquity and English constitutional history to produce, in 1765, an inflammatory blast, saturated with provincial pride, against the administration of the British Empire. What baffling ambiguities for the imperial mind to comprehend lay in the outlook of this Bostonian! Adams was proud of his region above all others because its people, as he told his wife, were of "purer English blood" and "descended from Englishmen too, who left Europe in purer times than the

[11] For Hopkinson and Rush see Sachse, *op. cit.*, pp. 4, 26.

present, and less tainted with corruption than those they left behind them." Puritans had, after all, he argued in his "Dissertation on the Canon and Feudal Law," fled "the ridiculous fancies of sanctified effluvia from episcopal fingers" to a better world. Yet Englishmen had only to revive the spirit of Magna Charta and of those brave enemies of Stuart tyranny, Hampden, Vane, Milton, Harrington, Sidney, and Locke, to "endear us to them for ever, and secure their good-will." Were not "the foundations of British laws and government in the frame of human nature, in the constitution of the intellectual and moral world?" The colonists, in view of what seemed to be a "direct and formal design on foot to enslave all America," would study them carefully to see, for if they had no such basis, then "the superstructure is overthrown of course."[12]

That devastating "of course" made Adams more radical than most of his countrymen at that time. Most colonials would not yet have envisaged the possibility that the argument from history and precedent might eventually have to be abandoned as a solid basis for colonial rights. In Virginia, Thomas Jefferson also was in advance of his fellow-citizens, as was Benjamin Franklin, unofficial spokesman for America in England. Yet what is striking about the position even of the radicals is their anxiety to think of the colonies in terms continuous with the European past.

Jefferson's "A Summary View of the Rights of British America" was, even in 1774, far too bold for most Americans, but its radicalism was subtly linked to ancestral piety. Comprising, as they did, his instructions for the delegates from Virginia to the proposed first Continental Congress, his resolutions were passed over for what he later called "tamer sentiments." Certainly there was nothing tame about his argument that the American settlements had been established at the expense of individuals and hence belonged unreservedly to those who had spent their substance and spilled their blood in making them: "For themselves they

[12] Letter to Abigail Adams, October 29, 1775, in Adrienne Koch and William Peden, eds., *The Selected Writings of John and John Quincy Adams* (New York, Knopf, 1946), p. 46; "Dissertation on the Canon and Feudal Law," *ibid.*, pp. 16, 21, 23, 22.

fought, for themselves they conquered, and for themselves alone they have right to hold." There was no provincial timidity either in his patronizing opinion of George III, admittedly the one common link of the empire, but, after all, "no more than the chief officer of the people . . . circumscribed with definite powers, to assist in working the great machine of government," who, if he heeded American advice and opened his breast to "liberal and expanded thought," need have no fear that his name would be "a blot on the page of history." But even this uncompromising document was curiously inhibited by Jefferson's lawyer-like attempt to show that the precedent for Americans holding title to their land by right of occupancy could be traced back to "our Saxon ancestors" before the feudal system had been introduced by William the Norman after his conquest of England in 1066.[13] Assertion of American pre-eminence in history, mingled with piety for the past, was neatly symbolized in Jefferson's proposed seal of the new United States which, according to John Adams, pictured the children of Israel in the wilderness led by a cloud by day and a pillar of fire by night; and, on the other side, Hengist and Horsa, the Saxon chiefs, "from whom we claim the honor of being descended, and whose political principles and form of government we have assumed."[14] Jefferson was to become one of the fathers of American isolationism, but in 1810, two years before the second war with England began, he could still say that American laws, language, religion, politics, and manners were "so deeply laid in English foundations that we shall never cease to consider their history as a part of ours, and to study ours in that as its origin."[15]

Benjamin Franklin, who came to embody, as few other Americans ever have, the very quintessence of the national character

[13] Adrienne Koch and William Peden, eds., *The Life and Selected Writings of Thomas Jefferson* (New York, Random House, 1944), pp. 294, 293, 310, 307.

[14] Quoted by John Adams to Mrs. Adams, August 14, 1776, in Daniel J. Boorstin, *The Genius of American Politics* (Chicago, University of Chicago Press, 1953), p. 93.

[15] Letter to Colonel William Duane, August 12, 1810, *Life and Selected Writings*, pp. 605–606.

for both Europe and America, was in nothing more representative of his time than in his affiliation with both the New World and the Old. English in his immediate ancestry, Puritan in his devotion to the gospel of work, and cosmopolitan in his intellectual interests, he brought to his mastery of a complex inheritance a rare poise of mind, maintained with remarkable shrewdness and wit. His Crown appointment as postmaster for America over a score of years and his lengthy services as colonial agent in England for four colonies gave him unmatched qualifications for mediating the disputes between England and her plantations across the sea. His ultimate failure is powerful evidence that by 1776 the differences had become unmanageable. Yet, as long as he decently could, Franklin stuck to his imperial concept of America as the brightest jewel in the crown of empire. When French Canada fell to British arms on the Plains of Abraham he rejoiced, as he told his Scottish friend Lord Kames in 1760, not merely as a colonist, but as a Briton. "I have long been of opinion," he said, "that the *foundations of the future grandeur and stability of the British empire lie in America;* and though, like other foundations, they are low and little now, they are, nevertheless, broad and strong enough to support the greatest political structure that human wisdom ever yet erected."[16]

Franklin was distressed to discover that few Englishmen had his wisdom. The population of the New World, as he had explained in his "Observations Concerning the Increase of Mankind" (1751), was expanding by geometric proportions, doubling every twenty-five years, in a land-rich continent. Such growth augured well for his dream. When the hated Stamp Act was passed in 1765, while he was in England as agent for the Pennsylvania Assembly, he suffered a rude shock, surprised at the obtuseness of the British government in passing it and at the violence of colonial indignation against it. The human wisdom needed to erect the great political structure he envisaged seemed lamentably scarce. Alarmed, he groped for a solution. Perhaps,

[16] January 5, 1760, in Carl Van Doren, ed., *Benjamin Franklin's Autobiographical Writings* (New York, Viking, 1945), p. 122.

he speculated, the colonies should be represented in Parliament. This idea he expounded in the House of Commons when, as the man who could speak best about American conditions and complaints, he was invited to testify during the debate over the question of repealing the Stamp Act. To his questioners, both sympathetic and hostile, he persuasively explained colonial objections to Parliamentary taxation without representation, an oppression which the colonists would never accept unless by submission to superior force of arms. Repeal of the Stamp Act brought temporary quiet, but the crisis had stirred Franklin's doubts that his vision of imperial unity would ever be fulfilled. Parliament, he observed to a friend in 1766, was too proud to accept American representation; "and when they will be desirous of granting it, we shall think too highly of ourselves to accept it."[17]

As he struggled to find a formula of reconciliation, his concept of the empire was transformed. The sovereignty of the Crown he could understand; the sovereignty of the British legislature out of Britain, he did not understand. By March 13, 1768, he was convinced, as he wrote his son, that "no middle doctrine can be well maintained" between the omnipotence or the impotence of Parliament's legal power over America. Between these extremes he had no difficulty in making a choice. What seemed to him most reasonable was the notion of a federation in which the colonies would be "so many separate states, only subject to the same king, as England and Scotland were before the union."[18] This theory of an imperial bond with the mother country only through a sentimental respect for a common sovereign—the modern form of dominion status—was as yet beyond the grasp of most men in either England or America. By 1776 it was the unspoken theoretical premise, as Carl Becker has brilliantly demonstrated, of the Declaration of Independence in which Jefferson had expressed "only the commonsense of the matter."

Between the lines of that sonorously phrased document ran a subtle argument: Regrettably, the King had badly neglected his

[17] Letter to Cadwallader Evans, May 9, 1766, quoted by Carl Van Doren, *Benjamin Franklin* (New York, Viking, 1938), pp. 354–355.
[18] March 13, 1768, quoted by Van Doren, *ibid.*, p. 378.

duties and woefully abused his powers. The colonists were thus morally and legally quitted of his claim on their loyalty which formerly had held the empire together. "A decent respect for the opinions of mankind" required that these depressing facts be submitted to "a candid world." Independence was a last, but necessary resort. "In this gingerly way," as Becker said, "did the deputies lift the curtain and peer down the road to revolution."[19] Rarely has a people broken away from its colonial past with such little eagerness. Thereafter Americans would feel profound sympathy for other rebellions against imperial bonds; but, unfortunately for their understanding of themselves and the world, the discriminating eye of history would seldom find much basis for the recurrence of "the spirit of '76," despite its influence.

The American Revolution was, in fact, less a popular revulsion against an alien tyranny than it was a tragic civil war. The colonists had challenged their oppressors by appealing to the glorious traditions of English history. Whatever revolutionary theory they had devised was borrowed from England's own John Locke, who had rationalized the settlement of 1688. To their disillusionment they ultimately found that the ideals they revered were better cherished in the New World than in the Old World that had given birth to them.

This disenchantment, like so many American feelings, was symbolically dramatized in Franklin's experience. For England he had felt genuine love. On the eve of the change in colonial policy which was to poison American relations with the mother country for a dozen years, he wrote an English friend that though reason bade him return to America, inclination prompted him to stay in England: "You know which usually prevails. I shall probably make but this one vibration and settle here for ever." If England

[19] Carl Becker, *The Eve of the Revolution*, Allen Johnson, ed., The Chronicles of America, vol. 2 (New Haven, Yale University Press, 1918), p. 214. For the Commonwealth theory of empire see Randolph G. Adams, *Political Ideas of the American Revolution*, 3rd ed., Introduction by Merrill Jensen (New York, Barnes and Noble, 1958), pp. 65–85.

was a "petty island, which, compared to America, is but a stepping stone in a brook," nevertheless, it had "in almost every neighbourhood, more sensible, virtuous, and elegant minds than we can collect in ranging a hundred leagues of our vast forests."[20] As a highly civilized man, a member of the Royal Society and the Society of Arts, Franklin had a thorough appreciation of these delights, which he had enjoyed for eighteen years while his home had been on Craven Street, Strand, London. But his dream of settling in England, like his vision of an empire strengthened by an expanding America, grew dimmer as the relations between his two countries worsened.

By accident he precipitated the event which finally turned him in bitterness against the British government. He dispatched to America, for limited circulation among certain patriots, some letters written to English authorities by colonial officials, among them Thomas Hutchinson, Governor of the Massachusetts Bay Colony. Franklin hoped that the letters, lamenting the seditious tendencies of the colony, would convince the colonists that the British ministry had been misguided rather than ill-intentioned. Instead, the instructions were violated and the letters, widely publicized in the newspapers, whipped up a demand for a petition to remove the Governor and Lieutenant Governor. Summoned early in 1774 before a committee of the Privy Council to explain his role in the affair, Franklin was charged with malice and bad faith, abused with rude sarcasm, and eventually relieved of his postmastership. Deeply wounded, he suffered the common fate of intermediaries in being considered, as he was unhappily aware, "too much of an American" in England and "too much of an Englishman" in America. By February of the following year he had buried his hopes of imperial union when he rejected Joseph Galloway's plan for tying the colonies to the Crown. Franklin had but one fundamental criticism of it: "When I consider the extreme corruption prevalent among all orders of men in this old, rotten state,

[20] Letter to William Strahan, August 23, 1762, *Autobiographical Writings*, p. 136; letter to Polly Stevenson, March 25, 1763, *ibid.*, p. 139.

and the glorious public virtue so predominant in our rising country, I cannot but apprehend more mischief than benefit from a closer union."[21]

These were the terms, defining an antithesis between the virtue of the New World and the vice of the Old, that colonial Americans were increasingly beginning to use as the long affiliation to the mother country finally atrophied. By 1776 they were prepared to respond enthusiastically to Thomas Paine's *Common Sense* with its blistering scorn of the absurdity of a great continent being dependent on a puny island bogged in the swamp of monarchy, that very "popery of government," which in its mystery-mongering complexity resulted in the seating of "asses," not lions, on the thrones of the world.

It was no colonial son who spoke with such unsentimental bluntness, but a crusading republican, only recently bankrupt and dismissed from the excise service as a troublemaker, and whose sense of injustice under English authority had been festering long before he came to the colonies. Paine arrived barely a year before the fighting broke out on Lexington Green. By a nice irony this "ingenious, worthy young man," utterly free of the colonial bonds which still enthralled Americans, was introduced by a letter of Benjamin Franklin, on whose heart these ties had for so long and so painfully exerted their filial force.

Those Americans for whom these ties were reinforced by their shock at the violence and democratic aspirations of many of the patriots had no choice but to become Tories. In their despair many of them accepted, or had forced upon them, exile to England. Before the end of the Revolution there were several thousand such *émigrés* living in London or Bristol. Most of them, at leaving, would have shared the bitterness of Judge Jonathan Sewall who felt that the dose of harsh conduct he had received at the hands of his countrymen had been too stiff for forgiveness: "God mend and bless them—but let me never be cursed with a

---

[21] Letter to Joseph Galloway, February 25, 1775, quoted by Van Doren, *Benjamin Franklin*, p. 517. The theme of Franklin as an Anglo-American is lucidly developed in Verner W. Crane, *Benjamin Franklin: Englishman and American* (Baltimore, Johns Hopkins University Press, 1936).

residence among them again."[22] Yet the exiles came to discover (almost as soon as they had lost it), that they had, after all, a native country. Most of them gladly returned to New Brunswick or Bermuda after the Revolution.

Only a narrow line, if a crucial one, had divided them from their countrymen during the crisis. The Tories had accepted the authority of Parliament, but they seldom had accepted its wisdom. Even Governor Hutchinson had been opposed to the expediency of the imperial measures which alienated the colonies. Like him, pathetically marooned in English society, in which (for all its "high life" an important official might enjoy) there was no compensation for the loss of his humble cottage at Milton, the exiles could not conceal their pride in the bravery of American troops or their resentment of the proprietary conceit with which Englishmen spoke of the colonies. Like Samuel Curwen of Salem, they experienced the same disillusionment the rest of their countrymen had suffered. Amidst "the dissipation, self-forgetfulness, and vicious indulgences of every kind, which characterize this metropolis," they felt a yearning for a simpler society without that tempting luxury "which (thank God) our part of America is ignorant of."[23] In nothing more than this disenchantment did they reveal their fundamental Americanism. The New World had found its dark antithesis in the Old. It was a division that came to be deeply engraved in the American imagination as the United States set out on its independent career.

The success of the Revolution, fully realized in the Treaty of 1783, gave the new nation a consciousness of its unique mission. The United States, as Ezra Stiles, President of Yale, preached in an election sermon at Hartford that year, was "God's American Israel." There was something new in the world. "But a DEMO-CRATICAL polity for millions, standing upon the broad basis of the people at large, amply charged with property, has not hitherto

[22] Quoted by Lewis Einstein, *Divided Loyalties* (London, Cobden-Sanderson, 1933), p. 204.

[23] Letter to Reverend Thomas Barnard, July 22, 1775, in George Atkinson Ward, ed., *The Journal and Letters of Samuel Curwen*, 4th ed. (Boston, Little, Brown, 1864), p. 33.

been exhibited." This country would now enter a new era of communication with all nations as an independent, self-supporting adult, no longer a colonial child. But it would do so with the challenging self-respect of a people convinced that Europe and Asia would "hereafter learn that the most liberal principles of law and civil polity," as well as "the true religion," were "to be found on this side of the Atlantic," far removed from "the rust and corruption of ages."[24] In that same year Noah Webster in his famous speller (*A Grammatical Institute of the English Language*) made an appeal for a national tongue because for America to adopt Old World standards would be to betray the bloom of youth: "Europe is grown old in folly, corruption and tyranny—in that country laws are perverted, manners are licentious, literature is declining and human nature is debased."[25] The New World would have to create its own culture.

Yet this self-conscious nationalism could not suppress a nostalgia for the idealized past. "Oh, England!" cried Ezra Stiles, "how did I once love thee! how did I once glory in thee!" Now it was farewell "to all this greatness," but perhaps some day the "hardy hosts" of England's American sons might "leap the Atlantic" to "rescue an aged parent from destruction" and then return in triumph "to this asylum of the world, and rest in the bosom of liberty."[26] In the rhetoric of this sermon was a prophecy that the relation of the New World to the Old would be troubled with a baffling mixture of defiant independence, righteous good will, and humble piety.

This American discovery of an Old World, to which by future definition (not by history) Americans did not belong, was itself a link to Europe. For Europeans, like Abbé Raynal, Condorcet, Crèvecoeur, Chateaubriand, and Hegel, the dualism between Europe and America was a fundamental axiom. Hegel's description

---

[24] Ezra Stiles, *The United States Elevated to Glory and Honor* (New Haven, Thomas and Samuel Green, 1783), pp. 7, 17, 56.

[25] Quoted by Ruth Miller Elson, "American Schoolbooks and 'Culture' in the Nineteenth Century," *Mississippi Valley Historical Review*, 46 (December, 1959), 432.

[26] Stiles, *op. cit.*, p. 32.

of the New World was both an American and a European dream: "It is the land of desire for all those who are weary of the historical lumber-room of Europe. . . . It is for America to abandon the ground on which hitherto the History of the World has unfolded itself."[27] In discovering themselves as an anti-Europe the Americans were fulfilling in their own way a European dream which had even antedated their Revolution. It would be a long time, as Carl Bridenbaugh has said, before the average citizen of New York, Boston, Philadelphia, Charles Town, and Newport—the major centers of colonial culture—would once again, as in the colonial age, feel "so much aware of his membership in the Atlantic community."[28]

[27] Quoted by Gilbert Chinard, "The American Dream," in Robert E. Spiller, Willard Thorp, Thomas H. Johnson, and Henry Seidel Canby, eds., *Literary History of the United States*, rev. ed. (New York, Macmillan, 1953), p. 214.

[28] Carl Bridenbaugh, *Cities in Revolt: Urban Life in America, 1743–1776* (New York, Knopf, 1955), p. 421. See also Michael Kraus, *The Atlantic Civilization: Eighteenth-Century Origins* (Ithaca, Cornell University Press, 1949), for American links to Europe.

CHAPTER

2

A MERIDIAN OF PARTITION

THE COMMON CONVICTION that the United States had a unique
mission in history which put it in fundamental opposition to
Europe was compounded of three national purposes: abstention
from the system of European politics and wars, expansion of republican institutions across the North American continent, and
the maintenance of a standing example of freedom for oppressed
peoples everywhere. These aims, generally combined together
but seldom without tension, implied the idea of Europe as, re-
spectively, an alien stranger, a threatening enemy, and a potential
pupil. To an important extent these conceptions were solidly
rooted in appreciation of historical fact. The new nation had
everything to gain in protecting itself for its own development
by staying out of Europe's internal conflicts and avoiding the
fate of becoming a satellite of some stronger power. On the soil
of North America there were still European footholds; in the
minds of European governments there were still hopes for fulfill-

ing imperial dreams in the New World. In the first half of the nineteenth century American diplomats were thus compelled to negotiate warily with the French, the British, the Spanish, and the Russians to secure their country's safety, freedom of action, and steady expansion of settlements. For European liberal movements the United States was a continuing inspiration for political and humanitarian reform.

Yet in the pursuit of these rational purposes a subtle mythologizing process was sometimes at work which tended to obscure the complexities and realities involved in America's relation to Europe. In later times it became possible to canonize the Founding Fathers of American diplomacy as the heroes of a mythology in which the New World is the dialectical antithesis of the Old. In this legend America is the land of the Future, where innocent men belong to a society of virtuous simplicity, enjoying liberty, equality, and happiness; Europe is the bankrupt Past, where fallen men wander without hope in a dark labyrinth, degraded by tyranny, injustice, and vice. In this context the traditional foreign policy of what came to be called "isolationism" was transformed into an absolute renunciation of Europe. The qualifying limitations of early definitions of the policy were gradually forgotten. In the intensely nationalistic rhetoric of Thomas Jefferson and John Quincy Adams isolationism had already acquired overtones of myth. What began as a pragmatic measure was on its way to becoming a fundamental presupposition of the national consciousness. (For those twentieth-century statesmen who felt compelled to depart from isolationism, this tradition was to prove an embarrassing burden—as it was to be a powerful source of inspiration for their opponents.)

Certainly the thirteen original colonies had not been isolated in fact from Europe's strife. Between 1689 and 1763 four European wars had repercussions on the continent of North America, which are known in American history books as King William's War, Queen Anne's War, King George's War, and the French and Indian War. If most of these struggles arose out of European conflicts, the last one had been a contest between the English and the French for mastery of North America itself. It was partly because the patriots of the American Revolution had such keenly unpleasant memories of these involvements that they pressed so insistently for a policy of independence from European entanglements. One of Tom Paine's shrewdest arguments in *Common Sense* was his assertion that American trade was hurt by colonial dependence on Great Britain, which "tends directly to involve this Continent in European wars and quarrels, and set us at variance with nations who would otherwise seek our friendship, and against whom we have neither anger nor complaint."[1]

Yet the leaders of the Revolution were well aware that without foreign aid their cause would perish; they were persuaded to declare themselves independent in 1776 because they knew that to obtain the aid of France it was necessary to make it clear that they were not fighting to restore relations with France's enemy, Great Britain. The memory of colonial wars inspired John Adams to urge on the floor of the Continental Congress in September, 1775, that concessions and commitments for French aid be limited to a treaty of commerce. It should be, he felt, a "first principle and a maxim never to be forgotten, to maintain an entire neutrality in all future European wars" lest "we should be little better than puppets, danced on the wires of the cabinets of Europe."[2] Though Adams's fears largely controlled the treaty plan which American commissioners brought to France in 1776, they were ultimately forced, out of dire need for sustained aid in achieving independence, to sign a treaty which bound France and America in "perpetual alliance." Both powers were guaranteed mutual protection forever of their present possessions in North America and of any fruits of the eventual treaty of peace. Desperate for further aid, the new nation was unable to wring assistance from Spain, though John Jay spent over two years seeking it, and when help came it was through the back door of a secret alliance made with Spain by France.

[1] Arthur Wallace Peach, ed., *Selections from the Work of Thomas Paine*, American Authors Series (New York, Harcourt, Brace, 1928), p. 21.

[2] Adrienne Koch and William Peden, eds., *Selected Writings of John and John Quincy Adams* (New York, Knopf, 1946), p. 40.

When John Adams learned of this humiliating arrangement he voiced a fear of America's being duped by wily foreigners that was to become a characteristic piece of national cant: "The subtlety, the invention, the profound secrecy, the absolute silence of these European courts, will be too much for our hot, rash, fiery ministers, and for our indolent, inattentive ones, though as silent as they."[3] Americans were fully justified in looking upon European diplomacy with a cold eye, but they displayed no evidence whatever of being "taken in"—except by their fear of being "taken in." It was true that no European power had any interest in underwriting American independence to the extent of making it the dominant power on the continent of North America—both the French and the Spanish hoped to keep the Americans cooped up well east of the Mississippi. American diplomats had no illusions on this score. Jay, Franklin, and Adams did not hesitate to violate their Congressional instructions, not to mention the spirit of the French alliance, by making separate peace negotiations with the British. Yet the son of John Adams could write his father in 1795: "I have been accustomed all my life to plain dealing and candor, and am not sufficiently versed in the art of political swindling to be prepared for negotiating with an European Minister of State."[4] This confession of innocence was, of course, only a paradoxical way of claiming an American superiority over Europe. The success of America's "shirtsleeve diplomacy" was a remarkable demonstration of the worldly shrewdness implicit in American "innocence."

The American fear of Europe almost resulted in a resignation from foreign affairs. The Virginia Assembly in 1783 instructed its state representatives in Congress to vote against sending any ambassadors to Europe. In 1789 a motion to have only a tem-

[3] Quoted by J. Fred Rippy and Angie Debo, "The Historical Background of the American Policy of Isolation," *Smith College Studies in History*, 9 (April-July, 1924), 102. In his diary Adams admitted that he had found "more intrigue and *finesse* among my own countrymen at Paris, than among the French." See *Works*, ed. Charles Francis Adams, III (Boston, Little, Brown, 1851), 226.

[4] Quoted by Samuel Flagg Bemis, *John Quincy Adams and the Foundations of American Foreign Policy* (New York, Knopf, 1949), p. 66, n. 1.

porary Secretary of Foreign Affairs was seriously debated; but the next year the plunge was made by setting up a Department of State with a Secretary and five clerks. To Americans it was clear that Nature herself in the form of the immense Atlantic had ordained the separation of the New World from the Old. What Nature had put asunder, no man, least of all an American, should join together.

It seemed to be a matter of primary political logic that the New World and the Old were different systems of interest, and European powers had themselves given sanction to the idea in the sixteenth and seventeenth centuries by the practice of often maintaining formal friendship in Europe while conflict among their subjects raged in the New World. This concept became official American gospel in the Monroe Doctrine of 1823. Paine had appealed to the idea in his flaming arguments for American independence; Washington and Hamilton in the Farewell Address of 1796 had counseled American abstention from "the ordinary vicissitudes" of European politics and alliances; and Jefferson in 1820 had prophesied the need for a formal "meridian of partition through the ocean which separates the two hemispheres, on the hither side of which no European gun shall ever be heard, nor an American on the other. . . ."[5] By Monroe's message to Congress the young republic reaffirmed its policy of nonentanglement with Europe and boldly warned the Old World to keep its hands off the New.

To Americans, not only geography and interest, but also freedom and morality divided their country from Europe. The Monroe Doctrine was in part an ideological challenge to the Holy Alliance of monarchical powers that were bent on stemming the

---

[5] Letter to William Short, August 4, 1820, Adrienne Koch and William Peden, eds., *The Life and Selected Writings of Thomas Jefferson* (New York, Random House, 1944), p. 699. For discussion of eary American isolationism see Richard Van Alstyne, Introduction, *American Diplomacy in Action*, rev. ed. (Stanford, Stanford University Press, 1947), pp. 9–26 and Albert K. Weinberg, "Washington's 'Great Rule' in Its Historical Evolution," in Eric F. Goldman, ed., *Historiography and Urbanization: Essays in American History in Honor of W. Stull Holt* (Baltimore, Johns Hopkins University Press, 1941), pp. 109–138.

tide of liberalism swelled by the French Revolution. Jefferson spoke for his countrymen in the year of the Doctrine when he wrote Monroe:

Our first and fundamental maxim should be, never to entangle ourselves in the broils of Europe. Our second, never to suffer Europe to intermeddle with cis-Atlantic affairs. America, North and South, has a set of interests distinct from those of Europe, and peculiarly her own. She should therefore have a system of her own, separate and apart from that of Europe. While the last is laboring to become the domicile of despotism, our endeavors should surely be, to make our hemisphere that of freedom.[6]

In this context the gulf between America and Europe was made unbridgeable; no good American could cross it without losing his political and moral integrity.

The isolationist tradition thus acquired a sanctity which inspired a fierce belief, easily transformed into pharisaical righteousness and blind bigotry, that America was the favorite child of God, Nature, and History. Convinced that he was blessed with special privileges and unique virtues, the American's relation to Europe was bound to be uneasy. The Old World would inevitably have the fascinating aura of evil to those who had virtuously renounced it.

The cool realism as well as the intoxicating pride of the early shapers of the policy of nonentanglement in Europe's politics are eloquently summed up in the careers of Thomas Jefferson and John Quincy Adams. Both men had many years of experience abroad as diplomats; both had sustained the responsibilities of Secretary of State and the Presidency; both were men of refinement. In their blood flowed the warm stream of a forthright Americanism, tempered by a sensitive appreciation of Europe's culture. In the thought of both men a clear line cannot always be drawn between their pragmatic relation to Europe and their sense of a contrast of nearly metaphysical significance between America and Europe. In this respect they were more character-

[6] Letter to James Monroe, October 24, 1823, *The Life and Selected Writings of Thomas Jefferson*, p. 708.

istic representatives of their country than was Benjamin Franklin, who, for all his legendary status as the quintessential American, was a cosmopolitan man of the world, remarkably free of parochial inhibitions and prejudices. With calculated shrewdness he wore his fur cap in France, not only to keep his head warm and to conceal his scalp disease, but to confirm the French liberals in their fond belief that in him Rousseau's Natural Man had, in the glorious New World, triumphantly become the God-like Legislator, the Philosopher-King, and Solon of the Wilderness. For the sympathetic people of France, her military enthusiasts for the Revolution, her liberal nobles, and her men of science, he became a culture-hero of mythical proportions, embraced as such by Voltaire in the famous meeting at the French Academy of Sciences in 1778—the year Franklin's prestige helped bring the decisive support of France to America's side. With his worldly wit, enjoyment of persiflage, spiced with flirtation, and his profound interest in science, the good Doctor Franklin was thoroughly at home in the social and intellectual pleasures of Paris. This urbanity, all the more astonishing in a man whose start in life was as a printer's apprentice in Boston, was proof that the American dream could have a hero whose whole life was an ironic commentary, almost a joke, on the primitivistic coloration of the national mythology.

Adams and Jefferson had their own mixture of sophistication and simplicity, but they had also a certain tenseness in their Americanism—especially when challenged by Europe—much more typical of their countrymen. Franklin, comfortable, secure, and rich in public honors as he was at Philadelphia after his return from France, could still write Madame Lavoisier in 1788 that none of these "blessings of God" could make him forget his nine years of happiness in Paris: "And now, even in my sleep, I find that the scenes of all my pleasant dreams are laid in that city, or in its neighbourhood."[7] Both Jefferson and Adams were con-

---

[7] Letter to Madame Lavoisier, October 23, 1788, Carl Van Doren, ed., *Benjamin Franklin's Autobiographical Writings* (New York, Viking, 1945), p. 761.

sumed by the passionate American conviction that only bad dreams could come true in Europe.

To Jefferson the division between the New World and the Old was both momentous and invidious. The natural barrier of 3000 miles of ocean was, in his eyes, valuable protection from the contagion of Europe's germs of corruption. With abundant room, a scanty population, and a "redundant soil" offering "the means of life and happiness" America's circumstances favored an agricultural economy in contrast to Europe's urban, manufacturing civilization. From Paris, where he had been sent as Minister Plenipotentiary in 1784 to assist Franklin and John Adams in making commercial arrangements with Europe, Jefferson anxiously listened for news of the movement to form a more durable, powerful government in America. Eagerly he corresponded with his close friend and collaborator in liberal politics, James Madison, to reassure himself that the new constitution would not hurt America's virtue and integrity. From Madison, fresh from his labors in the Convention at Philadelphia, he learned with apprehension that the Constitution did not limit the number of terms a president might serve. Jefferson feared that without provision for rotation in office the President would, in effect, be elected for life and thus became a focal point of foreign influence and pressure through the efforts of other governments to sway American policy. Such an invitation to foreign invasion of American affairs appalled him. Yet, as an adherent of majority rule, he told Madison he would abide by the results of the ratifying conventions, confident that the people could be trusted because they were "virtuous." While there was vacant land in America their virtue would remain. "When we get piled upon one another in large cities, as in Europe," he added, "we shall become corrupt as in Europe, and go to eating one another as they do there."[8] Fortunately, this corruption of the American dream was so distant as to seem then a mere figure of speech. By wise policy, Jefferson believed, the Republic could leave manufacturing largely

[8] Letter to James Madison, December 20, 1787, *The Life and Selected Writings of Thomas Jefferson*, p. 441.

to Europe. As a matter of pure theory and personal wish, he would even prefer that his country practice neither commerce nor navigation, but "stand, with respect to Europe, precisely on the footing of China."[9] But he knew theory had to give way to the decided taste (undoubtedly inherited from England) which his countrymen had for these pursuits. This much contact with Europe was a sad necessity.

The social order of the Old World was to Jefferson a Calvinist hell, "a true picture of that country to which they say we shall pass hereafter, and where we are to see God and his angels in splendor, and crowds of the damned trampled under their feet."[10] To this self-styled "savage of the mountains of America" (an ironic estimate which Franklin in his fur cap would have appreciated) the "physical and moral oppression" of Europe's masses and the "intrigues of love" and "those of ambition" which occupied the ruling class were very much inferior to "the tranquil, permanent felicity with which domestic society in America blesses most of its inhabitants" and to "that degree of happiness which is enjoyed in America, by every class of people." It was necessary for the American to be on perpetual guard against adopting European manners.

Even education abroad held out dangerous temptations to corrupt American virtue. To a young American, sent to Europe because of his poor health, Jefferson gave advice bristling with warnings of the danger of a French education to the youth's spiritual welfare. In everything except modern languages and medicine a student could learn as much at William and Mary College as in Europe, and he would not run the enormous risks of being corrupted by Old World manners and morals. "Let us view the disadvantages of sending a youth to Europe," Jefferson wrote him from Paris. "To enumerate them all, would require a volume. I will select a few." A "fondness for European luxury and dissipation," a fascination with "the privileges of the European

[9] Letter to Charles Van Hogendorp, October 13, 1785, *ibid.*, p. 384.
[10] Letter to Charles Bellini, September 30, 1785, *ibid.*, p. 382.

aristocrats," a partiality for monarchy, "a spirit for female intrigue" or "a passion for whores"—these were merely the most
poisonous fruits of European education. These debased tastes
would destroy the American's integrity by giving him "a contempt for the simplicity of his own country," an abhorrence for
"the lovely equality which the poor enjoy with the rich" in the
New World, and a pitying scorn for "the chaste affections" of
American women. Whatever doubts Jefferson may have had before he went to Europe about the evils of a European education,
they had been banished during his residence there, his experience
proving more than he had ever suspected in America. His conclusion was as inclusive as it was absolute. "It appears to me, then,
that an American, coming to Europe for education, loses in his
knowledge, in his morals, in his health, in his habits, and in his
happiness."[11]

This malignant darkness of life in Europe was in Jefferson's
vision the simple consequence of the institutional structure of its
social order. All Europe was "loaded with misery, by kings, nobles, and priests, and by them alone."[12] These were the vivid
symbols of a feudal system, the simple tokens of all those evils
America was blessed for not having. Jefferson himself, as a member of the Virginia House of Delegates, had between 1776 and
1779 devoted his extraordinary talents to legislation designed to
eliminate the last elements of feudalism from the law, education,
and church-state relations. That vestiges of the old order could
in a few years be wiped out by mere legislation was striking evidence of the weakness of whatever feudal roots had been planted
in America. The Declaration of Independence had been more
than a justification of America's separation from England; it had
been an eloquent announcement that the New World had turned
its back forever on European feudalism and had dedicated itself
to liberty and the inalienable rights of man.

Jefferson's five years in Europe confirmed him in this view of

[11] Letter to J. Banister, Jr., October 15, 1785, *ibid.*, p. 387.
[12] Letter to George Wythe, August 13, 1786, *ibid.*, p. 395.

the relationship between the Old World and the New. Only in Europe could a true perception be gained of the horrors which flow from a rigidly class-stratified society. From America they had seemed undesirable; in Europe they seemed anathema. Amusing himself abroad by "contemplating the characters of the then reigning sovereigns," he concluded that Louis the XVI was a fool, like the Kings of Spain, Naples, and Sardinia; the Queen of Portugal an idiot, like the Kings of Denmark, Sweden, Austria, and England; and the King of Prussia "a mere hog in body as well as in mind." Inbreeding, sensuality, luxury, and indolence had produced "these animals" as the inevitable results of hereditary monarchy—"And so endeth the Book of Kings, from all of whom the Lord deliver us . . ."[13] To Washington he wrote his fears that the Cincinnati organization of veteran officers of the Continental Army might mark the introduction of feudal hereditary principles into America. So far the common sense of the people was solidly established by their fortunate separation from "their parent stock, and kept from contamination either from them, or the other people of the old world, by the intervention of so wide an ocean."[14] This immunity to the influence of feudalism must become, he felt, the precious axiom of American development.

In these unqualified terms the mythical conception of a Europe whose every charm is the vicious opposite of an American virtue clearly emerges in Jefferson's thought. His rhetoric transformed Americans into a group of idealized sculptured figures. On one side stand Liberty, Happiness, Innocence, and Simplicity, pointing towards the Future, while separated by a pool of water and facing them with menacing mien stand Despotism, Misery, Corruption, and Sophistication, wrapped in the shrouds of the Past. Frozen in conventional attitudes and linked together by a dramatically satisfying relationship of antithesis the New World thus

[13] Letter to Governor John Langdon, March 5, 1810, *ibid.*, p. 604.
[14] Letter to George Wythe, August 13, 1786, *ibid.*, p. 394. On his view of the Cincinnati see Dumas Malone, *Jefferson and the Rights of Man* (Boston, Little Brown, 1951), pp. 153–156.

eternally confronts the Old. It was a set piece easily and frequently envisaged by the nineteenth-century American imagination.

Nevertheless Jefferson's relationships to Europe were much more complicated than this classic image suggests. Like many illustrious Americans after him, he was capable of promoting in all sincerity the currency of a symbolic feudalized Europe, shaped by American pride and fear, while relating himself practically to a Europe that could not be realistically comprehended in such simple terms. For all his dread of contamination by the contagion of Old World evils, he was too civilized a man and too intelligent a nationalist to blind himself to European values. This happy inconsistency was to be repeated in the lives of others equally fascinated by the Jeffersonian symbol of a corrupt Europe.

Even as a young man he had longed to make an extensive tour of Europe. This aim, which led him to defer plans for marriage, lost him an impatient girl. Later, his wife's sickness forcing him twice to refuse a post abroad, he wrote Lafayette to lament lost opportunities for "seeing countries whose improvements in science, in arts, and in civilization" it had been his fortune "to admire at a distance, but never to see." Many years after he had returned from Europe Jefferson wished that he were twenty years younger so that he might go with young George Ticknor, then starting out on his *Wanderjahre*, on a "classical voyage to Rome, Naples and Athens." He recommended a European tour as a means of improvement by which a good American might return home, "charged like a bee, with the honey gathered on it."[15]

This simile precisely describes Jefferson's own attitude as a traveler. His notebooks, recording his journeys in Southern France, England, Northern Italy, Holland, and the Rhine Valley, reveal a man determined to glean from his experience every possible advantage for his country. He took the advice he once gave two of his fellow Americans, Mr. Rutledge and Mr. Shippen, to observe with care in Europe agriculture, plants, useful animals

[15] The letters to Lafayette (August 4, 1781) and to Ticknor's father

and mechanical arts, gardens, architecture, and the condition of the laboring masses. But he had too keen an aesthetic sense to follow his own rule of dismissing painting and statuary as mere luxuries unsuited to America. He made his own collection of European pictures and sculpture and commissioned both French and American artists to commemorate the heroes of the Enlightenment. "Were I to proceed to tell you how much I enjoy their architecture, sculpture, painting, music," he wrote from France, "I should want words."[16] To America he brought back his own accumulation of honey. Hopefully, he sent back home the seeds of foreign grasses, olive trees, and Italian rice to be planted in the New World. When he lived in Paris, he devoted every afternoon he could take from his duties to the principal bookstores, diligently "putting by everything which related to America, and indeed whatever was rare and valuable in every science."[17] Making orders for books in four other major European cities, he built the library which would one day become the nucleus of the Library of Congress. When he returned to America he brought with him over fifty cases of luggage and over eighty packing cases of furniture and books purchased in Paris. To the task of remodeling a house in Philadelphia, to his personal attire, to his food, plate, and choice of servants and cooks, he introduced European innovations.

Most significantly of all, he enriched the artistic growth of his country by the fruits of his love for classical architecture. Jefferson's brief episode of romance in Paris with Maria Cosway, the beautiful wife of a fashionable English painter, was a charm-

---

(December 12, 1816) and to Governor Rutledge (July 12, 1788) on the virtues of a European tour are quoted by Edward Dumbauld, *Thomas Jefferson American Tourist, Being an Account of His Journeys in the United States of America, England, France, Italy, the Low Countries, and Germany* (Norman, University of Oklahoma Press, 1946), pp. 22, 146, 153.

[16] Letter to Charles Bellini, September 30, 1785, *The Life and Selected Writings of Thomas Jefferson*, p. 383. Cf. "Traveling Notes for Mr. Rutledge and Mr. Shippen, June 3, 1788," *ibid.*, pp. 147–149.

[17] Letter to Samuel H. Smith, September 21, 1814, *ibid.*, p. 651. For Jefferson's cultural explorations of the European scene see Dumbauld, *op. cit.*, pp. 60–163 and Marie Kimball, *Jefferson, the Scene of Europe 1784 to 1789* (New York, Coward-McCann, 1950).

ing flirtation; his interest in antiquity was an abiding passion. The dome of Monticello, modeled on the Hôtel de Salm in Paris; his plans for the state capitol at Richmond, a tribute to the Roman grandeur of the Maison Quarrée in Nimes, at which he had gazed for hours "like a lover at his mistress"; and the gracious harmony of the University of Virginia, designed and organized by this American Leonardo who also hired the school's European professors—these are permanent monuments to Jefferson's appreciation of European culture.

If to secure the useful benefits of European civilization the American had to sacrifice his pride and prejudice for the sake of his country's advantage, so also, in Jefferson's view, a diplomatic policy of isolation from the quarrels of Europe had to be qualified by a realistic assessment of American national interest. No one was a more faithful disciple of Washington's gospel of nonentanglement and nonintervention in Europe's "ordinary vicissitudes" than Jefferson; and, like Washington, his purpose was to preserve his country's power to grow and to exercise its independent capacity to "choose peace or war, as our interest, guided by justice, shall counsel." If pursuit of this goal required some entanglement with Europe, then the end justified the means.

As Ambassador to France, Jefferson stressed the need for accurate and extensive knowledge of European affairs in order that American policy might better calculate the opportunities for taking advantage of the strategic weaknesses of particular European powers. For a time his sympathy with the French Revolution and his friendship for liberal aristocrats like Lafayette led him much further than the mere acquisition of information about French conditions. He entangled himself in foreign politics to the extent of drawing up for Lafayette's friends a plan for a new Charter of Rights that the King might submit to the people. To the "Patriots" of the Reform Party Jefferson played host one night, while they used his house for a discussion forum. Yet, after his disillusioning experience in America as Secretary of State, when French efforts to influence American affairs had violated Washington's Neutrality Proclamation and shocked public opinion, he wished with renewed ardor that his country might remain neutral to all nations. So deep was his dread of all foreign influence in 1797 that he confessed: "I can scarcely withhold myself from joining in the wish of Silas Deane, that there were an ocean of fire between us and the old world."[18]

Intensely fearful as he was of any involvement in European affairs, he was (unlike some latter-day disciples of the isolationist creed) ready to bridle his fears and curb America's isolation whenever aloofness from Europe seemed no longer beneficial to the national interest. If, for example, the French ever took possession of New Orleans, he envisaged the distasteful necessity of a marriage with the British fleet and nation to protect America's Western interests. During the Louisiana negotiations of 1803 he was even prepared, for all his hopes of future westward expansion, reluctantly to agree to a guarantee to France of the west bank of the Mississippi. No friend to English politics or society, he could propose to President Monroe in 1823 that, because England could do America the most harm, it was the part of wisdom to "most sedulously cherish a cordial friendship" with her, especially if she offered to help establish "the American system," barred to foreign interference. For this reason he urged Monroe to accept the English offer of a joint declaration concerning nonintervention in South America. Ultimately, it was Jefferson's conception of an "American system," with a hemisphere of its own, not his willingness to make bilateral agreements, that found reflection in the Monroe Doctrine. But his advice illuminates the nature of his limited isolationism. As a philosopher of Americanism Jefferson spoke as if his country was meant to be an Arcadian haven of refuge from a naughty world; as a practical statesman his policy of isolationism was a limited instrument for securing the positive, active goals of an expanding power.[19]

In Jefferson's imagination the conception of a menacing Old

[18] Letter to Elbridge Gerry, May 13, 1797, *The Life and Selected Writings of Thomas Jefferson*, p. 543.
[19] On the limited nature of Jefferson's isolationism, as well as Washington's, see Van Alstyne, *American Diplomacy in Action*, pp. 48–49.

World was inextricably linked to a vision of America's greatness. This deep sense of a peculiar national mission bound together his isolationism, his sympathy for the French Revolution, and his utilitarian gathering of the "honey" from European culture. His two Inaugural Addresses as President are radiant with the conviction that America is a "chosen country," like "Israel of old," destined to be an example to the world. Retired from politics at Monticello, he wrote his friend John Adams that "before the establishment of the American States, nothing was known to history but the man of the old world, crowded within limits either small or overcharged, and steeped in the vices which that situation generates." America was the world's barrier against "ignorance and barbarism," while "Old Europe" would have "to lean on our shoulders, and to hobble along by our side, under the monkish trammels of priests and kings, as she can." For him the significance of the French Revolution had been its living proof that the American example was truly "a ralliance for the reason and freedom of the globe."[20] In his intense consciousness of a fundamental cleavage between America and Europe, between "the dreams of the future" and "the history of the past," Jefferson gave lyric form to a characteristically American idea.

This Jeffersonian image was also projected by John Quincy Adams, even though his political loyalties had been formed in the Federalist tradition. Adams, even more tenaciously nationalistic and anti-European than Jefferson, exhibited that tense Americanism abroad which so often made European residence a source of such exaggerated anxiety for his countrymen. Because of his father's diplomatic services Adams had spent much of his adolescence in Europe, and no Secretary of State ever had better preparation for his job in terms of prior diplomatic experience in foreign embassies. Yet for him, as for his father, it was a trial of conscience to be separated from his homeland. He believed that an American could not live long in Europe "without losing in some measure his national character," yet his own example was

[20] Letters to John Adams, October 28, 1813, and August 1, 1816, *The Life and Selected Writings*, pp. 633, 677.

overwhelming proof that his fears were groundless. His foreign experience only increased the fervor of his attachment to his country, which he held, as he said, in "as constant veneration as that with which the most faithful disciple of Mahomet presents his face towards the tomb of his prophet."[21] As if to prove it, he named his first child George Washington, certainly ample compensation for the fact that the boy had been born in Berlin of a half-English mother.

Like Jefferson, Adams was convinced that an American in Europe "breathes an atmosphere full of the most deadly infection to his morals." At fourteen he had been smitten with an infatuation for a child-actress who performed at the Bois de Boulogne near Passy, where he was staying with Franklin and his father. For two years he was tortured with the desire to meet her ("merely to tell her how much I adored her"); but from this ungratified longing he drew the puritanical lesson of the immense moral importance of never forming an acquaintance with an actress, a rule of his life which he impressed severely upon his sons. Yet he could later candidly confess that as a young man in Europe he had acquired "a taste for the fine arts" which contributed to "much of the enjoyment" of his life.[22]

For Adams the evils of Europe were more a matter of prior American assumption than concrete experience. On his first London mission Adams quite mistakenly became convinced that Lord Grenville was laying a snare for him. As a gesture of conciliatory good will the English diplomat had introduced Adams to the privileges of court society without regard to the technical qualification that he was by title Minister Resident of the United States at the Hague in Holland, rather than a regular, resident-representative accredited to Great Britain. Interpreting this courtesy as a subtle plot, Adams obstinately insisted upon the use of his precise

[21] Letter to John Adams, July 27, 1794, *Selected Writings of John and John Quincy Adams,* p. 240.
[22] Letter to Skelton Jones, April 17, 1809, *ibid.,* pp. 265–266. Cf. letter to Francis Calley Gray, August 3, 1818, *ibid.,* p. 294; letter to Louisa Catherine Adams, August 28, 1822, *ibid.,* pp. 340–341.

title and his welcome soon deteriorated to thinly veiled hints that his usefulness there had come to an end.

This strained consciousness in the proud American abroad was noted with much curiosity by such sharp-eyed European observers as Alexis de Tocqueville. The American, he remarked, was seldom at ease in a society marked by unfamiliar class distinctions and ceremonies, but was ever fearful of being ranked either too high or too low:

He is like a man surrounded by traps: society is not a recreation for him, but a serious toil: he weighs your least actions, interrogates your looks, and scrutinizes all you say lest there should be some hidden allusion to affront him. I doubt whether there was ever a provincial man of quality so punctilious in breeding as he is: he endeavors to attend to the slightest rules of etiquette and does not allow one of them to be waived towards himself; he is full of scruples and at the same time of pretensions; he wishes to do enough, but fears to do too much, and as he does not very well know the limits of the one or of the other, he keeps up a haughty and embarrassed air of reserve.[23]

As Tocqueville observed, the American found his situation abroad complicated by the disconcerting discovery that Europeans were not so engrossed as he in the splendid destiny of the United States and the virtue of its inhabitants. Watching the assertive surge of Americans across the continent, usually with careless contempt for Indians, Mexicans, and Negroes, the Europeans might be forgiven if they failed to take American estimates of their own peculiar innocence at face value. When Adams heard that in England and France the opinion was commonly held that Americans were an ambitious, aggressive people, he was roused to anger. He told his colleagues in the Cabinet that to scotch such talk it would be necessary to familiarize the world with the idea that "our proper dominion" was the continent of North America. Ultimately, he felt, Spanish and British possessions there would be annexed to the United States, not because of any

---

[23] Alexis de Tocqueville, *Democracy in America*, Phillips Bradley, ed. (New York, Knopf, 1946), II, 173.

"spirit of encroachment or ambition," but because it was "a physical, moral and political absurdity" that these outposts of such
distant powers could permanently exist "contiguous to a great,
powerful and rapidly-growing nation."[24] His own astute policies
did much to fulfill this prophecy of continental expansion, but
the simplicity of his argument masked, even to himself, the ambitious acquisitiveness animating the spirit of "Manifest Destiny."

Pride in American nationalism and enmity to Europe often
moved Adams to a tone of truculent defiance that would seem
quaintly jingoistic in a modern statesman. It was this animus of
intellectual aggression against Europe that inspired his impas-
sioned Fourth of July Address in 1821, given from the rostrum
of the House of Representatives with the European diplomatic
corps in attendance. For their ears, as well as for the "wise and
learned philosophers of the elder world" who had poured condescending scorn on America, Adams celebrated the Declaration
of Independence—which he read with dramatic effect from the
original historic text itself—as an emblem of the Republic's unprecedented devotion to the rights of man. For Britain's cham-
pions, those "chivalrous knights of chartered liberties and the
rotten borough" and "spawners of fustian romance and lascivious
lyrics," he saved his final challenge: "GO THOU, AND DO LIKE-
WISE."[25] The British Minister, Stratford Canning, as proud and
as stubborn as Adams, wisely used the occasion for a side-trip to
Harper's Ferry, thus sparing himself the edifying spectacle of a
vigorous twisting of the lion's tail by an American Secretary of
State.

Adams was a decisive influence in making the Monroe Doctrine unilateral instead of an Anglo-American joint declaration,
but only the unofficial, unsolicited, and tacit support of English

[24] John Quincy Adams, *Memoirs*, November 16, 1819, quoted by Bemis,
John Quincy Adams, p. 367, n. 11.
[25] John Quincy Adams, *An Address Delivered at the Request of a Com-
mittee of the Citizens of Washington; on the Occasion of Reading the
Declaration of Independence, on the Fourth of July, 1821* (Washington,
Davis and Force, 1821), pp. 29–31.

policy, backed by the British fleet, gave reality to the proud claim. The Doctrine itself was no proof of potency. Adams could be confident because he knew that, in view of British resolve not to let France intervene in Spanish America, the Holy Alliance could not successfully restore Spanish dominion over the revolted colonies. These realities behind the resounding document were soon made clear to the South Americans. When Colombia sounded out Adams for an alliance to implement the principles of the Doctrine, he replied that any manifest threat of force against the new republics could be met only after prior American negotiations with European powers to obtain active cooperation in the cause of defending the hemisphere from attempts to restore foreign rule. Despite republican claims of the New World for itself, the British had the consolation of the continuation of monarchy in Brazil after its separation from Portugal. Finally, the brave sentiments of Monroe's famous message to Congress did not guarantee the fruits of continental expansion. For actual acquisition and control of the territory included in their present continental boundaries, Americans were compelled to negotiate, purchase, or fight.[26]

The complacent belief in the special virtue and primordial innocence of the United States also became increasingly illusory as the cancer of slavery and industrial conflict wracked the Republic. Ironically, Jefferson's own embargo policy of 1807, formulated in pursuit of his Arcadian dream of an agricultural America isolated from European evils, had done much to force Americans to turn to manufacturing; and continental expansion, so vigorously fostered by Adams, finally precipitated a struggle over slavery that shook the country to its foundations. By 1813 Jefferson was running looms and spindles on his own farms; and by 1842, John Quincy Adams, for ten years the "old man eloquent" of the antislavery cause in the House of Representatives, was urging his constituents to oppose the annexation of Texas for fear it would only further swell the dominion of the hateful sys-

[26] See the penetrating discussion of the Doctrine by Bemis, *op. cit.*, pp. 381, 386, 404–406 and Van Alstyne, *op. cit.*, pp. 26–29, 36–49.

tem of human bondage in America. In the innocent New World, the evils of social and economic conflict, considered indigenous to Europe, had sprung up on the sanative soil of God's American Israel.

CHAPTER

3

GROUNDS OF HOPE FOR OTHERS

AMERICANS WERE CONFIDENT that the success of their struggle for independence offered "grounds of hope for others." Less than two weeks before his death, on the fiftieth anniversary of the Declaration of Independence, Jefferson expressed with characteristic eloquence the American idea that the Fourth of July would become for all the world, "(to some parts sooner, to others later, but finally to all), the signal of arousing men to burst the chains under which monkish ignorance and superstition had persuaded them to bind themselves, and to assume the blessings and security of self-government."[1] This widely shared concept of the American example inevitably affected and complicated American attitudes towards Europe.

It was a natural impulse for Americans, despite their isolationist inhibitions, to feel sympathy for the efforts of oppressed peoples

[1] Letter to Roger C. Weightman, June 24, 1826, Adrienne Koch and William Peden, eds., *The Life and Selected Writings of Thomas Jefferson* (New York, Random House, 1944), p. 729.

to overthrow their despots. If Europeans wished to imitate the American model, this sincere flattery could hardly fail to find a warm response in the American heart. Yet an inherent tension between the stern dictates of isolationism from the contagion of Europe and a generous empathy with foreign manifestations of the revolutionary spirit often divided the American soul. This dilemma was sharpened by the fact that European revolutions easily became symbolic in the fierce domestic strife of America's internal politics. To take sides on European issues was to take sides on domestic issues, and thus images of Europe were linked with associated images of America. In time the concern with foreign revolutions seemed likely to exact only too great a price in terms of embroilment in alien problems at the expense of national unity. As the principles of the Republic lost their novelty and acquired the sanctity of tradition, while the possibility of European imitation of the American example seemed ever less imminent, the American's familiar consciousness of a gulf between the New World and the Old was intensified. The American example was to shine as an isolated beacon in a dark world.

While the delegates at Philadelphia were soberly drawing up the Constitution of the new nation, in Paris a desperate mob, intoxicated with revolutionary fervor, was storming the Bastille, hated monument to the oppressions of the Old Regime. As a symbol of the link between the American and French Revolution, there now hangs on a wall at Mount Vernon the key to the Bastille prison which Lafayette sent to his former comrade-in-arms, George Washington, through Thomas Paine, veteran agitator of two revolutions. American enthusiasm for the French Revolution reached such a peak that Bastille Day became a holiday in this country.

When citizens of the United States looked upon the stirring events in France as a reflection of their own radiant example of the light of liberty, they reciprocated the feelings of most French liberals. Condorcet, one of the greatest philosophers of the Enlightenment, spoke for them all when he wrote of the new discovery of the "title-deeds" of the human race:

But it is not sufficient that these deeds be written in the books of philosophers and in the hearts of virtuous men. It must be possible for the ignorant or feeble man to read them in the example of a great people. America has given us that example. The state paper which declared their independence is a simple and sublime exposition of rights so sacred and so long forgotten. In no nation have they been so well known nor preserved with such perfect integrity.[2]

Through the efforts of Benjamin Franklin the state constitutions of America had been officially published and widely read in France, and the political ideas of both Franklin and John Adams had been discussed in the French National Assembly itself. When the beloved Dr. Franklin died in 1790, the Assembly displayed its piety for America by voting to wear mourning for three days. When Lafayette sought advice for the Declaration of the Rights of Man, provisional text for the famous document adopted by the Assembly in August, 1789, he naturally turned to Jefferson; and the American proudly wrote his friend Madison that among the liberal nobles of the Patriot group, who had met under Jefferson's own roof, the American example had been "treated like that of the Bible, open to explanation but not to question."[3] In historical fact, when the French set up their new political institutions, the American Constitution was severely questioned. Centralization of power in a single assembly, necessary to overturn a feudal order scarcely existent in America, was the favorite device of French liberals, as it was the favorite horror of Jefferson and John

[2] Quoted from Condorcet's *Influence de la Révolution de l'Amérique sur l'Europe* by Lewis Rosenthal, *America and France: The Influence of the United States on France in the Eighteenth Century* (New York, Henry Holt, 1882), p. 144. For Franco-American relations in this period see also Howard Mumford Jones, *America and French Culture 1750–1848* (Chapel Hill, University of North Carolina Press, 1927), 245–290, 500–568; Charles Downer Hazen, *Contemporary American Opinion of the French Revolution*, Johns Hopkins University Studies in History and Political Science, extra vol. XVI (Baltimore, Johns Hopkins University Press, 1897); and Bernard Faÿ, *The Revolutionary Spirit in France and America*, translated by Ramon Guthrie (New York, Harcourt, Brace, 1927).

[3] Letter to James Madison, August 28, 1789, quoted by Dumas Malone, *Jefferson and the Rights of Man* (Boston, Little Brown, 1951), p. 231.

Adams. But the mutual feeling that the two revolutions were related by blood ties soared above fact to the level of a sublime myth.

In its early stages the French Revolution was more popular with Americans as a whole than the American Revolution had ever been until it was over. Late in 1792, after the abolition of the monarchy and the creation of the first French Republic, public enthusiasm for the French cause became widespread. As news of French victories against the Austrians and Prussians filtered to America, celebratory feasts and processions were held throughout the United States. At Faneuil Hall in staid Boston Sam Adams, hero of the American Revolution, presided over a typical banquet in the middle of the winter of 1793 in which mass fervor for Liberty and Equality, mingled with a voracious appetite for food and liquor, so moved the people that in an ecstasy of civic good will the city's criminals were liberated from prison for a day. When Citizen Genêt, minister of the new Republic to the United States, arrived in the spring of that year, seeking American aid, he was greeted with elaborate enthusiasm, and his journey from Charleston was so studded with fetes and ovations that it took him twenty-eight days to reach Philadelphia.

But by the time of Genêt's mission the Revolution had begun to divide American opinion, already splitting into the factions which later became the basis of the Federalist-Republican party antagonism. Secretary of State Jefferson and Secretary of the Treasury Hamilton were assuming their roles as symbols of the liberal-conservative polarity in domestic politics. Jefferson's successor as Ambassador to France was a portent that there would be no unanimity about the Revolution. Gouverneur Morris, stylist of the American Constitution and conservative defender of the rights of property, was at first convinced that generosity, gratitude, and interest joined together to give the United States a stake in the success of the French Revolution. But stumping about the salons of Paris on his wooden leg, recording in his diary the conquests he had made of aristocratic ladies who lived by a code of sexual conduct delightfully un-American, Morris concluded that

France was in "an utter Prostration of Morals," having reached a "Degree of Depravity" difficult to convey to "an American Mind."[4] These materials were a poor "Edifice of Freedom." Hostile, like a true conservative, to political theorizing about the rights of man, he was certain that in France, at least, "Distinctions of Order" were necessary. "Our American Example has done them good," he judged; "but like all Novelties, Liberty runs away with their Discretion, if they have any." He added shrewdly, if not quite accurately, "They want an American Constitution with the exception of a King instead of the President, without reflecting that they have not American Citizens to support that Constitution."[5]

Morris could divide the world in two. What made sense in America was folly in France; what was vice in America was pleasure in France. On these principles he asked for a lock of the Queen's hair, made his house a refuge for aristocrats wanted by the revolutionary Committee of Public Safety, advised the King on modes of escape, and acted as trustee for the fleeing monarch's funds. With his extraordinary blend of American Federalism and French Royalism, he seems an exotic bloom unaccountably sprung from American soil, but his distrust of leveling theories and his abhorrence of violent revolutions were qualities well-appreciated in America. The execution of the King early in 1793 and the ensuing Reign of Terror under Jacobin rule began the process of American disenchantment with the Revolution, and disillusionment would have come even faster if it had not been for the entanglement of the issue in American politics.

Jefferson's case was symptomatic. While in France he had been a most cautious sympathizer with the enemies of the old regime. The Charter of Rights he proposed to Lafayette in June, 1789, did not even provide for equality of rights between the two priv-

[4] Letter to General Washington, April 29, 1789, Beatrix Carey Davenport, ed., *A Diary of the French Revolution*, I (Boston, Houghton Mifflin, 1939), 61. For a biography of Morris see Daniel Walther, *Gouverneur Morris: Witness of Two Revolutions*, translated by Elinore Denniston (New York, Funk and Wagnalls, 1934).

[5] Letter to William Carmichael, July 4, 1789, *ibid.*, p. 136. Cf. his diary notation recording his opposition to Jefferson, June 12, 1789, *ibid.*, p. 113.

ileged groups, the nobles and clergy, and the bourgeoisie. More conservative than leaders of the National Assembly, he urged them to woo freedom gradually by imitating not the American example, but the English constitution. Concerned with the political and legal problems of reform rather than with the economic or social issues, so much more pressing in France than in America, he tempered all his advice by his practical sense of how much liberty he thought the French "able to bear, soberly and usefully to themselves."[6] In one of his last official communications to the American government from Paris he expressed his confidence that probably no blood would be spilled in the Revolution, but if it was shed, the moderate royalists and moderate republicans would carry the day.

Back in America his fears of domestic reaction, led by the Hamiltonian Federalists, shaped his view of the Revolution in France. "I feel," he wrote a friend in August, 1791, "that the permanence of our own leans in some degree on that; and that a failure there would be a powerful argument to prove there would be a failure here."[7] In his anguish for the purity of the American example (menaced by a Hamiltonian fondness for merchants and capitalists) Jefferson deluded himself into believing that the Jacobins of France were the Republican patriots he had known in Paris. Distance not only lent enchantment to the revolutionaries; it dulled his conscience to their violence, injustice, and ruthlessness. "It was necessary to use the arm of the people, a machine not quite so blind as balls and bombs, but blind to a certain degree," he wrote early in 1793.[8]

For Jefferson, as for his supporters, the conflict of forces in the

[6] Letter to General Lafayette, February 14, 1815, Gilbert Chinard, ed., *The Letters of Lafayette and Jefferson*, Johns Hopkins Studies in International Thought (Baltimore, Johns Hopkins University Press, 1929), p. 368. He admitted that the French were, in advance of his own advice, able to "bear" the Constitution of 1791.

[7] Letter to Edward Rutledge, August 25, 1791, quoted by Gilbert Chinard, *Thomas Jefferson, the Apostle of Americanism* (Boston, Little, Brown, 1929), p. 282. Chinard clearly highlights the contrast between Jefferson's rhetoric and his cautious action.

[8] Letter to William Short, January 3, 1793, *The Life and Selected Writings of Thomas Jefferson*, p. 522.

French Revolution was a symbolic touchstone of American issues. Saturated in the native atmosphere of a society without deep feudal roots or a desperate proletarian populace, he lifted the Revolution out of its European habitat and domesticated it for American usage. Democratic Societies sprang up to link friendship with France and enmity to England with the Republican virtues of decentralized government, the interests of farmers, mechanics, immigrants, and small businessmen, and the right of free navigation of the Mississippi to Westerners. Opposing them, proponents of strong centralized government, merchants, shipowners, the established clergy, and conservative lawyers rallied their forces to cry up the virtues of England against the fearful anarchism of American Jacobins. Newspapers and theaters joined the partisan struggle with enormous enthusiasm.

Amidst all the excitement neither side recognized the fundamental ludicrousness of this sentimental re-enactment of the French Revolution in a society where the conservatives had no aristocracy to defend and the liberals no rabble to incite. Viewing their own conflicts through the distorting image of France, Americans indulged in the wildest suspicious surmise about their party opponents. Jeffersonian propagandists were convinced that every Federalist yearned for monarchy and English domination, while Federalist propagandists detected subversive revolutionaries everywhere. By a chain of crude links, forged on the principle of guilt by association, hyper-Federalists connected the secular philosophers of the Enlightenment with a general conspiracy against thrones and altars, allegedly instigated by a Bavarian anticlerical organization called "The Illuminati," which was supposed to have its insidious offshoots in the Masons, the Jacobins, and the Democratic Societies.

For defenders of the established churches in New England, which had survived the movement for separation of church and state, the fierce anticlericalism of the French revolutionaries was reincarnated in the mild Deism of Jefferson. The staunch Connecticut Federalist, Theodore Dwight, showed how political use of this issue could be made in a Fourth of July Address at Hartford in 1798. Dwight was not sure who belonged to the dread Illuminati in the United States, but if he were to make proselytes to Illuminatism, he would "in the first place apply to Thomas Jefferson, Albert Gallatin, and their political associates."[9] After Republican victory at the polls in 1800 the growing extremism of the hyper-Federalists disgraced their cause. By their opposition to "Mr. Madison's War" with England, courting treason in aborted plans for secession, while nursing their grievances against a Republican policy that had badly hurt the commerce of New England with Europe, they committed political suicide in an increasingly bitter indulgence of antidemocratic rhetoric.

For their part the Republicans gradually lost their naïve identification with the revolutionaries. Citizen Genêt's efforts to use American ports for condemning British ships as prizes, to fit out privateers against France's enemies, and to enlist Americans for military expeditions against Spanish and British territory on the North American continent threatened to involve the young Republic in Europe's quarrels. Even before presenting his credentials to Washington he had commissioned privateers and granted military commissions in preparation for an expedition of Kentuckians to capture New Orleans and Louisiana from Spain. When he aimed to intervene in American elections and threatened to appeal to the people over the heads of the government, Genêt's giddy public welcome was transformed into a frigid reception by Washington's administration. Even Jefferson was alarmed and irritated by this brazen interference with American sovereignty.

When enthusiasm for the effect of the American example abroad conflicted with the desire to keep the beacon of liberty isolated from European darkness, there was no doubt what the choice of responsible American leaders would be. Washington's Neutrality Proclamation of 1793 was the result. Popular sympathy

---

[9] Quoted by Vernon Stauffer, *New England and the Bavarian Illuminati*, Columbia University Studies in History, Economics, and Public Law, LXXXII, no. 1 (New York, Columbia University Press, 1918), 253. For the partisan struggle over the French Revolution see also Charles Warren, *Jacobin and Junto* (Cambridge, Harvard University Press, 1931) and Eugene Perry Link, *Democratic-Republican Societies, 1790–1800* (New York, Columbia University Press, 1941), as well as Hazen, *op. cit.*

for the Revolution, stimulated by the Republicans in their opposition to the Federalists, persisted; but as the events in France seemed destined to culminate in a harsh dictatorship, and while intrigues of French officials in American affairs continued, the pro-French faction dwindled. Increasingly the Revolutionary Republic looked strange to American eyes. Their humanitarian feelings and a reverence for the law were shocked at the execution of the King and the savage ruthlessness of the Terror. Their respect for religion was offended by the crude anti-Christian polemics of the French rationalists. Their commercial interests were damaged by the depredations of France's privateers. Talleyrand's arrogant attempt to intimidate an official American mission to France into granting a loan to the Republic (and a bribe to himself and the dictatorial clique of the Directory) was humiliating even to the most ardently pro-French Republicans. By 1800, realizing that the Revolution had ended in the military dictatorship of Napoleon, Jefferson was moved to anguished lament: *"I have never seen so awful a moment as the present."* He never lost his faith that "the American example had kindled feelings of right in the people."[10] But he had, like so many of his countrymen, deepened his pessimism about the possibilities of imminent reform in the feudalized and urbanized precincts of Europe.

Even with respect to the American half of the globe the policy of the United States was extremely wary of any commitments to revolutionary forces challenging the rule of European empires. The revolts in Spanish America provided a clear illustration of this caution. From his retirement in the mellow atmosphere of Monticello Jefferson wrote John Adams that one day "rank, and birth, and tinsel-aristocracy will finally shrink into insignificance, even there." But he added with characteristic caution: "This, however, we have no right to meddle with."[11] In 1811 the American government meddled to the extent of making appropriations for provisions of relief to Venezuela, but they arrived too late,

[10] Letter to Dr. William Bache, February 2, 1800, *The Life and Selected Writings of Thomas Jefferson,* p. 556; letter to John Adams, October 28, 1813, *ibid.,* p. 634.
[11] *Loc. cit.*

the revolutionary regime having collapsed, and the royalists intercepted the aid. After the war with England, Speaker of the House Henry Clay, voice of the West, traditionally hostile to Spain, took up the cause of the South American struggle for liberty. He had to contend with strong currents of public opinion, especially in New England, that looked upon the South Americans as hopelessly alien, schooled in feudal religion and politics, their energies sapped by a tropical climate into indulgent effeminacy, their characters debased by an obsession with the precious metals of their mines.

This southern corner of the New World was for Americans a remnant of the Old. The "American Hemisphere" was as yet only a quartersphere. Jefferson, an early advocate of the idea of a Pan-American system of republicanism isolated from Europe, was depressed by what he felt were the difficulties of illuminating the priest-ridden darkness of South America with the light of the United States. The doubts of John Quincy Adams were even more deeply rooted. Liberals in Europe and South America, as well as in the United States, might dream of an American system, with a hemisphere of its own, established on different principles from those of Europe; but Adams vigorously objected in 1820: "As to an American System, we have it; we constitute the whole of it; there is no community of interests or of principles between North and South America."[12]

The gap between Clay and Adams was not as wide as either imagined. Clay's farewell speech at Lexington, Kentucky, in 1821, on the occasion of his brief retirement from politics, urged that "a sort of counterpoise to the holy alliance" be formed in the two Americas "to operate by the force of example."[13] But he was arguing mainly for recognition of the republics and his concept

[12] Letter to President Monroe, September 19, 1820, quoted by Samuel Flagg Bemis, *John Quincy Adams and the Foundations of American Foreign Policy* (New York, Knopf, 1949), p. 366.

[13] Speech at Lexington, May 19, 1821, quoted by Arthur Preston Whitaker, *The United States and the Independence of Latin America, 1800–1830* (Baltimore, Johns Hopkins University Press, 1941), p. 345. For relations with Latin America see also Whitaker, *The Western Hemisphere Idea: Its Rise and Decline* (Ithaca, Cornell University Press, 1954).

of American aid did not include armed force. Secretary of State Adams, having by his own negotiations safely annexed the Floridas to the United States and wiped out Spanish claims to Oregon territory, was himself ready to move towards recognition, which would not now antagonize Europe or threaten embroilment in wars that might once again bitterly divide American opinion. But in his fiery Fourth of July Address in Washington, shortly after Clay's Lexington speech, he was anxious to tie recognition to neutrality and pin down the precise meaning of the American example. With all the fervor of his Puritan ancestors Adams saw America as "a city upon a hill," which might ultimately regenerate the world by the saving luster of its own purity. But this messianic spirit was paradoxically mingled with an equally intense and rigid devotion to isolationism. America's heart, benedictions, and prayers, he asserted, would always be with those who unfurled the standard of freedom and independence, but "she does not go abroad in search of monsters to destroy." Much as it might be imitated, the American example of 1776 could never be repeated: "It stands, and must for ever stand, alone, a beacon on the summit of the mountains, to which all the inhabitants of the earth may turn their eyes for a genial and saving light till time shall be lost in eternity, and this globe itself dissolves, nor leave a wreck behind." Pithily, Adams defined the narrow significance of the American example: "She is the well-wisher to the freedom and independence of all. She is the champion and vindicator only of her own."[14]

During the negotiations and discussions which led to Monroe's Doctrine, Adams had the consolation of toning down the missionary tenor of Monroe's original draft. The final document omitted both a rebuke to France for her invasion of Spain to quell the republicans there, as well as a broad recognition of the independence of the Greeks from their Turkish oppressors.

[14] *An Address Delivered at the Request of a Committee of the Citizens of Washington; on the Occasion of Reading the Declaration of Independence, on the Fourth of July, 1821* (Washington, Davis and Force, 1821), pp. 22, 29. For the full context of the speech see Bemis, *op. cit.*, pp. 355–362. For Adams's role in the Monroe Doctrine see *ibid.*, pp. 363–408.

To Adams these were alien issues likely only to entangle the United States in European passions. If he had modified his isolationism to the extent of championing, at least by declaration, the independence of the southern half of the hemisphere, he had never compromised the fundamental distinction between the New World and the Old. These remained separated by a yawning abyss. Congress, after inconclusive debate, tacitly went along with Adams and Monroe. In the Senate there was not even a debate. Without specific Congressional endorsement or modification the Monroe Doctrine passed into history to the general applause of most Americans.

Belief in the redemptive influence of the American example persisted throughout the nineteenth century as a host of insurgents inspired in Americans the hope that revolutions would bring republicanism to monarchical Europe; but as they watched with anxious sympathy the repeated failures of these revolts, citizens of the New World gradually became skeptical and disillusioned. The Greek Revolution, for example, enlisted the ardor and funds of respectable merchants and clergymen, as well as the more romantic enthusiasm of college students and classical scholars, like Harvard's Professor of Greek, Edward Everett. Mass meetings held throughout the country in 1824 raised money for the rebels fighting the Turks, who were widely condemned in America as barbarian infidels. Prominent American statesmen, like Monroe, Calhoun, Webster, and Clay, were warm advocates of the Greek cause. "From Maine to Georgia, from the Atlantic to the Gulf of Mexico," as Clay orated, sentiment for the embattled Greeks, who made a point of describing their efforts as an imitation of the American example of 1776, "blazed with the rapidity of electricity."[15]

After 1848, however, the Yankee caution of John Quincy Adams had become a general mood. With the French Revolution

[15] Quoted by Myrtle A. Cline, *American Attitudes toward the Greek War of Independence, 1821–1828* (dissertation, Atlanta, 1930), p. 195. See also Stephen A. Larrabee, *Hellas Observed: The American Experience of Greece 1775–1865* (New York, New York University Press, 1957) for cultural relations with Greece.

of that year setting off a general European conflagration, American sympathy was inhibited by fears and vexed by politics. Statesmen, sensitive to the ethnic diversity and internal conflicts of the United States, were hard pressed to take positions that did not alienate significant groups of voters. Slavery was already a deeply divisive issue, insinuating itself into any discussion of liberty, whether European or American. Swelled with immigrants from Ireland and Germany, the country could not be either indifferent or consistent, with respect to European developments. If German-Americans did not balk at the idea of joining England to quell oppressors of their homeland, Irish-Americans did. New England abolitionists could feel as enthusiastic about liberating Rome from the Papacy as they did about freeing the slaves; but Southerners and Catholics had their reasons for curbing sentiments which threatened revered institutions.

To most Americans the new prominence in European revolutions of socialistic radicalism, supported by an urban proletariat, was ominous and strange, troubling their easy confidence that a Washington, an Adams, or a Jefferson could also be bred on foreign soil. Europe, classically illustrated in the case of France, seemed to be caught in an un-American cycle of revolt, dictatorship, and restoration. When news of the French Revolution of 1848 reached America public enthusiasm was qualified by the caution of leading statesmen, like Calhoun, Webster, and Clay. Americans had accepted the July Monarchy of Louis Philippe in 1830 largely because their hero Lafayette had supported him. But what would the new change ultimately bring? Though the Second Republic had been speedily recognized by the State Department, Congressional congratulation was delayed by the debate caused by the North's stress on the new French policy of eliminating slavery in the colonies. The doubts of leading officials in the stability of the Republic were reflected in their conspicuous absence from the public celebration in Washington.

This relative coolness was reciprocated by the French Assembly itself. In its debates on the new constitution liberals were lukewarm, radicals skeptical, and socialists hostile to the frequent citation of the American example. Only the supporters of Louis Philippe, the high bourgeoisie, were ardently pro-American, finding their conservative interests best served by an appeal to the economic individualism and complexly-balanced system of political powers prevailing in the United States. The American Minister to France, Richard Rush, who took the initiative in recognizing the Republic, defended the American bicameral, federal system to influential Frenchmen, but when he saw the new constitution "with but one Chamber, and other anomalies to an American," he despaired of "any encouraging prospects of its durability."[16] The gulf between the New World and the Old was being dug from both sides.

In Germany, the Frankfort Parliament of 1848 seemed at first about to profit from the American example. President Polk, in answer to a German request, sent an American naval officer, empowered to join any new national navy that should be established, and in addition the facilities of the Brooklyn Navy Yard were offered for the equipping of an ex-mail packet purchased from the United States by Germans. Hopefully, an American mission was established at Frankfort. But when the Whig Party, committed to caution in international affairs, came into office the next year the Frankfort mission was recalled and the navy yard closed to German use. For his part, the naval officer sent to Germany had soon concluded that a federal union and a navy were both unlikely to materialize. When the German Assembly, conscious of its weakness, finally offered the executive office to the Prussian king, who would have the title of Emperor, American disappointment was bitter. One of America's roving diplomats, special agent to Germany, expressed a common disillusion in his belief that by

[16] *Occasional Productions, Political, Diplomatic, and Miscellaneous etc.*, ed., his executors (Philadelphia, J. B. Lippincott, 1860), p. 491. For American reactions to French Revolutions after 1789 see Eugene N. Curtis, "American Opinion of the French Nineteenth Century Revolutions," *American Historical Review*, 29 (January, 1924), 249–270, and his *The French Assembly of 1848 and American Constitutional Doctrines*, Columbia University Studies in History, Economics, and Public Law, LXXIX, no. 2 (New York, Columbia University Press, 1918); and Elizabeth Brett White, *American Opinion of France from Lafayette to Poincaré* (New York, Knopf, 1927).

this act the German legislators had shown themselves "utterly unworthy of the sympathies of a people so free as those in America."[17] With the Prussian army moving into the Rhineland it became clear that the American dream of a federal parliament for Germany erected on a popular basis was doomed to frustration.

Hope shifted to Hungary where the Magyars' revolt against Austrian oppression seemed to make them "the Americans of Europe," led by their General Washington, Louis Kossuth. Sympathy for the Hungarians was intensified as a kind of compensation for American disenchantment with the "wretched specimens" of republicanism in France and Germany, excoriated in one important journal as "a compound of socialism, agrarianism, anarchy and infidelity."[18] Russian intervention soon crushed the rebellion, and Kossuth began his campaign to enlist American aid. From his exile in Turkey he was brought to America in 1851 with the blessings of Congress on a vessel officially provided by the government of the United States. Met in the large cities with a warmth of public welcome that no foreigner since Lafayette had received, Kossuth nourished hopes that the election of 1852 would bring to power a candidate committed to enlist American power in the cause of Hungarian independence. In sober reality Kossuth discovered that public opinion was far from unanimous in supporting him, that he and his cause were political symbols to be manipulated in the great game of American politics, and that responsible officials dreaded any involvement with European affairs.

In the Northwest, with its German immigrants, and in New England, with its reformers and abolitionists, Kossuth was embraced with all the ardor even he could wish for, but in the South he encountered a chilling lack of enthusiasm. In Washington President Fillmore made it plain that his government had no intention of abandoning the tradition of nonintervention. Though Daniel Webster boasted in a grandiloquent note to the Austrian

[17] Quoted by Arthur James May, *Contemporary American Opinion of the Mid-Century Revolutions in Central Europe* (Philadelphia, University of Pennsylvania, 1927), p. 19.
[18] *New York Journal of Commerce*, July 21, 1849, p. 4, col. 1.

chargé d'affaires that "the prevalence on the other continent of sentiments favorable to republican liberty is the result of the reaction of America upon Europe" and drank a toast at a dinner for Kossuth to "an American model on the lower Danube," his pious sentiments were more related to domestic politics than to events in Europe.[19] For Webster, rhetorical support of European liberalism had conservative uses in the United States. His ties to New England manufacturing interests and his defense of the Fugitive Slave Law of 1850 had made him "Black Dan" to many men of principle; a touch of idealism was helpful to any presidential aspirant. To pluck the chords of national pride at a time of internal discord over slavery might also serve to keep the Union in harmony.

A few senators supported Kossuth to the point of urging a break of diplomatic relations with Austria, but in a divided Congress and country the caution of Henry Clay, no longer a young "War-Hawk," was a truer resolution of the forces disturbing the American mind. From his sickbed the venerable legislator told the Hungarian patriot that the failure of the French Revolution and the *coup d'état* of Napoleon the Third "teach us to despair of any present success for liberal institutions in Europe." America must look to herself for the preservation of the holy fire of freedom. "Far better it is for ourselves, for Hungary, and for the course of liberty," he said, "that . . . we should keep our lamp burning brightly on this western shore as a light to all nations, than to hazard its utter extinction amid the ruins of fallen or falling republics in Europe."[20]

A different kind of despair weighed down intellectual libertarians in America. To the disillusionment of a Samuel Gridley Howe or a Margaret Fuller the sobriety of Clay seemed increasingly to pervade the highest councils of government. Howe, philanthropist

[19] See Merle Curti, *Austria and the United States 1848–1852*, Smith College Studies in History, XI, no. 3 (April, 1926), 141–206 and "The Impact of the Revolutions of 1848 on American Thought," in Edward N. Saveth, ed., *Understanding the American Past* (Boston, Little, Brown, 1954), p. 250.
[20] Calvin Colton, *The Last Seven Years of the Life of Henry Clay* (New York, A. S. Barnes, 1856), pp. 223–224.

and abolitionist, was a veteran of liberal campaigns in the "vile old Babylon of Europe." He had fought with the Greeks against the Turks, cheered the July Revolution of 1830 in Paris, and spent a month in a Berlin jail as a suspected spy because of his services in bringing American aid to Polish refugees along the Vistula. Inevitably, he was an enthusiast for Kossuth. Sadly, Howe saw his hero spurn the efforts of abolitionists to entangle him in their cause, while the government smiled as little on Kossuth's attempts to influence American affairs as it had on the more brazen activities of Citizen Genêt. When pressed, Howe himself admitted that Kossuth's demands could not at the time be granted. Even in the name of human brotherhood the partisans of Hungarian independence would not rightfully plunge the United States into dubious battle with Russia. But (like many others over a hundred years later who witnessed the brutal Russian repression of another Hungarian revolution) he was shocked at the passivity of democratic powers. The self-imposed renunciation of all pressure on Austria or Russia would, he feared, encourage the despots in their ambition to "cut the throat of every liberal in Europe."[21]

In Rome Margaret Fuller, Boston bluestocking, feminist, and correspondent for the *New York Tribune*, shared Howe's feelings. The first stirrings of revolt in Italy convinced her that reform had to be based on popular institutions, not on "an old ivy-covered church long since undermined, corroded by time and gnawed by vermin." To resume her ancient glory Rome had to give up "all this gorgeous mummery," whose artistic charms she well appreciated, but "whose meaning is all of the past, and finds no echo in the future." The struggle for the Roman Republic in 1848 inspired her to believe that "the cry of the American eagle" was more vivid in Italy than in the United States. Celebrating Washington's birthday in Rome with two American friends, she was struck with a fresh awe at the glory of the American Revolution and its heroes. That spirit which alone made her coun-

[21] Letter to Charles Sumner, January 7, 1853, Laura E. Richards, ed., *Letters and Journals of Samuel Gridley Howe*, II (Boston, Dana Estes, 1906), 386.

try and its future valuable in her eyes seemed to her to have fled America, darkened by slavery and the Mexican War, to Italy. "My country," she wrote indignantly on the anniversary of the Battle of Lexington and Concord, "is at present spoiled by prosperity, stupid with the lust of gain, soiled by crime in its willing perpetuation of slavery, shamed by an unjust war, noble sentiment much forgotten even by individuals, the aims of politicians selfish or petty, the literature frivolous and venal."[22] In Rome she gave her life courageous dignity by consecrating herself to the cause of the Republic. Working in a hospital to care for the wounded, calmly awaiting Austrian bombardment of the city, which most Americans had fled, she married the Marquis Ossoli, republican Captain of the Civic Guard, and wrote a history of the Revolution. Though it perished with her and her family in a tragic shipwreck on her return voyage, her restless, ardent spirit found its home in the cause of Italian liberalism.

In America, meanwhile, a cautious government, much to Margaret Fuller's disgust, delayed recognition of the Roman Republic out of doubts of its survival and solicitude for Catholic feelings. The cause of Hungarian independence was also left to fend for itself. On July 14, 1852, Kossuth departed the United States under an assumed name, having raised nearly a hundred thousand dollars from private citizens, most of it according to his own accounting, spent on his fabulous tour. He left behind him a town in Wisconsin and a county in Iowa named in his honor. Some Hungarian refugees, in the expectation of getting free land from the government, settled a New Buda in hospitable Iowa, but the aid never came. When the Hungarian leader left the country, the relief of the Administration was as palpable as the sorrow of the liberals.

Unhappily, events in Europe justified official fears rather than liberal hopes. Reaction triumphed all over Europe. Increasingly,

---

[22] Letters 17 and 24, October 18, 1847 and April 19, 1848, Arthur B. Fuller, ed., *At Home and Abroad, or Things and Thoughts in America and Europe,* 3d ed. (Boston, Crosby, Nichols, 1856), pp. 243, 326–327. There were nearly 900 Americans in Rome during this period, according to Howard R. Marraro, "American Travellers in Rome, 1848–50," *Catholic Historical Review,* 29 (January, 1944), 470–509.

support for interventionist opinion in America came from irresponsibles, like the fantastic George N. Sanders. This brash Kentuckian, agent for capitalistic enterprises and promoter of revolutions, was the firebrand of the "Young America" political faction which had hopes of making Stephen A. Douglas and the Democratic Party the voice of a missionary ardor for the spread of American liberty in Europe to the ultimate benefit of American trade. Having induced a steamship magnate to purchase antiquated muskets from the government, Sanders set out for Paris. Although cheered by popular ovation in the city's streets, he arrived too late to make a deal with the revolutionaries of '48 before they were defeated. Back in America he toyed with a plan of providing Kossuth with armed merchant ships. An adept schemer, Sanders managed to wrangle himself an appointment as consul to London in June, 1853. Soon he was presiding at dinner over a meeting of nearly all the leading exiled revolutionaries of Europe—Kossuth, Garibaldi, Ledru-Rollin, Mazzini, and Herzen. (It was on this extraordinary occasion that the American Minister, Buchanan, asked his hostess if she had any fears of an explosion from the presence of so much combustible material.) The consul soon proved inflammatory enough even for "Young America." Learning that he had sent the exiles' dispatches to the continent in American diplomatic pouches and had used the columns of the London *Times* to advise the assassination of Louis Napoleon, Congress understandably failed to confirm his appointment. The temper of the country, if not that of Sanders and his friends, had considerably sobered since 1848.[23]

Official American reaction to the struggles of Spanish Republicans in 1868 was tempered with the new restraint. Senator Charles Summer, who had just successfully sponsored joint resolutions of sympathy with Crete in its troubles with the Turks, followed up this vague gesture with a more specific proposal for extending American sympathy to Spanish liberals, urging the formation of democratic institutions, and advising the elimination of

[23] See Merle Curti, " 'Young America,' " *American Historical Review*, 32 (October, 1926), 34–55 and "George N. Sanders—American Patriot of the Fifties," *South Atlantic Quarterly*, 27 (1928), 79–87.

slavery throughout the empire. Secretary of State Seward was anxious to restrict official recognition to governments which had been legally and overtly approved by their people. The dust had not yet settled in Cuba; therefore he would refuse premature recognition. The Senate Foreign Relations Committee cooperated with Seward by dropping the resolution. Certainly there was not sufficient interest in the Congress to keep the issue alive, and it expired quietly.[24]

Though reformers, like Horace Greeley and Elizabeth Cady Stanton, saluted Spanish Republicanism with traditional American optimism, there were skeptical voices even in liberal circles. E. L. Godkin, editor of the liberal *Nation*, followed the Spanish conflict attentively in his columns, but he was astutely critical of the naïve belief that the American example and American advice were directly relevant to the Spanish situation. National habits, character, and prejudices, not propaganda from foreign countries, he pointed out, do most of the work in shaping national destinies; Americans had enough to do in putting their own house in order. Its condition, he tartly reminded his readers, was a rather embarrassing reflection on American competence to lecture others on the felicities of republican virtue.[25]

Godkin's rebuke was understandable. America's own house was then messily disarranged by the recent impeachment proceedings against President Johnson, the manipulations of Gould and Fiske in seeking to corner the gold market, the violence of the Ku Klux Klan, the plunderings of New York's municipal treasury by the infamous Tweed Ring, and the bribing of Administration officials with stock in the dishonest Credit Mobilier corporation. In the harsh crude light of the Gilded Age the American example had a tawdry look. American zeal for European imitation of the Re-

[24] See Julius Goebel, Jr., "The Recognition Policy of the United States," *Columbia Studies in History, Economics, and Public Law*, 66 (1915), 199–203.

[25] "The Spanish Revolution," *Nation*, 7 (December 17, 1868), 496–498. For an old-fashioned libertarian salute to the Spanish Republicans see "Address of American Citizens to the Spanish Government and People," *Historical Magazine*, Second Series, 5 (March, 1869), 188–189.

public had never been easily embarrassed, but its fervor was at least diminished by the pressure of domestic difficulties.

Godkin ironically noted that most of the propagandist advice to Spain came from the French, "who as republicans have proved the greatest failures of modern times." By 1870 this judgment was widely shared. American recognition of France's Third Republic in 1870 produced no public demonstrations. The Franco-Prussian War had divided American sympathies (largely because of French hostility to the North in the Civil War), and Congress had voted for a relief ship to give impartial aid to both sides. The organization of Paris by the socialist and anarchist radicals of the Commune in 1871 aroused American fears of a revolutionary spirit alien to their own. Even traditionally pro-French newspapers lost their enthusiasm for what the *Providence Journal* called "this irrepressible passion for insurrection and for street barricades."

To Americans there seemed to be no solution to France's problems because the American model had no natural setting there. "The spirit of '76" could not cross the Atlantic. French radicals seemed to be intoxicated by a peculiarly European vintage. "They gave themselves up to their appetites," moralized the *Richmond Dispatch*, "philosophized (as they called it) away everything that restrained them, abolished God, Christianity, Home, and the Family institution, custom, law, everything."[26] As bloody civil war broke out between the Commune and the Assembly, the American Minister, Elihu Washburne, courageously sticking to his post in besieged Paris, witnessed in horror the reign of the Commune, which he later described as "the absolute force of desperate and wicked men, unlimited, unchecked and unrestrained by any human power."[27] The defeat of the Communards and the stability of the Third Republic did not restore American confidence in the future of liberty on European shores. Visiting the Old World in 1873, the editor of the *Baltimore American* summed

[26] Both newspaper items are quoted by White, *American Opinion of France*, p. 209.

[27] *Recollections of a Minister to France 1869–1877*, II (New York, Scribner's, 1899), 192.

up his widely reprinted impressions of his tour: " 'Liberty, fraternity, and equality' are unmeaning words in most European countries, and are merely used to gull the ignorant and to cover up the designs of ambitious masters."[28]

Unable to fathom a social order and a pattern of revolution so different from their own, Americans experienced a double alienation from Europe. To the old regime they were hostile by national self-definition. In the course of the nineteenth century they lost much of their spontaneous enthusiasm for the revolutionary forces challenging that order. When the American Minister to France in 1881 drove the first rivet into the Statue of Liberty, the gift of the French people to America, the solidarity of the two nations was widely toasted as symbolically established. But the monument had a deeper symbolism: the site, base, and pedestal of the Goddess of Liberty were supplied by the Americans. In thinking about freedom abroad they seriously doubted if the foundations of freedom existed anywhere but in the harbor of the New World.

The American attitude towards European revolutions was puzzling. It was the national pride and premise that Europe was simply defined as feudal oppression; yet the idea of the American example necessarily implied a more complex Europe which included the liberal forces for whom the example was supposed to be relevant. But if America was in truth a New World with an already liberalized society as a setting for its Revolution, then its direct relevance could not be realistically insisted upon—as Jefferson and Adams shrewdly understood. But why then should Americans condemn European liberals for radicalism in their struggle with more oppressive enemies than any Americans had ever known? If this response seems unfair, it smacked of smugness to elevate a prudent isolationism into a higher righteousness that preserved the American dream as an example for others only on

[28] Charles Carroll Fulton, *Europe Viewed Through American Spectacles* (Philadelphia, Lippincott, 1874), p. 309. American travelers in France from 1830 to 1860 ran through the same cycle of hope and disenchantment, increasing after 1848. See Robert C. L. Scott's dissertation (unpublished) *American Travelers in France, 1830–1860, a Study of Some American Ideas Against a European Background* (Yale, 1940).

the condition that it remain in actuality an exclusively American possession. The tactic was too convenient to resist: it neatly resolved the conflict of the American pride in the New World and the American hope for the Old.

CHAPTER

4

THE PURE FOUNTAINS
OF WISDOM

FOR AMERICAN WRITERS, ARTISTS, AND SCHOLARS the contrast between the Old World and the New was as vivid as it was for any American statesman. Yet for them the terms of that antithesis were colored by their awareness of the value of Europe to a young country struggling to create a civilized culture. Europe was inevitably a training ground for literary, artistic, and scholarly development. For the society that prided itself on its break with the past, it was a richly endowed museum of the treasures of Western Civilization, suffused with the romantic haze of antiquity. It was the former home of a nation of immigrants susceptible to nostalgic yearnings for what they had gladly left behind. It was, too, a social order of fascinating complexity and sophistication which subtly posed a dangerous temptation to the representatives of a society blest or cursed (it was often hard to say which) with a more rugged natural setting, a simpler social system, a more democratic code of manners, and a narrower standard of morality. For these reasons the Old World was both an inspiration and lure to Americans, even while it remained in political terms the incarnation of the enemy.

In their schoolbooks Americans told themselves that Europe had merely the embellishments of a morally inferior civilization to recommend itself; but even the nationalistic McGuffey Readers, which helped civilize the nineteenth-century frontier, drew heavily for their texts from English literature and quoted Daniel Webster's tribute to Europe: "Her obligations to Europe for science and art, laws, literature, and manners, America acknowledges as she ought, with respect and gratitude."[1] After the War of 1812 the discovery of Europe was aided by the new convenience of a regular transatlantic packet service, which by 1848 competed with steamship lines. These pre-Civil War voyagers were, however, not tourists of a modern style; they were pioneers, blazing the trails of a new Europe which opened up necessary and liberating sources of training and education. Scholars and artists brought home the rich loam of culture to fertilize the green shoots of American civilization. In this earnest and sympathetic response to foreign life there was no betrayal of devotion to the American, only a better equipped pursuit of it. "Had I remained at home," wrote Benjamin Silliman, Yale's great teacher and promoter of science, reflecting on his year abroad at London and Edinburgh in 1805–1806, "I should probably never have reached a high standard of attainment in geology, nor given whatever impulse has emanated from New Haven as one of the centers of scientific labor and influence."[2]

[1] "The Completion of the Bunker Hill Monument," Edwin P. Whipple, ed., *The Great Speeches and Orations of Daniel Webster* (Boston, Little, Brown, 1882), p. 149. The passage was used in McGuffey's *New Fifth Reader*, Lesson 77, which first appeared in 1844. For the use of English literature see Louis B. Wright, *Culture on the Moving Frontier* (Bloomington, University of Indiana Press, 1955), pp. 218–223. The denigration of European "embellishments" is pointed out by Ruth Miller Elson, "American Schoolbooks and 'Culture' in the Nineteenth Century," *Mississippi Valley Historical Review*, 46 (December, 1959), 411–434.

[2] Quoted by John F. Fulton and Elizabeth H. Thomson, *Benjamin Silliman: Pathfinder in American Science* (New York, Henry Schuman, 1947), p. 69.

The missions of these young scholars had the benevolent blessings of the patriarchs of the Republic. Before George Ticknor left for Germany with Edward Everett in 1815 he met with President Madison and Chief Justice John Marshall, received letters of introduction from John Adams and Jefferson, and borrowed John Quincy Adams' copy of Goethe's *Werther* to prepare himself for his education. One of his tasks was to buy books for Jefferson abroad and keep him informed of the state of European classical studies. If the sage of Monticello had been younger he would have leaped at the chance of accompanying Ticknor on a classical voyage; instead he hoped to acquire the young man upon his return for the faculty of the University of Virginia.

Enthusiasm for classical antiquity ran high in a new nation that could easily imagine that it had fallen heir to the wisdom of the ancient republics. For Ticknor Rome had the most eloquent ruins of Europe, and Everett's reverent tour of Greece inspired him to plan a poem on "The American's Pilgrimage" patterned after Byron's "Childe Harold."[3] But these affairs of the heart had to bow to the demands of discipline. Europe was essentially a preparation for a vocation. "The whole tour in Europe," Ticknor confessed, "I consider a sacrifice of enjoyment to improvement."[4] Ticknor gave up the law to pursue a life of letters; in Germany he accepted the post of professor of French and Spanish literature at Harvard, which sent him to Spain to ready himself for it. With similar foresight Harvard sent off Everett to prepare for a professorship of Greek literature; George Bancroft to study theology; and, later, Longfellow to become Ticknor's successor.

Germany, its culture wondrously illuminated by Madame de Staël's *D'Allemagne*, beckoned as a new world where a literary and philosophical renaissance was burgeoning. The universities at Göttingen, Heidelberg, or Berlin were obviously the place to

[3] See Stephen A. Larrabee, *Hellas Observed, the American Experience of Greece 1775–1865* (New York, New York University Press, 1957), pp. 33–34.

[4] Letter to Mr. Haven, July, 1814, *Life, Letters, and Journals of George Ticknor*, 8th ed., I (Boston, James R. Osgood, 1877), 23.

make American scholars. "We do not yet know what a Greek scholar is," Ticknor wrote his father from Göttingen; "we do not even know the process by which a man is to be made one."[5] In a spirit of enthusiastic dedication the young scholars from America explored museums, galleries, libraries, and monasteries to absorb as much learning as they could in a few years. Germany might be politically autocratic, but, they discovered, it had created a republic of letters and a spirit of free inquiry which represented a new kind of emancipation. "I have come to the pure fountains of wisdom," George Bancroft exulted to his pious mentor at Harvard (who feared for his protégé's soul in this dangerous atmosphere of speculation) "that I may drink of her unpolluted waters and be refreshed."[6]

Beneath the political mask of Europe, which always wore for these Americans a menacing look, there was a fair visage of intellectual vitality and social refinement. Secure in the recent victory over England, with the "era of good feelings" softening the partisan bitterness of America's domestic politics, these republicans could look beneath the mask without fear or guilt. Politics was not their pressing concern. Ticknor was vexed in 1835 to leave a stimulating company of English scholars "for so disagreeable a purpose" as that of being examined before a committee of the House of Commons on the subject of the ballot as managed in the United States. The Duchesse de Broglie even rebuked him for looking down on European politics and despising its republican efforts. A conservative Federalist by heritage, Ticknor once told Prince John of Saxony that Americans were not surprised that "no good" came from the revolutions of 1848. A republic, he told the Prince, unconsciously repeating the judgment he had heard from the lips of Metternich himself, was "a *truth* here; but what is it in France, or what *can* it be either there or in Germany?" When in Europe Ticknor had not been blind to Spain's

[5] November 10, 1815, *ibid.*, I, 73.
[6] Letter to Andrews Norton, September 5, 1818, quoted by Orie W. Long, *Literary Pioneers: Early American Explorers of European Culture* (Cambridge, Harvard University Press, 1935), p. 109.

systematized corruption and oppressive Inquisition, but he was without the republican anxieties of an Adams or Jefferson. To his eyes it was more remarkable that there was in Spain "more originality and poetry in the popular manners and feelings" than he found elsewhere.[7]

These pioneers, graciously received because they represented the New World in a teachable mood, were too much overwhelmed with the labors of their studies and the excitements of their social life to be absorbed with politics. They met everyone. Boston wits remarked that if Ticknor had been sent to Olympus he would have unhesitatingly presented his letters of introduction to Jupiter. As it was, he was hospitably ushered into the company of the nobility, the embassies, the artists, the scholars, and the fashionable. At the end of three separate European trips, totaling eight years abroad, his European acquaintances made a "Who's Who" of the Old World: scientists, like Sir Humphry Davy and Alexander von Humboldt; scholars, like Niebuhr and Malthus; poets, like Goethe, Byron, Chateaubriand, Wordsworth, Scott, and Coleridge; notables, like Madame de Staël, Lafayette, Talleyrand, and Prince Metternich; royalty, like the Duke de Laval, Prince John of Saxony, and Prince Lucien Bonaparte. He and his former fellow student at Harvard, Joseph Green Cogswell, of whom Goethe was fond, even had a private audience with the Pope.

In the midst of all these flattering attentions the young men remained Americans with the patriotism and naïveté of their countrymen. Jefferson was eager to know what effect Europe had had on Ticknor, and he answered, in tones that must have pleased the apostle of Americanism, that his experience had raised his country in his own estimation and attracted him to it even more. Even in 1837, after a year and a half of the delights of Europe on his second trip, the old American faith was strong in him: "Indeed, taken as a general remark, a man is much more

[7] For these reactions of Ticknor see *Life, Letters, and Journals,* I, 415, 311; II, 14, 236; I, 188.

truly a *man* with us than he is elsewhere; and, notwithstanding the faults that freedom brings out in him, it is much more gratifying and satisfying to the mind, the affections, the soul, to live in our state of society, than in any I know of on this side of the Atlantic."[8] It was characteristic that George Bancroft, whose later work as a historian was "to cast a vote for Jackson" and American democracy, should join in 1820 with a fellow-American student at Göttingen to celebrate the Fourth of July in their rooms with a patriotic oration and an exalted poem in honor of the happy land whose birth was "more glorious than other nations in their maturity." To assuage their loneliness these "forlorn pilgrims" drank a toast: "My countrymen, we are Americans. The arts and sciences of Europe cannot make us forget it. Thank God we are Americans."[9]

In nothing were they more American than in their prideful belief that America was purer than Europe. For all their respect for Goethe they did not conceal their scandalized conviction that much of his life and work reeked of immorality by simple American standards. Ticknor was still shocked by the French theater and the realism of Hugo, Balzac, and George Sand on his second journey, and Bancroft on his first told his spiritual guardian at Harvard that if only German literature could be transported to America, where it would be engrafted on a healthy tree of "high moral feeling," he was sure it would thrive more nobly.[10] There were, apparently, traps for the unwary in the pursuit of learning, but these defenders of the faith were proud to have avoided them.

Their quest had been a mission, not a sentimental journey or a vacation, and they returned full of the desire to do good works. Ticknor tried, with much frustration, to introduce the elective system at Harvard; Cogswell's friendship with Goethe secured the gift of the poet's works to the Harvard library, which the American soon organized on Göttingen lines. Everett and Bancroft,

[8] Letter to Richard H. Dana, February 22, 1837, *ibid.*, II, 75. For his response to Jefferson see Long, *op. cit.*, p. 46.
[9] Quoted by Long, p. 125.
[10] See *Life, Letters, and Journal*, II, 140 and Long, p. 113.

with some apologies, did their best to introduce the American public to the splendors of Goethe and German literature, a crusade which Longfellow later brought to triumph. Everett and Ticknor collaborated to establish the Boston Public Library; Cogswell organized the Astor Library in New York; and he and Bancroft joined forces to erect Round Hill School as a beacon of progressive education, guided by the latest European theories. There was even a gentle softening of the sturdy American manners; Bancroft had taken private lessons abroad in polite French, Italian, and dancing. Fresh off the boat from Europe, he greeted his old teacher Andrews Norton, a rock of conservative Unitarian piety, with a continental kiss on both cheeks, and a friendship was abruptly ruptured. If Harvard lost a theologian, the United States gained a historian. These scholarly explorers of the Old World had enriched both themselves and the New World.

For American painters and sculptors during much of the nineteenth century expatriation was a technical and practical necessity. There were at home no serious art schools or comprehensive collections of plastic art until well after the Civil War. It was necessary to go to school to Europe. At first they went to England, following the footsteps of Benjamin West, who in his London studio held court for American painters, including Peale, Copley, Stuart, and Trumbull, from the days of the Stamp Act crisis on throughout his presidency of the Royal Academy. Then Italy became the mecca of aspiring painters and sculptors. There, in Rome or Florence, over a hundred artists composed a shifting American colony between 1830 and 1875. Rich in ruins and artistic tradition, Italy was also wonderfully economical. Inexpensive marble, skilled craftsmen, and paying customers were rare in America, common in Italy. Above all, the American artist could there stand aloof from the pressures of practical affairs to enjoy the fellowship of a shared absorption in art against a background of a pastoral countryside and monumental cities. "To the American," as James Russell Lowell pointed out, "Italy gives cheaply what gold cannot buy for him at home, a Past at once legendary and authentic, and in which he has an equal claim with every other foreigner."[11] The particular fascination of old Italy for these Americans was caught on canvas in Washington Allston's *Italian Landscape*, with its glimpse of peasant life against the background of the Tiber River and the Alban Hills, mingled with antiquity's ruins and the figure of a medieval pilgrim, and in Thomas Cole's *The Architect's Dream*, with its grandiose vision of the monumental splendor of arched walls and columned temples.

"Dear, compact, bird's-eye, cheap, quiet, mind-your-own-business, beautiful Florence, how does my heart yearn for you!" exulted the sculptor Horatio Greenough.[12] By contrast American opportunities seemed woefully dim, and the public mind sluggishly indifferent or hostile. "Let us see if we can show Jonathan," Greenough wrote Fenimore Cooper from Florence, "that art is a noble vehicle of national gratitude and glory and that a man may be an *artist* without being ergo a blackguard and a mischievous member of society."[13] Jonathan was not easy to teach. On his return to Washington in 1851 Greenough, commissioned to design a statue of Washington for the capitol, discussed public buildings with one high official who, speaking as if his "mouth and tongue were clogged with bake beans," declared, " 'Well, we don't think it's of much importance who takes care of these things; there ain't much of 'em.' "[14] When there was an interest in art, it was either conventionally pious to tradition or naïvely

[11] Quoted by Otto Wittmann, Jr., "The Italian Experience (American Artists in Italy 1830–75)," *American Quarterly*, 4 (Spring, 1952), 11. For American artists in Italy during this period see also Oliver Larkin, "Two Yankee Painters in Italy: Thomas Cole and Samuel Morse," *American Quarterly*, 5 (Fall, 1953), 195–200; Madeline B. Stern, "New England Artists in Italy, 1835–55," *New England Quarterly*, 14 (June, 1941), 243–271; *Travellers in Arcadia* (catalog) (Toledo Museum of Art, 1951); and Albert Ten Eyck Gardner, *Yankee Stonecutters: The First American School of Sculpture 1800–1850* (New York, Columbia University Press, 1945).

[12] Letter to Henry Greenough, September 3, 1834, Frances Boott Greenough, ed., *Letters of Horatio Greenough to His Brother Henry Greenough, With Biographical Sketches and Some Contemporary Correspondence* (Boston, Ticknor, 1887), p. 99.

[13] August 22, 1832, James Fenimore Cooper, ed., *The Correspondence of James Fenimore Cooper*, I (New Haven, Yale University Press, 1922), 285.

[14] Letter to Henry Greenough, November 18, 1851, *Letters of Horatio Greenough*, pp. 236–237.

contemptuous of it. The public, the sculptor Hiram Powers complained, did not recognize beauty in anything unless it could "survey it with a telescope at a distance," to the detriment of "everything near by, everything domestic, everything consecrated by the air and spirit of America."[15] At the other extreme, even professional artistic opinion inclined to the complacent confidence that the American artist could find sufficient inspiration and power by merely casting his innocent glance at the natural contours of the New World. When James Jackson Jarves, indefatigable collector and promoter of art, whose own artistic awakening had been provoked by the glories of the Louvre, commended Americans who studied the world's masterpieces as the basis of their artistic education, he was severely chided by the editor of an art journal: "We do *not* 'need Art-students, men of sincerity and labor, who will not hesitate to go on their backs and knees, if need be in the dust, to read the soul-language of the mightiest minds in Europe,' we need only men who will, without any adoration of the works of 'the mightiest minds' of any country, stand with their brows bared and their eyes and hearts open before Nature, and tell us honestly what they see and feel, without reference to any previous art."[16]

In defiance of this Philistine public opinion these artists wanted a closer look than a telescope provides and were willing to get their knees dusty. They went to Europe, and a few made it their permanent home. Yet, like the scholars abroad, these artists were Americans with a mission, not alienated exiles. Samuel F. B. Morse, who yearned to be a great painter and succeeded in being a great inventor, assured his parents in 1814, "My country has the most prominent place in my thoughts. How shall I raise her name, how can I be of service in refuting the calumny, so industriously spread

[15] C. Edwards Lester, "Conversations with Powers in his Studio at Florence," *The Artist, the Merchant, and the Statesman of the Age of the Medici, and of Our Own Time,* I (New York, Paine and Burgess, 1845), p. 117.
[16] Quoted by Francis Steegmuller, *The Two Lives of James Jackson Jarves* (New Haven, Yale University Press, 1951), p. 151.

against her, that she has produced no men of genius."[17] Morse's master, Washington Allston, one of the first Americans to nurture his talent under Italian skies, returned to his country in 1818 out of homesickness, even though if he had stayed he might have succeeded Benjamin West as president of England's Royal Academy. Allston's patriotism during the War of 1812 irritated his friend Coleridge to complain that the painter was "not *an* American, but downright *American*."[18] For Greenough, ardent advocate of the American cause and friend to European republicanism, there was an eloquence to the United States deeper than politics. Returning from "the baked hills, the fierce sunlight, and the hard-hearted stone villages" of Pratolino to the verdant, active American world where "the up-going and down-floating sloops and brigs without number" entranced his aesthetic eye, he confessed to his brother, "My heart will always yearn after America."[19] Despite the obtuseness of the American public in matters of art, Greenough, like most of his fellow travelers, was hopeful that when the United States outgrew its dependency on foreign standards "pencils and chisels will be ready to echo in color and marble every noble cry of the American voice."[20]

The Old World did not and could not by itself make these men mature artists. Most of the sculptors fell too easily into a rather glib neoclassic style or dispersed their energies in contriving ingenious machines; and Allston, with his unfinished painting, *Belshazar's Feast*, begun in Italy and still incomplete on the day of his death twenty-five years later, was a notoriously pathetic case of unfulfilled genius. The vivid variety and abundance of Italian art and the elegant social pleasures of the international

[17] May 2, 1814, Edward Lind Morse, ed., *Samuel F. B. Morse His Letters and Journals*, I (Boston, Houghton Mifflin, 1914), 133.

[18] Quoted by Edgar Preston Richardson, *Washington Allston: A Study of the Romantic Artist in America* (Chicago, University of Chicago Press, 1948), p. 113.

[19] June 23, 1847, May 12, 1843, *Letters of Horatio Greenough*, pp. 205, 151.

[20] Letter to Robert C. Winthrop, November 26, 1844, *Letters*, pp. 182–183.

colony of expatriates could be a bewilderingly rich diet for the starved palates of some Americans. For William Wetmore Story, who first went to Italy as a young lawyer, elected by his fellow citizens of Cambridge to make a statue of his distinguished father, there was no recovery from its magical effects. After his return he found both the law and America distasteful, and he returned to Rome for good (in 1856) to dedicate himself to sculpture and poetry and enjoy the society of English friends like the Robert Brownings. But even Story, for whom "the golden air" of Italy had made America unlovely, did not expatriate himself in any ultimate sense. During the crisis of the American Civil War he was intensely angry at England's lack of sympathy for the North, and an articulate defender of Lincoln's unionist policy. Like his countrymen in the North, Story felt that republican institutions were on trial, their failure too great a loss to civilization for the world to permit. In his articles on "The American Question," published in an English newspaper, this exile, often painted as a dilettante lotus-eater, proclaimed: "Europe is a failure. It cannot be offered as an example to follow, but to avoid."[21] Even for her disgruntled children the Republic still had enormous prestige.

This group of artists left behind them a record of serious artistic work, if no impressive body of masterpieces. Perhaps James Jackson Jarves's great collection of early Italian "primitives," which Yale University acquired in 1868, represented the finest product of Italy's influence on an American heart and mind, and his treasures won practically no contemporary recognition. But whatever their limitations and disappointments, both the artists and the scholars had established the significance of a Europe which America would long need for its own purposes. Their descendants were the American graduate students who flocked to Germany in the late nineteenth and early twentieth centuries to

[21] *The American Question* (London, Manwaring, 1862), p. 68. For Story's attraction to Italy rather than America see Henry James, ed., *William Wetmore Story and His Friends from Letters, Diaries, and Recollections*, I (Boston, Houghton Mifflin, 1903), 253, 303. Appointed one of the U. S. Commissioners on the Fine Arts to the Paris Exposition of 1878, Story was irritated to discover that no American sculptures were exhibited, a sign of his country's parsimony in artistic matters.

learn the subtle secrets of historical criticism or seminar teaching and the American artists who, after 1870, found in Munich or Paris a necessary and vital stimulus. On these terms the Old World could be met without enmity or fear, but with a sympathy and gratitude that did not compromise allegiance to the New World. The traditional antithesis was not annulled. It merely took on a new meaning for those who could exploit the differences.

5

THE SHADOWY GRANDEURS
OF THE PAST

FOR THE AMERICAN LITERARY MIND of the eighteenth century the feudal darkness of the Old World had only a menacing political meaning. It stood for the iniquities of kings, nobles, and clergy who ruled by tyranny and superstition. The exciting prospects of the future opened up by the American Revolution were gloriously enthralling to the most ardent literary spirits of the age of Enlightenment. Philip Freneau, the new nation's first important poet, celebrated the New World against the Old as early as 1771 in a commencement ode delivered at Princeton on "The Rising Glory of America." By its happy emancipation from European evils America was destined, he prophesied, to become "a new Jerusalem" by "no second Adam lost" with no "dangerous tree" of "deathful fruit" or "tempting serpent to allure the soul" into a fatal loss of "native innocence."[1] Freneau was to become the poet

[1] Frederick Lewis Pattee, ed., *The Poems of Philip Freneau, Poet of the*

laureate of Jeffersonian Republicanism, and his rhetoric chanted with mythological force the theme of New World innocence, happiness, and liberty in contrast to Old World vice, misery, and despotism. He was seized with a passionate vision of the apotheosis of America through westward expansion. Nature and Reason would collaborate in the Western wilds to perfect the development of free man. In this way the eighteenth-century cult of Reason mingled with the agrarian cult of the soil to bolster the myth of a world geographically separated into the children of light and the children of darkness. By definition, history-laden Europe with its pomp and ceremony could never nurture that innocence peculiar to the American wilds where it was always "the morning of the world."

The hostile version of the American-European contrast, the literary analogue of political isolationism, was especially appropriate to the early days of the Republic. While the delegates were sitting in Constitution Hall at Philadelphia, New Yorkers were witnessing Royall Tyler's *The Contrast*, America's first professionally produced comedy with its vivid creation of the "true-born Yankee American son of liberty." Tyler's Jonathan, a rube from Bangor, and his master, Manley, a Revolutionary officer, were posed in virtuous contrast as honest provincials to the wily foppishness of Dimple and his slavish servant, who had been abroad to acquire "the polish of Europe." Tyler's comic Yankee later became widely popularized by the monologues of George Handel Hill and the newspaper sketches of the humorist Seba Smith, while the play spawned a swarm of imitations. One of the most popular successes of the nineteenth-century American stage, Anna Cora Mowatt's *Fashion*, which in 1845 did much to make theater-going socially respectable, was unabashedly derived from Tyler's formula. Mocking the fashionable aping of French manners, the play celebrated the triumph of Nature's Noblemen over foreign follies and bogus counts.[2]

American Revolution, I (Princeton, Princeton University Library, 1902), 80–81.

[2] The image of the Yankee is explored in Constance Rourke, *American*

At the same time, on a higher level of culture, a more sophisticated, if equally mythological, view of the American-European contrast developed in the nineteenth century. Influenced by the new sympathy for the medieval historical past and the fascination with folklore and ancient customs, which had been stimulated by the Romantic movement, the American literary imagination turned to Europe as a symbol of romance, hallowed by the charm of ivied ruins, picturesque scenes, and quaint customs. On these terms the contrast between the Old World and the New could be accented without tension. The Past became attractive by virtue of its very opposition to the Present. The New World remained unquestioned as the land of the free, the home of virtue, and the hope of the future, but its undecorated simplicity and bustling practicality stifled conventional romantic impulses.

This new attitude towards Europe was accentuated by a literary sense of cultural dependency on an older and richer civilization. Even Tyler, for all his pride in displaying his muse on native themes, had cleverly imitated the mannered style of English wits like Sheridan. While Americans were inspired by the outcome of the War of 1812 to redouble their energies in a patriotic crusade for an American literature redolent of the New World, their real literary pioneers went overseas to spend fruitful years in Europe, their minds deeply responsive to the authority and appeal of an officially alien culture.

Washington Irving began his literary career as a New York wit who collaborated in 1807 with James K. Paulding on the satirical sketches known as *Salmagundi*. Paulding alone produced the second series; Irving had left for Europe. While Paulding continued to exploit the vein of caustic, belligerent criticism of Europe, Irving moved on to discover a romantic Europe warmly appealing to the American mind. Sailing to Sicily on his first tour in 1805, "accustomed to our *honest* American hills and dales where *stubborn fact* presides and checks the imagination in its wandrings," he was full of enthusiasm for "that Island of fable and Romance"

Humor: A Study of the National Character (New York, Harcourt, Brace, 1931), chap. 1.

where "fiction has shed its charms o'er every scene."[3] Setting out again in 1815 for England on a matter of business, sick of his life as a literary man-about-town in New York, he became a seventeen-year expatriate and won a vast public for his graceful vignettes of the picturesque in English, Spanish, and German life and legend. Later, when he had become America's most prominent man of letters, Irving sometimes longed for the life that he had enjoyed in his wandering years. After a day spent with businessmen in Honesdale, New York, where they had named a cliff in his honor, he wrote to his niece in Paris that he had spent a commonplace day among commonplace people: "Good lord deliver me from the all pervading commonplace which is the curse of our country."[4]

Longfellow, whose own pilgrimage to Europe had been inspired by Irving's, piously joined the cry for a national literature. If it was not necessary that "the war-whoop should ring in every line," at least American poets should break away from bookish imitative poetry and remember that for Americans skylarks and nightingales "only warble in books." But for all this genuflection before the national creed he really believed that the torch of culture was "lighted at the old domestic fireside of England," and that English "solid sense" needed to be lightened by German tenderness, Spanish passion, and French vivacity.[5] He had himself gone to school not in "the forest primeval" or "by the shores of Gitchie Gumee," but at the University of Heidelberg.

If in America life was real and life was earnest, that was just the trouble for a romantic poet. "In truth it must be spoken and recorded," he noted in his journal in 1846, ". . . this is a dreadful country for a poet to live in. Lethal deadly influences hang over

[3] Letter to "Quoz," January 1, 1805, quoted by Stanley T. Williams, *The Life of Washington Irving*, I (New York, Oxford, 1935), 59. For Paulding's republican critiques of Europe see, for example, "A Trip to Paris," *The New York Mirror*, 8 (January 15, 1831), 220–221 and "Want of Excitement or a Trip to London," *ibid.*, 8 (January 22, 1831), 228–229.

[4] Letter to Mrs. Sarah Storrow, July 31, 1841, Williams, *op. cit.*, II, 97.

[5] Cf. his "Defense of Poetry," *North American Review*, 34 (January, 1832), 69, 75, with "Mr. Churchill's" opinion in *Kavanagh, The Prose Works of Henry Wadsworth Longfellow*, Riverside Edition, vol. 2 (Boston, Houghton Mifflin, 1899), 368.

him, the very 'Deadly Nightshade' of song. Many poetic souls there are here, and many lovers of song; but life and its ways and ends are prosaic in this country to the last degree."[6] As America's most popular poet, he was the singer of the pleasures of home and hearth, and as a good republican he once refused a decoration from King Emmanuel of Italy. "Please don't get expatriated," he could counsel others, reminding them that "life is not all cathedrals or ruined castles, and other theatrical properties of the Old World."[7] Yet it was just these theatrical properties that for long had fascinated him. From his house in Portland young Longfellow could see the Atlantic he longed to cross, and he was overjoyed when first Bowdoin College in 1826, then Harvard in 1835, sent him abroad to prepare for his professional duties. He later almost resigned his professorship at Harvard, where he had succeeded Ticknor, to go to Europe as a tutor to a young son of the Astor family, and he often dreamed of wrangling a post as secretary of the legation at Madrid. Like Irving, whose life and work he partly imitated, Longfellow was spellbound by the Old World.

The Europe that enthralled Irving and Longfellow was not quite the same Europe that had inspired Ticknor, Everett, Bancroft, and other scholars. It was not scholarship, but romance that these poetic voyagers were looking for, and they did not much cultivate that Spartan devotion to intellectual labor that characterized those other pioneers. If Irving doggedly toiled at a biography of Columbus in Madrid, and Longfellow took Ticknor's advice and settled down in Heidelberg to learn German literature before taking up the Smith Professorship at Harvard, these were episodes. Both men were essentially romantic artists, not students. For them the European past shimmered, as Irving put it, with "all the charms of storied and poetical association." For all the "youthful promise" of America, Europe offered "masterpieces of art, the refinements of highly cultivated society, the quaint pecularities of ancient and local customs" in which one could indulge

---

[6] Quoted by Lawrance Thompson, *Young Longfellow (1807–43)* (New York, Macmillan, 1938), p. 317.

[7] Quoted by Edward Wagenknecht, *Longfellow: A Full-Length Portrait* (New York, Longmans, Green, 1955), p. 195.

the desire to lose himself "among the shadowy grandeurs of the past."[8] "I, too, in a certain sense," wrote Longfellow in *Outre-Mer*, which paid Irving the compliment of imitating his famous *Sketch Book* in both form and format, "have been a pilgrim of *Outre-Mer;* for to my youthful imagination the Old World was a kind of Holy Land, lying afar off beyond the blue horizon of the ocean," which made the heart grow "swelled with the deep emotions of the pilgrim."[9]

Through the eyes of Irving and Longfellow the Old World became enchanted, in a compensating irony, by the very intensity of America's official commitment to the future. A new nation, composed of immigrants, was inevitably vulnerable to the impulse to take a wistful backward glance at the life left behind. The new image of Europe, saturated as it was with romantic nostalgia and drained of nearly all contemporary social significance, did not challenge native pieties, but complemented them. Through a dialectic generated by their position Americans could, in this romanticized Old World, vicariously enjoy the forbidden fruits of the past. To dream of a feudal past existing in America was not only impossible, but treasonable. It would have turned a splendid vision of man's republican destiny into a nightmare of reaction. To find that wistful dream incarnated in Europe was to appease American nostalgia for values alien to the national mythology without violating it.

The enormous popularity of both Irving and Longfellow owed much to their instinctive recognition and exploitation of this situation. Without the slightest compromise of his Americanism, Irving could describe for his avid readers a merry England, dominated by the rural gentry who lived with their estates and tenants in the ruddy afterglow of medievalism amid scenery "associated in the mind with ideas of order, of quiet, of sober well-established principles, of hoary usage, and revered custom."[10] As a diplomat, attached to the London legation and compelled to negotiate with

[8] *Sketch Book, The Complete Works of Washington Irving,* vol. 1 (Paris, Baudry's, 1834), 226.

[9] *Outre-Mer, The Prose Works,* vol. 1, 20.

[10] *Sketch Book,* p. 245.

these genial English squires over the West Indian trade, Irving was an adequate defender of the American cause, while in his role as the American romantic traveler he could deeply wish that John Bull's splendid mansion would not be meddled with by agitating "levellers" devoted to democratic progress.[11] Old England would lose its usefulness as an American symbol if it lost its antithetical charm. Its age was for Americans its novelty. To English eyes Irving, with his evident apprenticeship to the romanticism of Byron, Scott, and Moore, and his stylistic indebtedness to the felicity of the English essayists of the eighteenth century, was a pious traditionalist, "a bit of home," as Fanny Kemble exclaimed when she embraced him on her travels in America. To Americans he seemed fresh and original, creating a Europe peculiarly available to the native imagination.

With equal success Longfellow made the continent an American dream. The public responded eagerly to his pleasure in the color and traditionalism of French rural sports, fairs, dances, festivals, and ceremonies; his poetic reveries before the ruined temples and moldering aqueducts of Rome; his Irvingesque rhapsodies over the famed castle of Alhambra in Spain, like "the memory of a gorgeous dream," which was "a fortress, a palace, an earthly paradise, . . . a ruin, wonderful in its fallen greatness!"[12] A true son of the Romantic movement, he found delight in every vestige of the Middle Ages. At Rouen the ancient cathedral gave him such a vivid sensation of being "transported back to the Dark Ages" that he refused to visit it again for fear of losing his first impression of its "awful sublimity."[13] At the château of Chambord his imagination heard the clang of arms and sounds of revelry and wassail, while the epics and lyrics of the troubadour poets from the age of Charlemagne aroused his warmest poetic sympathies.

In his *Hyperion* (1839), which reflected the influence of Goethe and Richter and was widely used as a guidebook for travelers in Germany, he continued the account of his adventures

[11] *Ibid.*, p. 325.
[12] *Outre-Mer, The Prose Works*, vol. 1, 226–227.
[13] *Ibid.*, p. 30.

abroad in the guise of fiction. Paul Flemming's unrequited love for an English girl provides a sentimental framework for a romantic conflict between the charms of the past and the duties of the present, a theme especially significant for Americans. The heroine (recognizable as the American girl Longfellow later made his second wife) possesses a tender sense of the past; she has written sketches on the pageantry of the Middle Ages, with its ladies, knights, jousts, and minnesingers, so angularly pictured in illuminated manuscripts, and on the glory of the artist's life in Rome. Flemming's own nostalgia for the past is troubled by a consciousness of the claims of the present. A German Baron tells him, "It seems to me like falling in love with one's grandmother. Give me the Present, . . . warm, glowing, palpitating with life."[14] But for Paul the warm, glowing, palpitations of romanticized history are more appealing than the present. His crisis comes when he meets in a village church a tablet with an inscription urging man to forget the mournful past and "wisely improve the Present." The advice, symbolically, turns his thoughts "to his distant home beyond the sea." Renouncing his life as "a dreamer among shadows," he resolves to return to America to pursue "a life of action and reality."[15] But he leaves behind, along with the glories of the past, his beloved "Dark Lady," and so the book ends, in approved romantic fashion, on a note of melancholy.

Like his hero, Longfellow returned to America, but his dream of Europe remained as vivid as his professorial life was a burden. How could Portland, Cambridge, or even Boston compare with Nuremberg, lovingly described in his poem as "quaint old town of toil and traffic, quaint old town of art and song," with its "memories of the Middle Ages" when emperors lived in castles "time-defying, centuries old" while all around rose "the wondrous world of Art"? His conflict was not severe; he signed his peace gracefully. With characteristic mellowness his poetry dealt easily with either European or American themes. As Henry James,

---

[14] *The Prose Works,* II, 139.
[15] *Ibid.,* p. 277.

whose European experience was to be longer and deeper, won-deringly remarked, if Longfellow's life seemed "a piece of the old world smoothly fitted into the new, so it might quite as well have been a piece of the new fitted, just as intimately, into the old."[16]

Washingon Irving also came back from Europe to grow up with the country, throwing himself into the American life of his time with all the zest of an immigrant. He wrote an admiring biography of Washington, "roughed it" on a tour of the Western prairies, played the role of glorifying publicist for John Jacob Astor's fur trade, speculated on the stock market, lectured his nephews on the importance of sacrificing their fashionable life to the business of getting on in the world, and basked in the honor of having his name given to mountains, hotels, steamboats, public squares, and even cigars. He was, because of his European success, a literary Horatio Alger in the United States. He had not forgot-ten the national vision of the special destiny of the Republic and the hostile image of Europe it entailed. "I come from gloomier climes to one of brilliant sunshine and inspiring purity," he piously proclaimed at the welcoming dinner held for him in New York in 1832.

I come from countries lowering with doubt and danger, where the rich man trembles and the poor man frowns . . . where all repine at the present and dread the future. I come from these to a country where all is life and animation; where I hear on every side the sound of exultation; where every one speaks of the past with triumph, the present with delight, the future with glowing and confident anticipation.[17]

In a gesture to live up to his rhetoric he pledged himself, in the heat of the moment, to stay in America as long as he lived. Ten years later, when his friend Daniel Webster recommended him for Minister to Madrid, America's "Ambassador of Letters from the New World to the Old" once again gratefully set sail for Spain, where he had earlier occupied for a delightful month the

[16] *William Wetmore Story and His Friends from Letters, Diaries, and Recollections,* I (Boston, Houghton Mifflin, 1903), 311–312.
[17] Quoted by Williams, *op. cit.,* II, 334, n. 2.

royal apartments of the Alhambra castle, so rich in the romantic past of Moorish Spain.

If Irving's and Longfellow's reconciliation of the American myth of the New World with their affection for the Old World was achieved with few evident signs of personal strain, it was largely because their own vision of Europe was such a very complementary one. Only a society that had defined itself as a fresh start in history could have produced such nostalgic hungers for a Europe made enchanted by the traces of an ancient past. In their poetic image the traditional antithesis between the two worlds, far from being abandoned, was restated by being rediscovered in a romantic light.

This same romantic image of Europe was created for less sophisticated Americans by Nathaniel Parker Willis. Reared in Boston by narrowly pious parents, Willis left his local church, became a popular journalist in New York, and was sent to Europe in 1831 as a correspondent. For him it was a delightful liberation, and his widely copied letters to *The New York Mirror* bubbled over with his pleasure in the stimulation of the European scene. Snubbed at home by the guardian of the girl he had hoped to marry, he found abroad that he could swim in the most frothy currents of European social life, thanks to the quasi-diplomatic privileges he had secured from the American minister in Paris and the letters of introduction to Italian society he received from the editor of an English journal. The thought of returning to "naked America" from this fabulous world where there was "so much to fill one's mind and eye" depressed him. "I love my country," he explained, "but the *ornamental* is my vocation, and of this she has none."[18] In London he became, through the kindness of Walter Savage Landor, a member of Lady Blessington's *salon*. Willis was overwhelmed at his good fortune. "All the best society of London exclusives," he naïvely wrote his sister, "is now open to me—me! a sometime apprentice at setting types—me! without a sou in the world beyond what my pen brings one, and with not

[18] Quoted by Henry A. Beers, *Nathaniel Parker Willis*, American Men of Letters (Boston, Houghton Mifflin, 1885), pp. 122–123.

only no influence from friends at home, but a world of envy and slander at my back."[19] Lionized by fashionable society, admitted to the Athanaeum, given a pass to the opera, and presented at court, he seriously thought of becoming an expatriate. When attacked by some prominent English literateurs as a name-dropping snob who invaded the privacy of the aristocracy to write up "high-life" in his columns, Willis was undaunted. He returned to America five years later with the hand of an English girl, daughter of a General. It was a provincial triumph, rather incomprehensible to a present generation that sees more charm in his good looks than in his slight literary works.

His American success was quite understandable. Willis was a shrewd journalist who reported on his travels with the spontaneous colorfulness his public craved. Instinctively, he grasped and reported the forbidden charm of aristocratic life for republican America. "The Americans are queen-mad," noted the *Mirror* in 1838. "We have Victoria bonnets, Victoria shawls, Victoria songs, Victoria marches, Victoria mint-juleps, and somebody has just opened a shop in Broadway which he calls 'The Victoria Hair-Dressing Establishment.' "[20] It was this easily titillated public that took Willis to its heart when he confided to his readers that at Dalhousie Castle in Scotland "you may fatigue yourself in a scene that is formed in every feature from the gentle-born and the refined. The labor and the taste of successive generations can alone create such an Eden. Primogeniture! I half forgive thee."[21]

In his fiction half-forgiven primogeniture struggles seductively with manly republicanism until the issue, despite the author's intention, is dubious. The young American artist in Willis's novel *Paul Fane* returns from "the perfumed atmosphere of Europe," where by "arts of inhalation not elsewhere to be learned" his lungs have been given "their full trial of expansibility," to marry

[19] *Ibid.*, p. 140.
[20] Quoted by Frank Luther Mott, *A History of American Magazines 1741–1850* (New York, Appleton, 1930), p. 397.
[21] *Pencillings by the Way, The Complete Works of Nathaniel Parker Willis* (New York, J. S. Redfield, 1846), p. 196.

his childhood sweetheart.[22] The plot, however, is largely taken up with demonstrating Paul's success in bringing to his feet every European woman he meets whose beauty is hallowed by aristocratic lineage. As in cheap, popular fiction thereafter, Willis's literary image of Europe was a racy mixture of the vulgarized fascinations of art, sex, and high birth, crudely mixed in a casserole of genteel romanticism and low comedy.

It was the function of Willis, the traveler, as a reviewer remarked in 1855, to express "in the most apt and airy manner, the average natural sentiment of an intelligent American in Europe, just as Byron hits the general tone of romance in Venice and Rome." If it was true that "the eyes which see are set in a *tête exaltée* by early success, and the hands which record tremble a little with the pressure of the hands of famous wits, and noble lords, and lovely ladies," these were weaknesses which the public could more than half forgive. His success was natural, the explanation simple, as his reviewer said: "With desires and aspirations for the reverend and historically beautiful, forever unsatisfied at home, fed for years upon the splendid literature of all time, and the pompous history of the nations that have occupied and moulded the earth," yet separated "by the essential spirit of society around him" from them, "the American mind is solicited by Europe with unimagined fascination."[23] More perceptive writers, like Cooper, Hawthorne, and James, recognized that the romantic posture was superficial, but their concern with it as an American problem was tacit acknowledgment of its importance for the nineteenth century. It was a characteristic American way of sympathetically relating oneself to a Europe which by national self-definition was regarded as the alien opposite of the New World.

[22] *Paul Fane, or Parts of a Life Else Untold* (New York, Scribner's, 1857), p. 395. Christof Wegelin sees Willis's fiction as countering the snobbish tone of his newspaper reports, but there is ambiguity in both. See Wegelin, "Social Criticism of Europe in the Fiction of N. P. Willis," *American Literature*, 20 (November, 1948), 313–322. Willis does anticipate the "international theme" which Henry James exploits so much more seriously.

[23] "American Travellers," *Putnam's Monthly*, 5 (June, 1855), 570, 563–564.

CHAPTER

6

TROUBLESOME ENJOYMENTS

IRVING'S AND LONGFELLOW'S IMAGE OF EUROPE was reconciled to their belief in the promise of the New World with a blandness only occasionally ruffled by an outburst of ambivalent feelings. For writers with a stronger sense of actuality and a greater sensitivity to complexities, the problem of reconciliation was much more acute. All the major American writers of the nineteenth century from Cooper to James were fascinated with the American-European theme, which had a personal basis in their own experience abroad. The dream of a primitive innocent New World was thus brought into contact with the facts of a complex sophisticated society, and the encounter, unsettling to American poise, fostered the feeling for ambiguity which was to mark serious American literature in the nineteenth century. Emerson's "American Scholar" address at Harvard in 1837 celebrated the end of "our long apprenticeship to the learning of other lands" and a meager feeding upon "the sere remains of foreign harvests," but his stirring sermon on intellectual independence did not recognize

86

that brooding upon the American encounter with Europe, rather than upon "the meal in the firkin" or "the milk in the pan," would provide a powerful intellectual stimulus to American writers. Even in his own case this stimulus would produce the classic American analysis of England, *English Traits*, his most integrated book.

Herman Melville, giant of the early American novelists, would appear to be the striking exception to this rule, his metaphysical sea stories apparently having nothing to do with the "international theme." But just as Cooper's Leatherstocking tales, which familiarized every boy with the great national myth of the noble pioneer and redman, had before the nineteen thirties concealed his deep involvement with Europe, so has Melville's Calvinist imagination, which he shared with Hawthorne, muffled until recently the "international" overtones of some of his stories. In *Benito Cereno* the good-natured Captain Delano's republican image of a Spanish aristocrat is as relevant as his stereotypes about Negro slaves in blinding him to the mutinous conspiracy aboard the *San Dominick*. And *Redburn* is not only a prosaic narrative of a young sailor's first voyage; it is also the story of an innocent's initiation to experience through the shocking revelations of the brutal poverty of Liverpool and an unsettling night with an effeminate rake in a London gambling hell. Several of Melville's short pieces are diptycha making a cultural contrast between America and Europe: the exclusive, uncharitable atmosphere of a New York church set against the hearty, lower-class hospitality of a London theater; the pathetically self-respecting poverty of the American poor contrasted to the desperate grubbing acceptance of charity by London beggars, feeding upon crumbs from aristocratic tables at Guildhall; the snug and smug bachelor club life of London contrasted with the bleak sterility of New England factory girls.[1] Melville's stories never actually

---

[1] See "The Two Temples" (1854), "Poor Man's Pudding and Rich Man's Crumbs" (1854), and "The Paradise of Bachelors and the Tartarus of Maids" (1855) in Jay Leyda, ed., *The Complete Stories of Herman Melville* (New York, Random House, 1949), pp. 149–212. The relation of these stories and *Benito Cereno* to the "international theme" was suggested to me by the ingenious analysis in W. R. Thompson, " 'The Paradise of

board the "international theme," but they swim close enough to sight it.

James Fenimore Cooper and Nathaniel Hawthorne were the true forerunners of Henry James. They were remarkably honest in their reactions to Europe at a time when the national myth, encouraged by the enthusiasm for Jacksonian Democracy, was all against the relevance of their perceptions. "The West—not the East continually troubled with European visions—is ultimately destined to sway the country," prophesied Francis J. Grund in his contemporary portrait of Jacksonian America: "The sea does not separate America from Europe, but behind the Alleghenies is springing up a new life, and a people more nearly allied to the soil that nourishes them, than the more refined and polished population of the seaboard."[2] As a European, who had lived for over a decade in America, Grund was understandably disgusted by the affectations of genteel bourgeois Americans who aped the aristocracy and scorned the mob; Cooper and Hawthorne shared his politics without closing their eyes to the disturbing fascination of Europe.

Cooper went abroad with his family in 1826 to educate his daughters, improve his health, look after some business with his European publishers, and enjoy himself.[3] Seven years later, after an extensive tour of England, France, Italy, the Rhine, and Switzerland, he returned home to conduct a lover's quarrel with his country that finally turned him into a despairing skeptic, unable either to accept or reject America's confidence in its "manifest destiny."

Two years after Cooper's death, Hawthorne was rewarded for his political support of the Democratic Party by being made American Consul at Liverpool in 1853. This plum, a payment for

---

Bachelors and the Tartarus of Maids': A Reinterpretation," *American Quarterly,* 9 (Spring, 1957), 34–45.

[2] *Aristocracy in America, from the Sketch-Book of a German Nobleman,* introduction by George E. Probst (New York, Harper, 1959), p. 301. Originally published in 1839.

[3] He also had a nominal post as Consul to Lyons.

his campaign biography of his friend Franklin Pierce, not only provided a hardheaded writer with much-needed cash, but gave an old Yankee a chance to fulfill a cherished desire to see the land of his ancestors. After seven years abroad, including a year and a half in Italy with the American colony of sculptors, he had filled many volumes of travel journals, finished one novel, and projected another, all reflecting the disturbing impact of European life on the sensitive conscience of an American democrat of Puritan heritage. For Hawthorne, as for Cooper, foreign travel provided a new perspective on the traditional polarity of the New World and the Old: On the European scene "all past affairs, all home-conclusions, all people whom I have known in America, and meet again here, are strangely compelled to undergo a new trial."[4]

By American convention Europe was the past and hope resided with the future. Neither Cooper nor Hawthorne denied this patriotic premise, but their minds were too searching to accept it as a final judgment of value. Cooper began his journey in full commitment to the vision of America as a New World of freedom, goodness, and happiness. Profoundly irritated by the misinformed, haughty scorn poured on the United States by European travelers and the English quarterly reviews, he tried to set the record straight in *Notions of the Americans* by impersonating an English traveling bachelor, who is guided to the truth about America by a cicerone from New York. "The moral feeling with which a man of sentiment and knowledge looks upon the plains of your happiness," the New Yorker tells the visitor, "is connected with his recollections; here it should be mingled with his hopes." The few remnants of the past in America give rise to the idea of progress and "lead the mind insensibly to cheerful anticipations, which may penetrate into a futurity as dim and as fanciful as any fictions the warmest imaginations can conceive of the past." Americans might claim English triumphs of arms, art, liberty, and law as "portions of a birthright," but they were "no worshippers of

---

[4] Randall Stewart, ed., *The English Notebooks* (New York, Modern Language Association, 1941), p. 77.

stocks and stones."[5] Cooper was determined to avoid sentimental romancing over ruins, and he held his fancy in check with the stern reminder that "the greater force of the past than of the future on the mind" can only be the result of "questionable causes," because "our real concern with the future" is "incalculably the greater."[6]

Yet in all honesty he was forced to admit before he left Europe that if hope is a "livelier, and, on the whole, a more useful feeling" than that connected with memory, still there is "a solemn and pleasing interest clinging about the latter, that no buoyancy of the first can ever equal." Charmed by a seven-hundred-year-old castle, he tried to appease his American conscience by imagining equally inspiring pictures of the American future, but he had to confess, "though reasonably ingenious in castle-building," he could never do it. The past was a fact; the future, at best, "only conjecture."[7] In *Home as Found*, which dramatized his critical view of America as he found it after his travels, he put the conventional praise of the New World's emancipation from the heavy burden of the past in the mouth of Aristabulus Bragg, one of those typically restless, entrepreneurial Americans whom Cooper so intensely disliked. The happier people of France or Italy, Cooper discovered, did not waste themselves "in vain struggles to reach a goal that recedes as we advance."[8] The gospel of progress, by ruthlessly destroying old buildings to make way for economic enterprise, also sacrificed beauty and grace to a cold, naked utilitarianism. "I do not like to see these historical edifices converted into manufactories," Cooper complained, "nor am I so much of a modern utilitarian as to believe the poetry of life is without its correcting and useful influences."[9]

[5] *Notions of the Americans, Picked Up by a Travelling Bachelor*, I (Philadephia, Carey, Lea, and Carey, 1828), 250–251, 323.

[6] Robert E. Spiller, ed., *Gleanings in Europe: France* (New York, Oxford, 1928), p. 37.

[7] *Sketches of Switzerland, Part Second*, II (Philadelphia, Carey, Lea, and Blanchard, 1836), 173–174.

[8] Robert E. Spiller, ed., *Gleanings in Europe: England* (New York, Oxford, 1930), p. 359. Cf. *Home as Found, Works*, Mohawk Ed., vol. 14 (New York, 1896), 23.

[9] *Sketches of Switzerland, Part Second*, I, 156.

Hawthorne's relationship to the past was likewise ambiguous. As a good Democrat, in close touch with the "Young America" movement, which with crusading fervor envisaged a world made over in the light of the American example, he was eagerly responsive to the promise of the future. A ramble through the British Museum could stir his Americanism to the pitch of wishing that "the whole Past might be swept away" to make "a clean world for the coming generation."[10] With his "Western love of change," he was ultimately appalled by the tedium of English village life:

Rather than such monotony of sluggish ages, loitering on a village-green, toiling in hereditary fields, listening to the parson's drone lengthened through centuries in the gray Norman church, let us welcome whatever change may come,—change of place, social customs, political institutions, modes of worship,—trusting that, if all present things shall vanish, they will but make room for better systems, and for a higher type of man to clothe his life in them, and to fling them off in turn.[11]

For this child of provincial America the Italian scene was especially a staggering contrast. Dense with monuments that recorded a history far more ancient than the Gothic cathedrals that first gave him his sense of the European past, Rome was History incarnate. As a true believer in the hopeful promise of the New World, he felt his stomach sicken with a terrible despondency at the sight of faded frescoes with their pathetically dim evidences of a former brightness. The pathos of the past triumphed over his aesthetic feelings and made him wish that these remnants of glory were obliterated by whitewash. The awesome permanency and solidity of dirty buildings, some of them erected in Etruscan times, filled his mind with horrible imaginings of "death-scents, ghosts, murder-stains," and he concluded that "all towns should be made capable of purification by fire, or of decay within half-a-century or so; else they become the hereditary haunt of vermin

<hr>

[10] *The English Notebooks*, p. 243.
[11] *Our Old Home, The Complete Works*, Riverside Ed., vol. 1 (Boston, Houghton Mifflin, 1888), 79.

and noisomeness."[12] With good American logic he made Italy the guilt-ridden setting of his novel *The Marble Faun* because as a romancer, searching for "picturesque and gloomy wrong," he was convinced he could not find it in "the commonplace prosperity, in broad and simple daylight," of his own happy country.[13]

Even so Hawthorne too was sympathetically drawn to the past, and his notebooks record the contradictory impressions of a profoundly ambivalent mind, powerfully attracted by the very things which repel it. His "home-feeling with the past" grew naturally out of his family tradition, which had invested his earliest American ancestor (a Puritan soldier, legislator, and judge) with "a dim and dusky grandeur." Cherishing his New England roots, Hawthorne felt with uncommon intensity a common nostalgia for the English background from which his ancestor had come. In England he confessed that he felt

like the stalwart progenitor in person, returning to the hereditary haunts after more than two hundred years, and finding the church, the hall, the farm-house, the cottage, hardly changed during his long absence . . . while his own affinities for these things, a little obscured by disuse, were reviving at every step.[14]

Like many another American tourist of English descent, weaned on the great writers of English literature, he made a pious pilgrimage to Westminster Abbey, and scanned the gravestones and searched the Record Office for his family name. As Consul, he had a sympathetic patience for those Americans who came to his Liverpool office to pour out their pathetic fantasies of visiting the Queen or inheriting an English estate. In England he found an antidote to the restlessness of American life, and he was stimulated by the delicious feeling of having turned his back on progress to retreat into the past. It was pleasant to think of "the good life" which a man might lead in sleepy English towns, "linked to old

[12] Norman Holmes Pearson, ed., *The French and Italian Notebooks*, III (unpublished dissertation, Yale, 1941), 603–604. Cf. *ibid.*, II, 424; III, 443–444. Professor Pearson kindly permitted me to use his edition.

[13] *The Marble Faun, The Complete Works,* Riverside Ed., vol. 6, 15.

[14] *Our Old Home,* p. 83.

customs, welded in with an ancient system, never dreaming of change, and bringing all the mellowness and richness of the past down into the midst of these railway times, which never make him or his community move one whit quicker than of yore."[15]

America was dedicated to the liberal ideal of an individualistic, mobile, progressive society; in Europe both Cooper and Hawthorne discovered, to their surprise, the satisfying compensations of a settled, organic, and traditional society. Their European experience subtly qualified, without ever destroying, their basic democratic liberalism. Their journals and novels reflect the tensions engendered by their efforts to reconcile their conservative impulses with their liberal ideas.

Cooper forged for himself a democratic philosophy, despite his upbringing in an atmosphere that might easily have made him share Irving's happy enthrallment with the life of the English country squire. The son of a conservative Federalist, who was something of a feudal manor lord in Cooperstown, Cooper was educated by a clerical tutor who ardently supported the English Crown, Church, and nobility and lived in the secure confidence that Jefferson was a libertine and George the Third a model of deportment. Seldom has a teacher had less influence on an intelligent pupil. Even Cooper's marriage into the DeLancey family, with its Tory tradition, did not stop him from becoming a loyal Jacksonian Democrat, a defender of American institutions against European criticism, and a sturdy enemy of aristocratic and plutocratic privilege. He was a gentleman by breeding, a democrat by conviction.

Europe did not kill the democrat in him; in fact, as with Jefferson, it strengthened his liberalism. While in Europe, the American was in danger of getting behind the facts of democratic progress in his own country, but there was, he felt, even "more danger of his getting *before* it, as to opinion."[16] In Europe, he felt, the liberal could whet the edge of his philosophy against the hard resist-

---

[15] *The English Notebooks*, p. 586.
[16] *Sketches of Switzerland, Part Second*, I, iv. Cf. *Gleanings in Europe: France*, p. 357.

ance of the old order, while in America (democratic by fact, habit, and practice), there was all too often a lag between fact and theory. By this shrewd insight he explained the humiliating paradox that French rather than American reviewers praised his novels for their republican principles. Characteristically, he became convinced in his last four years abroad that it was the very essence of being a gentleman to let liberal opinions enter thoroughly into "the whole composition of his mind." If gentlemen in America refused to take the popular side, it was because they were victims of "vulgar feelings" and "contracted associations" and so made "a fundamental mistake *as gentlemen*."[17] Several Democratic presidents would have applauded his epigram that it takes a first-class aristocrat to make a first-class Democrat.

Much of Cooper's European experience was eloquent testimony to his stubborn defense of democratic America. Always on guard against European snobbery or American hypocrisy, disdaining to use his letters of introduction, he met the nobility and intelligentsia of Europe with the proud, blunt independence of an American gentleman-democrat. He was quite undazzled by the aristocracy, confiding to his journal that it took "a good deal of faith and more ignorance to entertain a very high respect for what is called an ancient family."[18] He irritably chastised in his journal pliant American travelers, like the one he met in Belgium, who, "as is the case with half of those who read English books," was republican in all his practices, "but deeply imbued with arguments against all his habits."[19] He quickly spurned the chance given him to obtain social distinction in the European hierarchy when his daughter had a proposal from a Frenchman of good fortune, fair looks, and noble family; Jefferson, who died the day Cooper landed in England, would have blessed him from the grave if he could have heard Cooper's firm refusal: "We mean to continue Americans."[20]

[17] *Sketches of Switzerland, Part Second*, I, 86.
[18] August 10, 1828, Journal II, James Franklin Beard, ed., *The Letters and Journals of James Fenimore Cooper*, I (Cambridge, Belknap Press, 1960), 283.
[19] August 3, 1832, Journal XIII, *ibid.*, II, 294.
[20] Letter to Richard Cooper, March 12, 1833, James Fenimore Cooper,

Seizing every opportunity to defend American government, he wrote at Lafayette's request an article on the economy of a republic for use in the budget debate in the Chamber of Deputies, though he was shocked to discover that his arguments were challenged by members of the American embassy in France, who gave support to the slander that democracy was expensive. In his fiction the character of the "dough-face" American with European principles, like Mr. Gilded Wriggle of *The Monikins*, was a familiar target of satire.[21] The crudeness of American life, Cooper maintained, was the consequence of its primitive circumstances, not of its republican principles. If America had "no annals for the historian; no follies (beyond the most vulgar and commonplace) for the satirist; no manners for the dramatist; no obscure fictions for the writer of romance; no gross and hardy offenses against decorum for the moralist; nor any of the rich artificial auxiliaries of poetry," these limitations were merely the reverse side of the coin in a society which substituted "plain good sense" for the "artificial absurdities of life."[22] The American novelist had, therefore, but one fig leaf to cover his nakedness: the peculiarity of America's distinctive political opinions. Cooper's three historical novels with a European setting, *The Bravo*, *The Heidenmauer*, and *The Headsman*, used their background to highlight the superiority of American republicanism. He came to history not to praise it, but to bury it. The ruins of feudalism aroused no yearnings in him for the old order, but put him in mind of the long span of events which had led to the discovery of America and of "the novel but irrefutable principle on which its government was based" and "the silent working of its example in the

---

ed., *The Correspondence of James Fenimore Cooper*, I (New Haven, Yale University Press, 1922), 314.

[21] Robert E. Spiller, ed., *Letter to General Lafayette: James Fenimore Cooper and Related Correspondence on the Finance Controversy*, Facsimile Text Society, Series 1, vol. 6 (New York, Columbia University Press, 1931). Cooper's *Monikins*, an allegorical satire against both England and America, and his European experience are analyzed in Robert E. Spiller, *Fenimore Cooper: Critic of His Times* (New York, Minton, Balch, 1931), a pioneering work, establishing Cooper as much more than the author of the Leatherstocking stories.

[22] *Notions of the Americans*, II, 108.

two hemispheres."[23] His stories were warnings that even the Old World's ancient republics had suffered from the evils of aristocracy and failed to grant sufficient power to the masses.

True to his belief in the American example, Cooper was stimulated by the revolutions of 1830 to an intense concern for European liberty. Working with his friend Lafayette, a splendid example of Cooper's definition of the aristocratic liberal, he became chairman of a committee of Americans, resident in Paris, organized to give financial aid to the revolution and shelter to escaping refugees. He urged Lafayette to work for a nominal monarchy that was a real republic, with the king subordinated to a popularly elected Senate and with no representation of property in the government. The danger was, both in Europe and America, that a new "vulgar aristocracy" of trade and capital would result from the modern challenge to the caste system. "Heaven knows which is the worst!" he exclaimed in his journal. "I have never yet been in a country," he said, "in which what are called the lower orders have not clearer and sounder views than their betters of the great principles which ought to predominate in the control of human affairs."[24]

If Cooper's European education had only served to make him a more articulate liberal democrat, his experience would have differed little from that of Jefferson. Cooper's mind also felt the impact of certain European values, but for him they put the United States in a harsh, critical light. His political loyalty to America was complicated by a growing awareness that politics was not all of life, that European civilization could not be written off merely as a symbol of reaction. This tension, clearly apparent in his last four years abroad, was aggravated by the bitter conflicts over his reputation and property rights that he suffered upon his return to his country. If he had been conventionally pious

---

[23] *The Heidenmauer, or the Benedictines, Works,* Mohawk Ed., vol. 29, xxi.

[24] August 20, 1832, Journal XVI, *The Letters and Journals,* II, 312; *Sketches of Switzerland, Part One,* I, 177. Cooper wrote an amusing satire of the French government party's "mixed-government" synthesis of monarchy, aristocracy, and democracy in "Point de Bateaux à Vapeur—Une Vision," *Paris, ou Le Livre des Cent-et-Un,* 9 (1832), 221–250.

toward America or Europe, or toward both at once in the spirit of Longfellow and Irving, he might have been spared. Instead he exhausted himself by prosecuting with relentless success an appalling number of libel suits against those American critics who, for reasons of party politics, had defamed his character. The sophistication of Cooper's position, which rejected both romantic nostalgia and provincial contempt for Europe, isolated him from his contemporaries. Behind his long, increasingly waspish quarrel with his country there sometimes seemed to lurk a half-suppressed suspicion that perhaps the dark Old World could alone guarantee the values so unhappily absent from American life. For an American who had with the passionate intelligence of a Jefferson served the myth of the New World as the center of a glorious civilization, that nagging doubt was a cancer.

He had to admit that by contrast with Europe American culture and society were blighted by a "vast expansion of mediocrity." In European towns the Church held a central place, while in America "half a dozen ill-shaped, and yet pretending cupolas, and other ambitious objects, half the time in painted wood, just peer above the village, while the most aspiring roof is almost invariably that of the tavern."[25] In Italy he had been charmed by the "grace of mind," produced by frequent contact with great art, that distinguished both nobles and populace from the relatively barbarous Anglo-Saxons. It was unpleasant for him to have to record the fact that the only country in which he found it a social disadvantage to be a writer was his own, because "blocks are not colder, or can have less real reverence for letters, arts, or indeed cultivation of any kind, than the great bulk of the American people." The Church in Europe was a constant spectacle to delight the eye and ear, while "of all these touching embellishments of life" America was naked. Though he hated the "shoving propensities" of English aristocratic society, he was forced to confess that in America, where no one knew or accepted his place, social climbing was endemic, the upwardly mobile always

[25] "American and European Scenery Compared," *The Home Book of the Picturesque, or American Scenery, Art, and Literature* (New York, G. P. Putnam, 1852), p. 69.

displaying the same snobbery to those beneath them that they condemned in those above them. A society without fixed status, however much of a relief from the pressures of European life, had the effect of promoting the prestige of money-making as the highest standard of success. From the perspective of Rome Cooper saw New Yorkers as a mere "congregation of adventurers, collected from the four quarters of the earth, that have shaken loose every tie of birth-place, every sentiment of nationality or of historical connexion" and "care less for any greatness but that which is derived from the largeness of inventories."[26]

In the harsh light of Cooper's criticism much of the splendor of the myth of America as a happy land of liberty, so prominent in his *Notions of the Americans,* faded away. Even those travelers who had found America homely in comparison with Europe had loved their country for her tolerance and liberty; but Cooper, an exacting lover, discovered flaws in these boasted charms as well. If Americans had more social freedom in matters of form than Europeans, they enjoyed far less freedom than Europeans in matters of personal opinion and conduct.

Here Cooper first touched upon what has since become a common theme: the tyranny of conformity that plagues American democracy. As a democrat, he tried—with only occasional success —not to let his hatred of the despotism of public opinion disillusion him with democracy. "He is, indeed," he could write, "a most sneaking democrat, who finds it necessary to consult a neighborhood before he can indulge his innocent habits and tastes." The tyranny of public opinion, he felt, did not come from "the humblest classes of society at all, but from those nearer one's own level." Yet in Europe he had lamented the absence in America of a class "accustomed to sustain each other in a high tone of feeling and thinking." After his return to the United States, finally, he conceded in *The American Democrat* (1838) that "the tendency

---

[26] For his Italian perspective on "grace of mind" versus New York see *Gleanings in Europe: Italy,* II (Philadelphia, Carey, Lea, and Blanchard, 1838), 238, 156–157. For the writer and the Church in Europe see *Sketches in Switzerland, Part Second,* I, 199, 185. For the "shoving propensities" of Englishmen and Americans see *Gleanings in Europe: England,* p. 54.

of democracies is, in all things, to mediocrity, since the tastes, knowledge and principles of the majority form the tribunal of appeal."[27]

Because of the antirent wars of the 1840s in New York, in which Cooper supported the cause of the landlords against the tenants, his hostility to democracy was intensified. Characteristically, he took up a fictional plea for the landlords that ran to three volumes. In the last of the trilogy, *The Redskins* (1846), the story ends with the hero, whose uncle has been expatriated for twenty years in Paris, setting out for Washington to obtain justice for the landlords. If he should fail, Cooper acidly commented, "he has the refuge of Florence open, where he can reside among the other victims of oppression, with the advantage of being admired as a refugee from republican tyranny."[28] For the author of *Notions of the Americans*, which upheld America as the beacon of freedom, it must have been an anguishing sentence to write.

With this disillusionment he gave up too his old championing of those movements abroad which once seemed brave struggles to realize the American idea. "These quarrels and bitter conflicts of which we hear so much in the Old World," he wrote in 1850, a year before he died, "like some of our own, have their rise in abstractions quite as much as in actual oppression; and the alternative offered by change half the time amounts to but little more than the substitution of King Stork for King Log."[29] Still, in these same pages, he could reaffirm his fondness for the old buoyant

[27] For Cooper's Tocqueville-like observations see *Gleanings in Europe: France*, pp. 355–356; *Sketches in Switzerland, Part Second*, I, 133; and *The American Democrat, or Hints on the Social and Civic Relations of the United States of America*, 3rd ed., introduction by H. L. Mencken and Robert E. Spiller (New York, Vintage Books, 1956), p. 68.

[28] *The Redskins, or Indian and Injun, Works*, Mohawk Ed., vol. 25, 506. Cooper's ambivalence with respect to Europe and America is highlighted by Marius Bewley, "Revaluations (XVI): James Fenimore Cooper," *Scrutiny*, 19 (Winter, 1952–1953), 98–125; "Fenimore Cooper and the Economic Age," *American Literature*, 26 (May, 1954), 166–195. Bewley concentrates on the later fiction.

[29] *New York*, introduction by Dixon Ryan Fox (New York, William Farquhar Payson, 1930), pp. 60–61. Part of an introduction to a work Cooper planned on the history of Greater New York City.

hope that unless Americans threw away their advantages their country would in fifty years take its place at the head of the civilized nations of the world. Dampened by doubts as it was, the flame of his confidence in America's destiny still flickered.

Like Cooper, Hawthorne did not shut his democratic eyes abroad, but he too found that he kept seeing out of their corners attractive things not fully comprehended in his liberal creed. His conscience did not slumber; it merely alternated with his nostalgic yearning for a traditional society. Like sentinels, they spelled each other in their duty of looking out over the ramparts at the scene below. His humanitarian feelings did not fail to note the debasement of the English working class, the coarseness of the bleary-eyed women, often scrambling for coal or dung in the streets, the gin shops where ragged children came to fill shaving mugs or broken teapots for their parents, the almshouses with their wretched inmates, resigned to their inevitable end in an unpainted box ten feet below ground in the pauper's cemetery. The glimpse of a wandering beggar-woman, haunting the grounds of an English estate, or the contrast of a crude mass wedding with an elegant aristocratic ceremony, provoked his suspicion that a system which could give some such desirable privileges, while it shut out "a million others from any home whatever," must have some basic flaw in it. For all the pageantry of English life there rang in his ears an ominous dull sound, "as if the old foundations of things were crumbling away."[30]

In Italy there was also much to repel him. With his Puritan background he found something too artificial or too sensuous in the great masterpieces of art. One can sense his heritage in the passage of *The Marble Faun* where he describes Hilda lost in the labyrinth of Rome, a young American innocent at the mercy of a city dominated by "a priesthood, pampered, sensual, with red and bloated cheeks, and carnal eyes," corrupted by "an indolent nobility, with no high aims or opportunities, but cultivating a vicious way of life, as if it were an art," and where no place in which man had standing room was "unstained with one or an-

[30] *Our Old Home*, pp. 362, 111.

other kind of guilt."[31] Nothing could be a more devout offering on the altar of national orthodoxy than the ending to his fragmentary manuscript, *The Ancestral Footstep*, in which the orphaned young American virtuously renounces his claim to an English estate and returns to America with a radiantly innocent American girl, the two of them destined to become "the Adam and Eve of a new epoch, and the fitting missionaries of a new social faith."[32]

But neither Hawthorne the man nor Hawthorne the artist could give himself up single-mindedly to the naïve simplicity of this democratic American response to Europe. He was much too attracted, even obsessed, by the Old World life he saw. Tired of progress, he felt an alluring continuity in English life that made American mobility seem disagreeable. By comparison with English homes, where the shades of departed ancestors had a rightful place by the family hearth, "making this life now passing more dense as it were, by adding all the substance of their own to it," an American home was but one of those "poor tents of a day, inns of a night, where nothing was certain, save that the family of him who built it would not dwell here, even if he himself should have the bliss to die under the roof, which with absurdest anticipations, he had built for his posterity."[33]

Hawthorne's feeling for continuity was vividly expressed in his unfinished novel, *Dr. Grimshawe's Secret*. With its disconnected structure, compulsive repetitions, and murky Gothic atmosphere, it vibrates with all the ambivalence of a dream told in the psychoanalyst's office. Exploiting the legend of a bloody footstep left by a Protestant martyr in the stone floor of Smithell's Hall, the novel tells the story of the attempt to claim an English family estate by an American descendant of an English exile who had fled long ago to America. In one version of the plot the bloody footstep (in which the hero obsessively fits his own foot)

---

[31] *The Marble Faun*, pp. 467–468.

[32] "The Ancestral Footstep," *The Dolliver Romance, Fanshawe, and Septimius Felton, The Complete Works*, Riverside Ed., vol. 11, 490.

[33] Edward H. Davidson, ed., *Doctor Grimshawe's Secret* (Cambridge, Harvard University Press, 1954), first draft, p. 97.

was made by a regicide who had trod in the King's blood. Had Hawthorne's forefathers "killed" their king in '76 and set this Yankee son's teeth on edge? The American hero is too proud to accept the aristocratic distinction to which he is legally entitled, but he cannot resist congratulating himself on being able to enjoy "as old a rank, as desirable a station as the best of them." With great sympathy Hawthorne describes the hero's feeling of being a missing link in the long chain of ancestors, "stretching from the medieval ages, and their duskiness, downward, downward," holding out "dim arms to welcome him." He knows that if he becomes an English aristocrat, "America has been discovered in vain," but he is deeply tempted by the seductive appeal of English life: "What could there be in the wild, harsh, ill-conducted American approach to civilization which could compare with this? What to compare with this juiciness and richness?"[34]

In a status society, Hawthorne discovered, there was "a closer feeling of brotherhood, a more efficient sense of neighborhood," as well as an absence of ridiculous pretension among those who knew their place. In America's mobile society, where there was no permanence to either success or failure, there was little charity for those who, according to the official creed, had by their own lack of abilities determined their lowly place; and there was widespread affectation of gentility by those who were really common.[35] Democracy paid a high price for its political virtues.

Even monarchy and aristocracy, those American symbols of oppression, had in Hawthorne's candid gaze an appeal which he found hard to resist. At Blenheim, the Marleborough's palatial family seat, he was so impressed with the ordered beauty of the

[34] *Ibid.*, p. 133; "The Ancestral Footstep," p. 495; *Dr. Grimshawe's Secret*, p. 161. Hawthorne's obsession with the European past struck English reviewers as an American distortion, as Christof Wegelin points out in "Europe in Hawthorne's Fiction," *ELH*, 14 (September, 1947), 245.

[35] See *English Notebooks*, pp. 41, 95, 116–117. American travelers in Germany made the same disconcerting discovery. See Ruth Ann Musselman, dissertation, *Attitudes of American Travellers in Germany 1815–1890: A Study in the Development of Some American Ideas*, U. M. S. 4321, (Michigan State College, 1952), pp. 111–112.

scene as a setting for aristocratic life that, swallowing his republican prejudices, he confessed to cherishing the idea that "noblemen lead noble lives, and that all this stately and beautiful environment may serve to elevate them a little above the rest of us." America was proud to have refused the tinseled raiment of monarchy, but Hawthorne was struck with how beautifully "the royal robe of monarchy" was embroidered. "Palaces, pictures, parks!" he exclaimed: "They do enrich life; and kings and aristocracies cannot keep these things to themselves—they merely take care of them for others." If the splendor of regal life was a mere bauble, he was at least glad that he had come to England while they were "still playing with such a toy."[36]

Hawthorne accepted, like the rest of his countrymen, the traditional contrast between the Old World and the New, but he qualified its terms. Each pole was bewilderingly charged both positively and negatively. One could never be quite sure which way the current would flow. This predicament in optimistic, nineteenth-century America had the dimensions of a crisis for Hawthorne. Quite apart from his flagging creative powers, it is understandable that he never managed to complete his novel on the ancestral footstep theme, but left instructions (fortunately ignored) to have his unfinished manuscripts burned.

His choice between the two poles could never again be clear cut. Early in his consulship he had, like a good patriotic American, hated English policy, dreamed of an American invasion of England, and joyfully envisaged a Yankee Commodore sailing up the Mersey River. When he left England for the continent in 1858 he had his journals sealed until 1900, confident that by then England would have become a minor republic under the protection of the United States. Yet, unlike Cooper, who had eagerly returned to America (only to be disillusioned with what he found), Hawthorne flirted several times with the idea of settling in England. If "our old home" were only a republic, he felt, Americans might easily settle there.[37] If he pitied the plight of

[36] *English Notebooks*, pp. 410, 424.
[37] *The French and Italian Notebooks*, III, 580. For his earlier anti-English

American artists in Italy, "hermetically sealed in a foreign substance," still there were times when the splendor of Rome captured his heart as "even London or even little Concord itself, or old sleepy Salem, never did and never will." When he left it, he could not say he hated it, perhaps he even loved it, but life was too short for such "questionable and troublesome enjoyments."[38] Watching his country become embroiled in crisis after crisis over slavery, he confessed to his publisher, "I shall never again be so free as I have been in England and Italy." The United States were fit for many excellent purposes, but they were certainly "not fit to live in."[39] It was surely a remarkable confession to come from an American democrat born on the Fourth of July.

Impressed by the unified loyalty of Englishmen to their Queen, he wondered how Americans in their loosely knit union could develop a personal affection for their country. When you try to make it "a matter of heart," he complained in his notebooks, "everything falls away except one's native State—neither can you seize hold of that, unless you tear it out of the Union, bleeding and quivering."[40] For himself Concord was his sole remaining heartstring to America. When he returned there in the summer of 1860, the campaign which split America's political parties wide open and carried the country to the brink of civil war was already begun. Soon the affections of those Southerners who formed the Confederacy were to lead them to tear their native states, "bleeding and quivering," out of the Union. There was, as Henry James remarked, a deep tragedy in this agony for all Americans compelled to witness "the best of all possible republics given over to fratricidal carnage."[41] For Hawthorne, whose loyalty to America

---

views see Lawrence S. Hall, *Hawthorne: Critic of Society*, Yale Studies in English, vol. 99 (New Haven, Yale University Press, 1944), 145–146. He had been on friendly terms with the crusading republican firebrand George N. Sanders, mentioned in Chapter Three.

[38] *French and Italian Notebooks*, II, 418; III, 611, 619, 657.

[39] February 10, 1860, *Letters of Hawthorne to William D. Ticknor 1851–1864*, II (Newark, Carteret Book Club, 1910), 96; April 14, 1858, *ibid.*, II, 72.

[40] *French and Italian Notebooks*, III, 579.

[41] "Nathaniel Hawthorne," Edmund Wilson, ed., *The Shock of Recog-*

was rooted in his belief that it was, with all its faults, a secure beacon of political freedom, the Civil War came as a trauma. As the war dragged on, his doubts of a beneficial result multiplied. The future was problematic, hope dubious. Filled with "a sense of infinite weariness," he wrote an English friend in 1863, "I want the end to come, and the curtain to drop, and then to go to sleep."[42]

Cooper and Hawthorne had the distinction of bringing into a different, sharper focus the familiar Old World-New World theme. They brought them into a relationship close enough to generate the precious light of national self-criticism. Hawthorne's *The Marble Faun* was the artistic expression of the new attitude. Part guidebook, and widely used as such, it drew heavily on his notebooks which reflected his daily experience and reflections in Italy. Part morality play, it was a parable of innocence coming to maturity through personal knowledge of good and evil. Though he was thoroughly conventional in choosing the Italian scene as "a sort of poetic or fairy precinct, where actualities would not be so terribly insisted upon as they are, and must needs be, in America," and was even more so in using this background to suggest all the evils of the gloomy past, he brought to this hackneyed contrast a fresh ironic vision.[43]

Through the character of Kenyon, a member of the American artists' colony, Hawthorne criticized the bleakness and conformity of American village life, compared with the splendor of Rome and the social freedom the artists enjoyed there. He also subtly used the Italian mirror to reflect the ambiguities of his moral theme. Hilda, the young painter from New England, trimming the Virgin's lamp in the shrine at the top of her tower amid the fluttering of doves, is an appealing symbol of tender innocence, just as Donatello, with his faun-like ears and sympathy with the

nition, the Development of Literature in the United States Recorded by the Men Who Made It (Garden City, Doubleday, Doran, 1943), p. 536.

[42] Letter to Henry Bright, March 8, 1863, copy shown to me through the courtesy of Norman Holmes Pearson.

[43] *The Marble Faun*, p. 15.

animals, symbolizes the charm of the child of nature. But both are transformed into greater maturity by their experience of evil. Significantly, it is Miriam, a sophisticated woman with an international background and a shadowed past, who is the moral catalyst for them both and who voices Hawthorne's philosophical theme. It is Miriam who gives Hilda her vicarious knowledge of evil and provokes Donatello into committing the crime of murder. By this encounter with sin both are humanized. She, no longer a mere copyist, gains a new depth of perception into art; her severity is softened by sorrow, which finds its catharsis in her confession to a Catholic priest in an alien Roman church. Donatello, by assuming his burden of "sin, care, and self-consciousness," has had his simple, imperfect nature ripened to "a point of feeling and intelligence which it could have reached under no other discipline."[44] Though Hilda never accepts this heretical departure from her simple faith in the clean-cut distinction between right and wrong, she has been changed.

By this ambiguity of the moral structure of the tale, so has the traditional antithesis between America and Europe been transformed. The Old World no longer stands as a mere negative symbol of the darkness of the past. Hawthorne's novel implies (even more, perhaps, than he intended) that Europe has an educative value for Americans because it stands for a complexity and sophistication of experience denied by traditional mythology to the New World. It was an idea that Henry James would develop into the major theme of his art.

[44] *Ibid.*, p. 491.

7

THE INNOCENTS ABROAD

THE AMERICAN MIND has traditionally rested its case against the Old World on the superiority of a democratic republic which drew its sustenance from the green breast of the New World. Even on the very brink of civil war, that confidence in America's superiority to Europe ran strong in the devotees of the mission of America. Between secession and Bull Run, for example, Henry James, father of the novelist, gave a Fourth of July address at Newport which reverberated with the old ardent faith. Though he scorned the easy trust in an inevitable, automatic "manifest destiny," he still believed that America had exalted "man himself unqualified by convention" in contrast to hierarchical Europe, where class lines stifled the "exquisite honor which is due to man alone, and this exquisite indifference which is due to persons."[1] Europe was the letter, which was nothing; America was the spirit, which was everything.

[1] "The Social Significance of Our Institutions," F. O. Matthiessen, ed., *The James Family* (New York, Knopf, 1947), p. 61.

This sublime confidence was put to severe trial in the tragedy of the Civil War. To Henry James, the novelist, the lesson for Americans of his father's faith was clear. In days to come the good American, schooled by bitter experience, would acquire "a certain sense of proportion and relation, of the world being a more complicated place than it had hitherto seemed, the future more treacherous, success more difficult."[2] It was a lesson, relevant to the American attitude toward Europe, that his art was eloquently to teach. Even Mark Twain, whose best work was transmuted out of his nostalgic memories of the prewar days and in whom there still lived much of the old-fashioned blunt hostility to the conservative Old World, had in the Gilded Age corroding doubts about the simple pieties that had made it seem just to contrast American innocence with the bad Old World.

The post Civil War era was not an epoch to inspire complacency in any sensitive, reflective American. If slavery had been eliminated and the Union restored, it had been done at the price of enormous bloodshed, sectional embitterment, and a collapse of standards. The Negro was set free of his chains without being genuinely liberated from dependency and inferior status. Political corruption spread like a cancer into the national and local governments. Large-scale industry produced a breed of business leaders who built their empires without the restraints of any deep sense of social responsibility for their power. The newly rich, bereft of culture and taste, despoiled Europe in a search for the emblems of refinement which might give prestige to a fortune made from the exploitation of steel, oil, railroads, or textiles.

Aggressively secure in the conviction that they had, like the heroes of the Alger stories, risen by luck and pluck to reap the just rewards of free enterprise, they were pathetically insecure in their hunger for a kind of established status that neither their origins, their code, nor their mobile society could naturally supply. Proud citizens of a nation that boasted of never having known the thralldom of feudalism, they wistfully emulated in their palatial

[2] "Nathaniel Hawthorne," Edmund Wilson, ed., *The Shock of Recognition* (New York, Doubleday, Doran, 1943), p. 536.

homes on Fifth Avenue or at Newport the splendor of Old World architecture, amassing a jumble of European styles, often appropriated in ignorance and consecrated to lavishness. These were the stunning products of what Henry James called their "witless dream"—the vast "white elephants," mostly "all cry and no wool," which he noted with horror on revisiting Newport in 1906. Hungering for the badges of culture, refinement, and social distinction, these new masters of capital crashed New York society, rivaled each other in their "conspicuous consumption," climbed spurious genealogical trees on the hunt for aristocratic ancestors, and on their grand tour of Europe bagged for themselves and their families treasures of art or a son-in-law of bluest blood. Witless as many of these raids were, some of them embellished the nation with first-rate collections of art, like those of J. P. Morgan or Isabella Stewart Gardner. Tutored by Harvard's Charles Eliot Norton to collect first editions of Dante and by her protégé Bernard Berenson to prefer Titian to Gainsborough, this "Serpent of the Charles" reigned with an iron glove at her *salons*, where such brilliant guests as Henry Adams, Oliver Wendell Holmes, and William James could enjoy this "Bostonian's dream of Italy."[3] Her Fenway Court, begun in 1900 at the height of the American ravaging of Europe, was symbolically graced with the greatest Titian in America—*The Rape of Europa*.

Europe was a school of instruction through amusement, as Grant Allen's guidebook *The European Tour* preached to its American readers. What the traveler was supposed to seek was a Europe defined as a museum. A year's tour, as Allen planned it, made Italy "the key by which you may unlock the secret of Europe"; bypassed Germany, except for a week in the medieval atmosphere of the Rhineland; neglected the French provinces for the sake of the Louvre, "*the kernel of Paris*"; and advised only a short final stay in England, because its historical treasures presupposed the continent, older and more novel to a young country.

[3] See Aline B. Saarinen, *The Proud Possessors, the Lives, Times and Tastes of Some Adventurous American Art Collectors* (New York, Random House, 1958), pp. 25–55.

"Several admirable and noteworthy things in Europe are more recent than the Crusades," this cicerone priggishly admitted. "My plan does not include them,—that is all," he explained; "and you can find out everything you need to know about them without my telling you."[4]

Italy was inevitably the essence of the Old World for a Protestant, prosperous, industrialized, democratic country. The popular architects McKim, Mead, and White understood the point with great success in the city and country houses they planned and decorated on Italian models in the 1880s; and William Dean Howells made his first literary triumph with popular guidebooks and fiction exploiting the years he spent as American Consul in Venice. It was, significantly, Howells' Italian experience that initiated him into the Dante-worshiping circle of the Cambridge literati—Longfellow, Norton, and Lowell. Italy was also an appropriate backdrop for the growth of the American literary type of the innocent, independent American girl, invented by Hawthorne, developed by Howells, and refined by Henry James. With the unification of Italy in 1860 and the Austrian annexation of Venice and seizure of Rome, American sympathy with Italian republicanism faded away in a fascination with Italy as a jewel in the Old World museum.[5]

Despite the narrow limitations of the orthodox Grand Tour, Americans displayed a broader zest in going to Europe. Colonies flourished in London and Paris, while over 2000 Americans in the decade of the eighties alone pursued the rigors of the higher learning at German universities in Berlin, Leipzig, Heidelberg, or Halle and discovered an academic freedom unfamiliar at home. By the early twentieth century there were already familiar signs of an American invasion of Europe—the noisy dazzle of Montmartre,

---

[4] Grant Allen, *The European Tour* (New York, Dodd, Mead, 1899), p. 295.
[5] See Van Wyck Books, *The Dream of Arcadia, American Writers and Artists in Italy 1760–1915* (New York, E. P. Dutton, 1958), pp. 238–239; James L. Woodress, Jr., *Howells and Italy* (Durham, Duke University Press, 1952); Annette Kar, "Archetypes of American Innocence: Lydia Blood and Daisy Miller," *American Quarterly*, 5 (Spring, 1953), 31–38; Roy M. Peterson, "Echoes of the Italian Risorgimento in Contemporaneous American Writers," *PMLA*, 47 (March, 1932), 220–240.

rising prices, cleaner hotels, soda fountains, cocktails, and the social triumphs of the organizationally-minded American woman.
In 1894 Du Maurier's *Trilby*, a sentimental picture of the Bohemian style of life in the Latin Quarter, became a national craze,
and Whistler's protest against its caricature of him made his reputation as the prophet of expatriation. The "young prophets of
culture," lamented a man of letters, think that the only modern
art is French or Japanese, find the most advanced literature in
Parisian realism, and believe "it is impossible for an intelligent
man to be contented in America."[6]

It was in this period that Europe became for Americans a playground in the modern sense. (In 1851 a minister setting out on
his European travels was unable to find guidebooks, written for
Americans, in the best bookstores of Boston and New York.)[7]
A writer in a popular journal noted in 1868 that Americans were
traveling to Europe no longer for truth or beauty, but merely for
pleasure, health, novelty, social prestige, or escape from the cares
of dull routine. One of the popular idols was Bayard Taylor,
world traveler and lecturer, whose restless peregrinations inspired
the remark that he had traveled more and seen less than any man
living. Europe was inundated by a new group of "passionless
pilgrims," as Henry James called them, who were disposed to
treat the Old World as "a vast painted and gilded holiday toy,
serving its purpose on the spot and for the time, but to be relin-
quished, sacrificed, broken and cast away, at the dawn of any
other convenience."[8]

[6] Norman Hapgood, "American Cosmopolitanism," *Literary Statesmen
and Other Essays on Men Seen from a Distance* (Chicago, H. S. Stone,
1897), p. 176. See also Rowland Short, "Americans in Paris," *Harper's
Weekly*, 54 (April 2, 1910), 13–14; Anglo-American, "Americans Abroad,"
ibid., 53 (August 7, 1909), 24 and "The American Colony in London,"
ibid., 48 (July 30, 1904), 1176; Charles Franklin Thwing, *The American
and the German University* (New York, Macmillan, 1928), pp. 42–43; John
R. Walz, *German Influence in American Education and Culture* (Philadelphia, Carl Schurz Memorial Foundation, 1936), p. 51; and Albert Parry,
Garrets and Pretenders, a History of Bohemianism in America, rev. ed.
(New York, Dover, 1960), pp. 110–137.

[7] He wrote one of his own: Rev. Roswell Park, *A Hand-Book for
American Travellers in Europe* (New York, G. P. Putnam, 1853).

[8] Preface to "The Reverberator," *The Art of the Novel, Critical*

Mark Twain's *The Innocents Abroad,* an immediate best seller, is an authentic reflection, as well as a criticism, of American tourists going to Europe for amusement. On June 8, 1867, he had himself sailed on the *Quaker City* excursion, writing up this "New Pilgrim's Progress" for the newspapers before he made a book out of his experience. Already known as a rough-and-tumble Western humorist, he shrewdly exploited the strategy of debunking the sentimental reactions of the pious pilgrim. He aimed to give an account that would "suggest to the reader how he would be likely to see Europe and the East if he looked at them with his own eyes instead of the eyes of those who traveled in those countries before him." Other travel books had humbugged readers by telling them what they *ought* to feel in Europe. This tactic was not new; another Westerner, J. Ross Browne, a friend of Mark Twain, had in 1853 recorded his journey to the Near East, with the explicit purpose of crusading against "the Mists of Fancy." He traveled with a group of Americans, "priding ourselves upon our superiority over all other nations in piety, morals, and railroads," who were "just popping in on Constantinople for a pastime."[9] Mark Twain simply raised this brand of Western humor to the level of art.

In his reactions there was something archetypal, a self-conscious strain of undiluted Americanism, Western style, struck with the pedal pushed to the floor for the sake of effect. With unabashed provinciality he labeled the Cathedral of Notre Dame a "brown old Gothic pile," preferred contemporary copies to the "mournful wreck" of "The Last Supper" in Milan, and was more impressed with Italy's "depots and turnpikes" than with its "vast museum of magnificence and misery." He was the man from Missouri who had to be shown. What was the Città Vecchia in unvarnished truth but "the finest nest of dirt, vermin, and ignorance we have

Prefaces, introduction by R. P. Blackmur (New York, Scribner's, 1934), p. 189. Cf. "Going Abroad," *Putnam's Magazine,* 1 (May, 1868), 330–338. James's story is a trenchant judgment on "passionless pilgrims."

[9] Cf. J. Ross Browne, *Yusef: or the Journey of the Frangi, a Crusade in the East* (New York, Harper, 1853), p. 117, with Mark Twain, *The Innocents Abroad or the New Pilgrim's Progress,* Uniform Ed. (New York, Harper, 1905), preface.

found yet, except that African perdition they call Tangier, which is just like it?"[10] In Paris the famous "grisettes" of the Latin Quarter were only another "romantic fraud"; they were not even delightfully immoral. These ugly creatures showed by their looks that they lived on garlic and onions. In this exhilarated spirit he deflated the "Europe" of the travel books.

In Mark Twain's democratic scales of judgment Europe was perpetually weighed and found wanting. In the Louvre his responses to art were perpetually distracted by his disgust with "the cringing spirit" of artists who had been complimentary to their "princely patrons." The Medici were too infamous a set of villains to be hallowed in paint. Rome with its beggars, its tyrannical priesthood, its standing army, and technological backwardness irritated and depressed him. Morse, Fulton, Daguerre—these were the real heroes, freed of superstitious ancestor worship, who had benefited mankind through their inventions. What Europe needed was a Connecticut Yankee whose common sense could cut through the medieval nonsense that had plagued Europe since the days of King Arthur, and liberate it with the blessings of free institutions, public schools, insurance policies, and modern inventions.

This naively invidious comparison of the New World with the Old, utterly untutored by either an aesthetic or historical sense, surely reflected popular American prejudice but Mark Twain was too sophisticated to accept it for himself without qualification. It is often difficult to tell when he is merely playing a role (like Franklin wearing his fur cap in the French *salons*, or Jefferson describing himself as a "savage of the mountains of America") and when he has actually accepted the mask as his own. When he peeps with shamed curiosity through his fingers at a Parisian Can-Can, is there flat statement or prudish irony in his conclusion that French morality is not of that "strait-laced" kind that is "shocked at trifles"? It is easy to be persuaded here that he has his tongue in cheek in picturing himself as an embarrassed peeper, but then what is one to make of his outraged protest against sen-

[10] *The Innocents Abroad*, I, 334.

timentalizing "a dastardly seducer like Pierre Abelard"? Certainly Tom Sawyer and Huck Finn were deliberate departures from the genteel and improving stories for boys produced by the bale in the Peter Parley or Rollo books, yet his criticism of Europe is much like those consummately orthodox juvenile tales. He could easily have written Peter Parley's *The Balloon Travels of Robert Merry and His Young Friends*, with its emphasis on French deceit, immorality and fickleness, its condemnation of St. Peter's for having its origins in pride, not piety; and its contrast of the "bright, youthful vigor" of America with time-worn Rome, "grovelling beneath the most degrading superstitions."[11]

Fortunately for modern readers, Mark Twain saw with the saving eye of the humorist the comic side of this confrontation of American utilitarianism with the European world of rank, feudal tradition, and high civilization. If he shared much of the tourist's complacent sense of superiority to Europeans, it was not without irony: "We generally made them feel rather small, too, before we got done with them, because we bore down on them with America's greatness until we crushed them."[12] Though they talked the best *Quaker City* French, they never could, he blandly remarks, succeed "in making these idiots understand their own language." The satirical edge of his humor clearly cuts both ways also in *A Connecticut Yankee in King Arthur's Court*. At times the figure of the Hartford mechanic, a "champion of hard, unsentimental common sense and reason" against the quixotic knight errantry and superstitious black arts of the medieval world, seems like an incredibly naive idealization of American technological know-how and depreciation of the forces of tradition, religion, and feudal institutions. To some extent Mark Twain was a devotee of this simple-minded faith in the glory of nineteenth-century civilization. He characteristically lost thousands of dollars investing in an impractical typesetting machine, and in his autobiography he finds it startling to reflect that household conveniences hardly existed in the world when Queen Victoria was born.

[11] Samuel Griswold Goodrich, *The Balloon Travels of Robert Merry and His Young Friends* (New York, J. C. Derby, 1855), p. 192.

[12] *The Innocents Abroad*, II, 438.

"The valuable part—to *my* thinking the valuable part—of what we call civilization," he declared, "had no existence when she emerged upon the planet."[13] There was probably less ambivalence for him than there is for a generation that has known Henry Ford in the humor of his Yankee's scheme of hitching up Simon Stylites on his pillar to a sewing machine, so that the energy wasted in making his prayers might be exploited in producing cheap shirts for the masses.

Yet there are undercurrents in the story quite subversive of any unambiguous reading of it. Not only are there critical references to the tariff, slavery and the stock exchange as American evils, but the Yankee himself is aware that the crowd's homage to the King is not entirely misplaced, for there is something "peculiarly grand" about the bearing of a King, after all. The Yankee's conversion of the knights into salesmen with sandwich boards advertising soap, in order to introduce the benefits of a "new deal" to the ignorant people, is a burlesque of both civilizations. It is, above all, highly significant that "The Boss's" effort to turn medieval England into a democratic republic ends in disastrous failure. After the Yankee introduces the blessings of modern industrial civilization, he longs to follow them up by overthrowing the Church and establishing universal suffrage. But a war, produced by bitterness over dishonest manipulations on the stock exchange (formerly the Round Table), forces the Yankee to defend his "new deal." Isolated with only fifty-two boys as supporters, the rest having joined the Church, nobles, and gentry, the Yankee faces defeat. Drawing on his experience in the arms factory at Hartford, where he learned all about guns, revolvers, cannon and "all sorts of labor-saving machinery," he sets about defending himself with Gatling guns, dynamite, torpedoes, and electrically charged wire fences. Increasingly absorbed in the fantasy of destroying the English nation by merely touching a button, the Yankee betrays something of the ugly character of a dictator, drunk with power. The ending is grotesquely and mor-

[13] *The Autobiography of Mark Twain*, I, introduction by Albert Bigelow Paine (New York, Harper, 1924), 208.

dantly ironic. "The Boss" becomes trapped in a cave, immobilized by the electrified mass of human beings his weapons have destroyed: "We had conquered; in turn we were conquered." Merlin the magician is left to proclaim his triumph over modernism by sentencing the Yankee to sleep for thirteen centuries. When he at last awakes, he is dying. He thinks he hears the bugle of the King's troops, and he shouts incoherent orders. "He was getting up his last 'effect'; but he never finished it." The distance between Hartford and Camelot is great in many ways, but human nature in the New World is not as innocent as it thinks.

Like Henry James, Sr., Mark Twain might have wondered what "the Lord will do with any European people." But he had much too uneasy feelings about modern life to join the elder James in his serene faith that "American disorder is sweet beside European order: it is so full of promise."[14] For other sensitive spirits in the Gilded Age, Europe was beginning to have the appeal of a refuge from American barbarism. For them the old terms of contrast between the New and the Old Worlds were being transvalued. Devotion to the gospel of work and the freedom to rise in a mobile society had, they felt, destroyed civilized leisure and made money-making the mark of success. The vaunted moral sense of a middle-class republic had produced a dreary conformity. The very solidity of the political foundations of the United States, strong enough to survive Civil War, had been secured at the price of a depressing absence of gracious superstructure. These themes, in varying degrees, began to appear in some serious novels as the century approached its end.

For these writers outright expatriation was still shunned, though only a bitter peace could be signed with America. In Henry B. Fuller's *The Chevalier of Pensieri-Vani* (1890) the American hero

[14] *The James Family*, p. 287. For the further development of Twain's doubts about the conventional contrast between Europe and America see the discussion of *The American Claimant* by Roger B. Salomon, *Twain and the Image of History* (New Haven, Yale University Press, 1961), p. 129. Salomon provocatively suggests also that Hank Morgan in *A Connecticut Yankee in King Arthur's Court* is much like the figure of Louis Napoleon III whom Twain sketched admiringly in *The Innocents Abroad*. See *ibid.*, p. 119.

returns from Italy to the provincial life he scorns, but he is a divided soul, attached by birth and habit to his homeland without being a "good American" and drawn by cultural aspiration to Europe without the hope of ever being "a good European." He is a man caught between two fires, "both of which scorched him." It was a plight the author understood out of the pain of his own troubled flutterings between Europe and Chicago. Robert Herrick's heroine of *The Gospel of Freedom* (1898) flees to Florence for emotional rejuvenation after a disillusioning marriage that had introduced her to the corruption and vulgarity of Chicago. But Herrick allows her no fulfillment there. She soon becomes equally disenchanted with the pettiness of the Bohemian community of artists in Italy and returns to the midlands to accept its harsh limitations as the sober setting for her search for love and freedom.[15]

To Americans of patrician background, who resented the inroads of the new vulgar aristocracy of raw wealth, the American scene looked especially bleak. The historian Henry Adams, who saw in President Grant's administration enough evidence alone to refute an optimistic belief in evolutionary progress, found a compensating intellectual pleasure in contemplating the medieval cult of the Virgin and the harmonized glories of Chartres Cathedral. "Paris delights me," he wrote John Hay, "but not for its supposed delights. It is the calm of its seclusion that charms; the religious rest that it diffuses, and the cloister-like peace that it brings to the closing years of life."[16] Adams enjoyed the historical dream of himself as respectable Norman farmer doing military service for his fief. He was sure (like his brother Brooks) that his ancestors had steadily declined since the building of the cathedrals. "They have lost their religion, their art and their military tastes," he wrote Brooks. "They cannot now comprehend the meaning of what they did at Mont St. Michel. They have kept only the qual-

[15] For Fuller see his *The Chevalier of Pensieri-Vani*, 4th ed. (New York, Century, 1892), pp. 57, 96, 105, 176–177; Elwood P. Lawrence, "Fuller of Chicago: A Study in Frustration," *American Quarterly*, 6 (Summer, 1954), 137–146. For Herrick see his *The Gospel of Freedom* (New York, Macmillan, 1898), pp. 265–266, 286–287.

[16] August 20, 1899, W. C. Ford, ed., *Letters of Henry Adams (1892–1918)* (Boston, Houghton Mifflin, 1938), p. 235.

ities which were most useful, with a dull instinct recalling dead associations. So we get Boston."[17] For Edith Wharton, who remembered with nostalgic affection the more honorable style of an earlier New York aristocracy, the Old World was a stable point of reference for "beauty and old-established order" in an age that seemed to have lost its compass.[18] By 1907, after so many crossings of the Atlantic that Henry James called her "the pendulum woman," she had settled permanently in the Faubourg St. Germain, the most aristocratic quarter of old Paris.

Henry Adams and Edith Wharton, like her mentor Henry James, were able to reconcile their conflicts with successful realization of their creative purposes. For less gifted and weaker souls, who also could not look upon the Gilded Age without a sensitive shudder, there were sadder outcomes. "We are," wrote George Cabot Lodge, "a dying race and really we've never lived."[19] Lodge had been reared in Washington in the hothouse atmosphere of mutual admiration and haughty disdain for the outside world so characteristic of the patrician circles his family moved in, and

[17] September 8, 1895, *ibid.*, p. 80. Ferner Nuhn relates Adams's medievalism to his problem of being an aristocrat in a democratic world in "Henry Adams and the Hand of the Fathers," *The Wind Blew from the East, a Study in the Orientation of American Culture* (New York, Harper, 1942), pp. 164–194. Nuhn ignores, however, the particular relevance of the especially crass conditions of post-Appomattox America. For Brooks Adams's cult of the Gothic see Arthur F. Beringause, *Brooks Adams* (New York, Knopf, 1955), pp. 136–138. Henry particularly admired Saint-Michel, Chartres, Coutances, Bayeux, and Caen, rather than the later Gothic which he found pretentious.

[18] Edith Wharton, *A Backward Glance* (New York, Appleton-Century, 1934), p. 44. In *French Ways and Their Meanings* (1919) she presented French civilization as a model for Americans, who lacked taste, reverence, belief in tradition, and intellectual honesty. See the analysis by Warren I. Susman, "A Second Country: the Expatriate Image," The University of Texas *Studies in Literature and Language*, 3 (Summer, 1961), 174–175. Constance Fenimore Woolson, a lesser writer, who also idolized Henry James, reveled in what she called "that old-world feeling" at Oxford, Florence, and Venice from 1879 to 1893. See John Dwight Kern, *Constance Fenimore Woolson, Literary Pioneer* (Philadelphia, University of Pennsylvania Press, 1934), p. 115.

[19] Quoted by Edmund Wilson, introduction "Henry Adams: the Life of George Cabot Lodge," *The Shock of Recognition*, p. 745. For Lodge's contempt for American society see letter to Langdon Mitchell, Spring, 1904, *ibid.*, p. 812.

despite his youthful promise as a poet, it was his fate to remain (as Edith Wharton noted) "in a state of brilliant immaturity." Homesick for America when in Paris or Berlin, he was bitterly resentful of American life and yearned for Europe when at home.

No one understood better these pilgrims, whether passionless or passionate, than the novelist Henry James. His life and work were profound assessments of the American-European relationship, and he was armed, more powerfully than either Cooper or Hawthorne had been, with a style and technique elaborately shaped to match the depth of his perceptions. He made "the international theme" the core of the fruit of his prodigious productivity. By the circumstances of his life he was uniquely qualified to analyze the attraction of Europe for Americans, as well as their limitations in coming to grips with it. Haphazardly educated abroad, in London, Paris, Geneva, Boulogne, and Bonn, he took to Europe with "unnatural precocity." As far back as he could remember he had carried in his side, "buried and unextracted, the head of one of those well-directed shafts from the European quiver" to which "tender American flesh" was "helplessly and bleedingly exposed." He had been hurried off to London and Paris as a baby and was ever after to feel the "nostalgic poison" in his veins; so much so that when he returned at the age of thirteen for prolonged exposure to Europe he felt as if he had been "restored to air already breathed and to a harmony already disclosed."[20] In America he counted as close friends Boston Brahmins like James Russell Lowell and Charles Eliot Norton, men who were widely traveled in Europe and keenly conscious of its cultural advantages. Not surprisingly, Europe had for James the magic of art, history, fame, and power—"the world in fine raised to the richest and noblest expression."[21] In 1869, at the age of twenty-six, a revisiting of England and a first glimpse of Italy had, in his own retrospect, determined his fate. He sailed for Paris in 1875 to make Europe his permanent residence, and forty years later, shortly before he died, became a citizen of the England in

[20] Preface, "The Reverberator," *The Art of the Novel*, p. 195.
[21] *A Small Boy and Others* (New York, Scribner's, 1913), pp. 346–347.

which, as master of Lamb House at Rye, he had become a personage of almost legendary significance, the very symbol of the dedicated, self-conscious artist.

Superficially, James seems, both as an artist and as a man, so opposite a case to Mark Twain that by facile comparison the Westerner makes the expatriate look like an un-American "sport" mysteriously generated on native soil. Mark Twain's fiction, drawing heavily on his experience in the small town of Hannibal, Missouri, or his rough-and-tumble life as a Mississippi steamboat pilot and a prospector in the Nevada mining camps, easily justifies his being called "the Lincoln of our literature." What could be more different from his unbuttoned frontier humor than the cultivated baroque style of Henry James with his passion for close scrutiny of motive and scruple and his cast of characters endowed with special privileges of money, education, or social position? James was as pungently evocative of the East and Europe as Mark Twain was redolent of the West and America, and in native mythology the West was a positive symbol of America's unique, ruggedly democratic nationality, just as the East was, by the logic of the legend, a negative symbol of an effete, class-conscious community subservient to Europe.

This neat antithesis, however, is the offspring of the myth-making propensities of the American mind which are so readily provoked by the encounter with Europe. For all his Western background Mark Twain made his home in Hartford in 1871, enjoyed at least a dozen trips to Europe, where he once lived for nine successive years, held court and *salon* for European intellectuals and dignitaries as if he were a visiting potentate, was inordinately proud of his honorary Oxford degree, and indulged in *The Prince and the Pauper* his suppressed romantic enthusiasm for medieval pageantry. If he was no simple provincial, neither was James a simple expatriate. He settled in "the denser, richer, warmer European spectacle" because he felt, as an artist, "it takes such an accumulation of history and custom, such a complexity of manners and types, to form a fund of suggestion for a novelist."[22] London was for him a "vast compendium of the world" which offered wider scope than America for his own sensibility to social forms and the blending of past and present in the life of a people. He advised other writers, like Hamlin Garland, Edith Wharton, or Amy Lowell, not to take his own choice as a general rule, and he always spoke guardedly about his own decision with full awareness of the difficulties, both artistic and personal, of living abroad. He had, by his formidable resolution and rare subtlety, made a triumph out of his self-imposed exile; others not similarly equipped might achieve only a dim disaster. "To be a cosmopolite is not, I think, an ideal," he wrote soon after settling in London in 1876; "the ideal should be to be a concentrated patriot. Being a cosmopolite is an accident, but one must make the best of it." Its advantage, which James exploited to the utmost, was that of forming the habit of looking "for the virtues that go with certain defects, and the defects that go with certain virtues."[23]

He had not rejected his country in anger, spite or indifference; he had merely found a new vantage point. "I know what I am about, and I have always my eyes on my native land," he reassured his brother. Symbolically the statement was true. His stories are the work of a writer who never lost touch with the values, however ironically appreciated, of his own native land. When he became an English citizen in 1915, it was from a sense of indebtedness to the country in which he had lived for forty years and whose civilization was threatened by the outbreak of war. If the United States had entered the war sooner, he explained, no personal act of his would have been necessary. His debt would

[22] "Nathaniel Hawthorne," *The Shock of Recognition*, p. 459.
[23] *Portraits of Places* (Boston, Houghton Mifflin, 1911), p. 75. The relevant letters for understanding James's choice of Europe as a place to work are quoted in Matthiessen, *The James Family*, under the heading "Europe and/or America?"; see pp. 296–297. For his becoming an English citizen see letters to Henry James, Jr., June 24, 1915 and July 20, 1915, Percy Lubbock, ed., *The Letters of Henry James*, II (London, Macmillan, 1920), 494–497, 508–509. For his advice to other writers see Bruce R. McElderry, Jr., "Hamlin Garland and Henry James," *American Literature*, 23 (1951–1952), 433–446.

have been paid. Since America delayed intervening, he tried to set it an example.

His knowledge of Americans in Europe was notably intimate and extensive. In the richly furnished and skillfully lighted gallery of his art their portraits are impressive to the documentary as well as to the aesthetic eye. He knew them all—the pathetically earnest and easily duped tourists, yearning for a picture-post-card "Europe"; the high-spirited young maidens from the provinces, heedless of alien proprieties and protected by the charmed circle of their innocence, out "to see Europe for themselves"; the snobbish daughters of the rich, seeking titled prey and preyed upon by down-at-the-heels aristocrats; the bookish young dilettantes, hoping to make an art out of life in "the real Europe"; the tired businessmen who smirk and wink when they think of Paris; the ardent pilgrims to an enchanted "Europe," lost in a fabulous museum, disoriented by the vivid abundance of their impressions. They are all there, painted with affectionate amusement, unsparing honesty, and calculated irony. If these traveling Americans now seem like familiar types, it is because Henry James made them so.

In his travel books James indulged his own appetite for the picturesque, reveling in the antique, the traditional, and the pastoral, like any other American tourist fascinated with the decorated, historical surface of an Old World so different from his own. He could go "reeling and moaning" through the streets of Rome in "a fever of enjoyment," cherish in England "the fine old ivied and cobwebbed improprieties" reformers wanted to sweep away, and find Gladstone's liberalism painfully prosaic in contrast to the imperial pretensions of self-conscious Toryism. Yet James always understood that these American predilections for the old and established order in any European country were the prejudices of the irresponsible, "sympathetic stranger." What the tourist sought in Europe was confirmation of his habitual distinction between two polar worlds. What made America unique and glorious was its being an anti-Europe; what made Europe aesthetically attractive to the nonpolitical eye was its being an anti-America. "To travel is, as it were, to go to the play, to attend a spectacle,"

James pointed out; "and there is something heartless in stepping forth into the streets of a foreign town to feast upon novelty when the novelty consists simply of the slightly different costume in which hunger and labour present themselves."[24] He could smile at himself for romanticizing "an harmonious little figure in the middle distance," picturesquely whistling as he climbed the hill overlooking an Italian town, who turned out to be an unemployed Italian radical instead of an operatic symbol of "sensuous optimism." Listening to the "drowsy old canons of Rheims," he could do full justice to the "enchanting perspective" and "dusky splendor" of the great cathedral, yet still deeply sympathize with the liberals and radicals for their hatred of the reactionary policy of the Catholic party and the unction of a clergy, acting as the "go-betweens of Bonapartism," which gave "daily evidence of its devotion to arbitrary rule and to every iniquity that shelters itself behind the mask of 'authority.'" As passionate a pilgrim to the Old World shrines as any of his characters, he was distinguished from them by his rare capacity for objectivity and detachment in analyzing his own feelings.

His fiction brilliantly illuminated the self-deceptions and weaknesses of the romantic attitude towards Europe. In "A Passionate Pilgrim" and "The Madonna of the Future," early stories which he felt were documentary "in the highest degree" of his own crucial tour of England and Italy in 1869, he sympathetically dramatized his young Americans' delirious aesthetic piety for the elaborate finish of the Old World.[25] Yet James presented with

[24] "Italy Revisited," *Portraits of Places*, p. 50. Cf. *ibid.*, pp. 52–53; "Rheims and Laon: A Little Tour," *ibid.*, pp. 105–106; "London at Midsummer," *ibid.*, pp. 226–227. On a fourth visit to Rome in 1877 he found its charm to lie in the mixture of antiquity and modernity. See "'Very Modern Rome'—an Unpublished Essay of Henry James," *Harvard Library Bulletin*, 8 (Spring, 1954), 125–140. The best examples of the travel writings of James as a "visionary tourist" are collected in Morton Dauwen Zaubel, ed., *The Art of Travel, Scenes and Journeys in America, England, France and Italy from the Travel Writings of Henry James* (New York, Doubleday, 1958).

[25] Preface, "The Reverberator," *The Art of the Novel*, p. 196. Both stories are in vol. 13 of the New York Edition (New York, Scribner's, 1908). This edition was organized, on the model of Balzac's *The Comédie Humaine*, as "Scenes of the International Life." See Leon Edel, "The

equal force the irony of their celebrations of formal order. Both the American claimant to the English estate, glorying in "distinctions and privileges the most delicious and invidious" denied to him in "the deadly dry air" of America, and the American artist, escaped to Florence from "our crude and garish climate, our silent past, our deafening present," are overwhelmed by their romantic impressions and reduced to ineffectiveness. The painter, blind to the aging of his model, lives in a state of "charmed inaction, for ever preparing for a work for ever deferred." Consumed by his extravagant ambitions for greatness, he lacks the facility of technique commanded by an Italian sculptor who turns out cheap and nasty erotic figurines for the tourist trade. The American descendant of the English family also ends in futility. He wins his claim just after he expires in the last stages of a consumptive disease, feverishly identifying himself and an English girl with the shades of ancient ancestors. Quietly the story makes the point that for the English, who live under the forms the American aesthetically admires, the social framework is inexorable, even oppressive. The hero's exiled ancestor had fled to America because he had loved a girl unacceptable to his family; the female ancestor of the heroine had been in disgrace for marrying a French fiddler. The down-and-out Oxford alumnus, who wheels the sick American about the grounds of the college, has had a younger son's meager portion and looks to America as a land of opportunity. Beguiled by the splendor of alien forms these pilgrims from America fail to grasp their actuality.

To be forced to awake from the enthralling dream of an enchanted Europe is the common fate of James's Americans—of the incorruptible Madame de Mauves, who has married into a thoroughly corruptible French family out of a deluded fascination with aristocratic pedigree; of the imaginative Isabel Archer, who is "ground in the very mill of the conventional" by a loveless marriage to a fake cosmopolitan; of the retired businessman Chris-

Architecture of Henry James's 'New York Edition,' " *New England Quarterly*, 24 (June, 1951), 169–178.

topher Newman, dazzled by the elaborate education of an Anglo-French beauty, "fashioned for exalted social needs," whose tribal loyalty to her Legitimist family is stronger in the end than her love for the American; and of the innocent, invalided heiress, Milly Theale, who is grossly deceived by English fortune hunters. "It is a complex fate, being an American," James knew, "and one of the responsibilities it entails is fighting against a superstitious valuation of Europe."[26] No one knew better the insidious attractions and devastating aftereffects of "the nostalgic poison" of Europe.

What gave trenchancy to his irony was his awareness that it was not only Europe Americans regarded with superstition, but their own country as well. In his own family he had evidence for the American's "superstitious valuation" of his innocence. This was the theme, as old as Jefferson or Royall Tyler, of his father's faith in the sweet disorder of American life, "so full of promise"; of his brother's love for America, "for her youth, her greenness, her plasticity, innocence, good intentions, friends, everything"; of his sister's reverence for America as a "huge chance for hemmed-in humanity . . . undraped by the illusions and mystery of a moss-grown, cobwebby past, but overflowing with a divine good-humour and benignancy . . . a heart of hope for every outcast of tradition." That so many of Henry James's heroes and heroines are transfigured by the radiance of a native innocence justifies his brother's remark that Henry was, for all his protective,

[26] *The James Family*, p. 290. The theme of the American being compelled to awake from his bewitchment with Europe is acutely explored in Ferner Nuhn, "The Enchanted Kingdom of Henry James," *The Wind Blew from the East*, pp. 87–163. See also Christof Wegelin, *The Image of Europe in Henry James* (Dallas, Southern Methodist University Press, 1958) for a comprehensive study, though he reads both *The American* and *The Portrait of a Lady* without finding the ambiguity and irony which I see in them. The conventional view of James as a disgruntled expatriate who romanticized European aristocratic life has been propagated by influential historians like Vernon L. Parrington and Charles A. Beard. It is an interpretation which cannot survive an intelligent reading of James's fiction, as Marius Bewley points out in *The Complex Fate, Hawthorne, Henry James, and Some Other American Writers*, introduction by F. R. Leavis (London, Chatto and Windus, 1952), p. 5.

Anglican coloration, "a native of the James family, and has no other country."[27] Yet, though his stories seem to have as their premise the traditional distinction between American innocence and European guilt, his evaluation of that contrast was far from pious. If in certain contexts "the grace of youth and innocence and freshness" gave value to his Americans abroad, in a different perspective these qualities were characteristic limitations of those "almost incredibly *unaware of life*—as the European order expressed life."[28]

In this lack of awareness James saw both the comedy and tragedy of American dealings with Europe. The comedy of *The Ambassadors* lies in the incongruous inadequacies of the provincial New England mind when it tries to comprehend a French society in which the forms of love are not exhausted by vagrant lust or domestic fidelity. Lambert Strether, agent of the family which is anxious to rescue its son in Paris from what it is sure are the clutches of a vulgar hussy, is something of a cosmopolite in Woolett, Massachusetts; yet even he is forced to make a double discrimination in assessing the situation. Not only has the son been improved to a lustrous polish under the tutelage of the elegant Countess de Vionnet, but he is, after all, having a serious affair, and not with the Countess's daughter, but with the lady herself. It is one of the finer ironies of the plot that the passion is, in fact, rather more ardent and genuine on her part than on his. Woolett was, in its hide-bound way, half-right in its suspicions, all wrong in its conclusions.

In James's vision American innocence, even when morally triumphant over European evil, has its chilling side since its victories are those of the renunciation of life. Euphemia in "Madame de Mauves" has a moral imagination vastly superior to that of her philandering French husband, but her unrelenting character drives her husband to suicide. Isabel Archer in *The Portrait of a Lady* chooses resigned acceptance of her loveless marriage as the grand-

---

[27] For his family's views of America in relation to Europe see *The James Family*, pp. 303, 304, 306.
[28] Preface, "The Reverberator," *The Art of the Novel*, p. 187.

est response to failure, but there is more than a hint that she is too proud to publish her mistake before the world by breaking the marriage, and, in a turbulent final scene, she flees the opportunity of accepting the love of the young businessman from Massachusetts, whose ardor has shown her that "she had never been loved before." In her act there is a fear of passion, both of her own and her lover's, that reveals Isabel to be incapable of any profoundly passionate commitment to life. She was prone to "the danger of keeping up the flag after the place has surrendered; a sort of behaviour so crooked as to be almost a dishonour to the flag."[29]

James saw, with the intense detachment of an American who had removed the blindfold of native pieties, that American innocence represented not only an ignorance of the European world, but a superficial grasp of experience itself. If for the American imagination the Old World was a dark one, evocative of guilt, evil, and harsh limitation, then there was a lesson to be learned there which was not taught in the primer of native mythology. The American thought of his New World as an Eden, but genuine human experience began only after Adam had eaten of the fruit of the tree of knowledge of good and evil and so lost his paradise. The American too easily conceived of experience as infinitely malleable. In a society whose folk hero of popular literature was Horatio Alger it was tempting to believe that wishes were horses and beggars could ride. To discover the limits of success the American needed to go to Europe.

In *The Portrait of a Lady* and *The American*, James examined with affectionate irony that confident approach to experience which Jefferson once defined: "It is part of the American character to consider nothing as desperate, to surmount every diffi-

[29] *The Portrait of a Lady*, vol. 4 of the New York Edition, I, p. 69. "Madame de Mauves" (vol. 13) is thematically very similar. Even in *The Ambassadors* (vol. 21), in which the role of Europe, in the form of France as art, passion, and drama, has the most positive educative effect on James's Americans, the awakened Lambert Strether renounces the opportunity to get some tangible, personal advantage from his education by his detached response to the overtures of Maria Gostrey. Here, however, the sacrifical note has no grimness.

culty by resolution and contrivance."[30] Handsome and rich, Isabel Archer has the means for living out her dream of "the free exploration of life," but she cannot fulfill her wish of doing it without touching "the poisoned drink" of "the cup of experience." This free spirit finds the idea of marrying an English peer, with the "splendid security" of his social world, or an American cotton manufacturer, whose energy of character and personal investment of it in her happiness is greater, she knows, than anyone else's, much too restrictive for her soaring imagination. By a severe irony she makes instead the tragic mistake of marrying Osmond, the hyperconventional fortune hunter, because he has an air of emancipated cosmopolitanism and gives Isabel a chance to play the role of Lady Bountiful with her money. She matures in the hardest possible way by having to recognize the enormity of her failure. If America is "innocence" and Europe "experience," the free spirit discovers in the Old World only at painful cost the necessity of learning to face the limits of life.

In *The American*, Christopher Newman, a true son of the New World as his name implies, is brought up short by a Europe he has never realistically taken into account. With his "general hospitality to the chances of life," his chivalry to women, and his amiable "democratic assumption of every one's right to lead an easy life," he is an appealing representative of his country's good-natured innocence. This mobile American, who has more than once climbed the ladder of commercial success according to type, has a simple integrity which puts in dark shadows the calculating snobbery of the reactionary Bellegardes, the quixotic honor and idle vices of their son, or the brazen opportunism of the Nioche family. In refusing, partly from disdain and partly from the indifference of his own tolerant nature, to take revenge against the Bellegardes for preventing him from marrying their daughter, he reaffirms the morality of his "good-humoured prosperity." Yet there is something of a judgment on him in his being forced to

---

[30] Letter to Martha Jefferson, March 28, 1787, Adrienne Koch and William Peden, eds., *The Life and Selected Writings of Thomas Jefferson* (New York, Random House, 1944), p. 418. For the novels see vol. 2 (*The American*) and vol. 4 (*The Portrait of a Lady*) of the New York Edition.

see the woman he longed to marry, "the skim of the milk of the old noblesse," shut herself up for life in a Carmelite convent, the melodramatic symbol of all those forces in the Old World which the New had rejected.

Success for Newman has always meant the ability to "gouge a fortune, the bigger the better," out of the New World. Though he has turned his back on the commercial world in coming to Europe for entertainment and diversion, he covets Claire as "a very expensive thing," quite "the best article in the market." He would like to take home this choice piece of Old World to hang on his belt like a scalp. It would give him a sense, as he says, of "the greatest victory over circumstances." He takes the Grand Tour, with the relaxed conviction that "Europe was made for him, and not he for Europe," in the spirit of Mark Twain himself. There is a flaw, however, in Newman's whole conception of life: "The world, to his vision, was a great bazaar, where one might stroll about and purchase handsome things; but he was no more conscious, individually, of social pressure than he admitted the claim of the obligatory purchase."[31] Any assumption of "a fatality in misery" irritated him more than anything else; he felt he could always wipe it out "with the sponge of his own prosperity."

When this easygoing pragmatism, with its confidence that life can be fixed up for one's own convenience, is challenged by the Bellegardes, who live in "the world of things immutably decreed," the American is forced to feel for the first time the hard contours of limitation. He has never taken seriously the fixed conventions of this European world that has so entertained him, but it is Claire's dutiful adherence to family authority and her ancient religion that cheats him of his coup. Even the happy citizens of the brave New World are not immune to a failure and a sorrow that have no remedy. That is the lesson the American learns in Europe.

If Henry James had brilliantly refined the process of American self-criticism generated by contact with Europe, he had also, quite as much as Irving, Longfellow, Cooper or Hawthorne, reaffirmed the traditional polar distinction between the New World and the

[31] *The American*, p. 87.

Old. These terms had been given new values and brought into new relationships, but the contrast remained fundamental. His readers might easily conclude that the scene of Europe was a decorated stage, a static refuge from the vicissitudes of history, but James himself had no such illusions. He had what he called "the imagination of disaster," and in his study of class conflict and radical politics in England, *The Princess Casamassima* (1886), he looked directly at the strains and corruptions of a world in unstable tension. But the background for James's international dramas was that of "the grand tour," and in those prewar years his Americans could pursue their dreams on the enchanted ground of a Europe that shimmered with an illusory stillness. "Their author, I am quite aware," he confessed late in life, "would seem struck with no possibility of contrast in the human lot so great as that encountered as we turn back and forth between the distinctively American and the distinctively European outlook."[32] This emphasis he now wished to qualify.

James felt that his last great works, especially *The Wings of the Dove* and *The Golden Bowl*, though they exploited to some extent the international contrast, could have expressed their subjects perfectly had all the persons concerned been only American or only European. He was increasingly impressed with "the multiplied symptoms among educated people, from wherever drawn, of a common intelligence and a social fusion tending to abridge old rigours of separation."[33] In this "eventual sublime consensus of the educated" the writer would find "the personal drama of the future." There was, to confound the novelist of manners, an increasing mixture of manners. When the First World War broke out, he recognized at once the end of the Europe his American

[32] Preface, "Lady Barbarina," *The Art of the Novel*, p. 198. In *The Princess Casamassima* James sought to give the effect of "society's not knowing, but only guessing and suspecting and trying to ignore, what 'goes on' irreconcilably, subversively, beneath the vast smug surface." See Preface, *The Princess Casamassima* (vol. 5 of the New York Edition), *The Art of the Novel*, pp. 77–78. The sociological veracity of the novel is brilliantly discussed by Lionel Trilling, *The Liberal Imagination, Essays on Literature and Society* (New York, Viking, 1950), pp. 58–74.

[33] Preface, "Lady Barbarina," *The Art of the Novel*, p. 202.

pilgrims had known: "The subject-matter of one's effort has become *itself* utterly treacherous and false—its relation to reality utterly given away and smashed. Reality is a world that was to be capable of *this*. . . ."[34] It was fitting that the supreme dramatist of the international theme should have anticipated the sound of the bell which would toll the dying relevance of the polar distinction between the New World and the Old.

[34] Letter to Hugh Walpole, February 14, 1915, *The Letters of Henry James*, II, 462. As Philip Rahv has noted, the character of Dr. Staub in "A Bundle of Letters" (vol. 14 of the New York Edition) represents, in its portrayal of Prussian militarism, "remarkable proof of his insight into the European situation" as early as 1879. See *The Discovery of Europe, the Story of American Experience in the Old World* (Boston, Houghton Mifflin, 1947), p. 270. For an admirably economical and intelligent study of James's life and writings see F. W. Dupee, *Henry James*, rev. ed. (Garden City, New York, Doubleday, 1956).

8

THE OLD SWEET
ANGLO-SAXON SPELL

As AN ARTIST, Henry James foresaw with some uneasiness the diminished significance of the traditional, national "rigours of separation" which had given life to "the international theme." By the end of the 1890's the globe was beginning to seem smaller to those Americans who yearned for imperial greatness under the Anglo-Saxon banner. At the same time the social fusion which James prophesied seemed then only to be a bewildering social incoherence, most vividly illustrated not in any "sublime consensus," but in the remorseless traffic across the Atlantic of alien-sounding names. For those who cherished what James called "the old sweet Anglo-Saxon spell" the new immigration to America from southern and eastern Europe provoked another ambivalent response to the Old World.

Returning to the United States in 1904 after a long absence, James was both a nostalgic native son and something of a foreigner, faced with the shocks of a dislocating experience. He had

132

been steeped in English life since 1876. The problems posed for him by this new flood of "Ninevites," who did not cherish England as their old home, were acute. Yet he was too imaginative merely to recoil in distaste, and he was himself the grandson of an immigrant from Ireland. These elements of his situation made for a complexity of perspective. Watching the swarms of newcomers at Ellis Island or riding with them in the packed East Side streetcars, he brooded over their implications for the American future. As a patrician New Yorker with close ties to the Brahmins of New England, he was bewildered and shaken at having "to share the sanctity of his American consciousness, the intimacy of his American patriotism, with the inconceivable alien."[1] He felt Americans had to go *"more* than halfway to meet them," and it gave him a sense of dispossession. These new citizens had shed their European manners, so attractive to the tourist abroad, without any apparent compensating gain. Yet the very scale of the whole gigantic process of assimilation fascinated him and aroused his sympathies. Doubtless, he conjectured, some echo of their old manners and amenities would, "the business of slow comminglings and makings-over at last ended," rise to the surface, "affirming their vitality and value and playing their part."[2] This confidence, very much alive in an American who had not lived in his country for a quarter of a century, was not widely shared among countrymen of his own native background. For them Europe, in the person of these representatives, wore the face of menace. They shamefully forgot the question Henry James asked in 1907: "Who and what is an alien, when it comes to that, in a country peopled from the first under the jealous eye of history? —peopled, that is, by migrations at once extremely recent, perfectly traceable and urgently required."[3]

[1] *The American Scene, Together with Three Essays from Portraits of Places*, introduction by W. H. Auden (New York, Scribner's, 1946), p. 85. Cf. his comments on the passing of "the old sweet Anglo-Saxon spell' in Preface, "Lady Barbarina," *The Art of the Novel, Critical Prefaces*, introduction by R. P. Blackmur (New York, Scribner's, 1946), pp. 207–209.

[2] *The American Scene*, p. 129.

[3] *Ibid.*, p. 124.

Political and social changes in the late nineteenth century subverted the satisfying simplicity of the New World-Old World antithesis, separating England from Europe while linking Americans with the British. Two great changes accounted for this strain on the conventional concept: the vast influx of immigration from southern and eastern Europe and the emergence of the United States as a power in world politics. By the end of the century there was mounting demand for a reversal of both America's traditional hospitality to immigrants and her policy of isolationist anticolonialism. These developments brought with them a new sense of Europe's menace and a new groping for Anglo-American friendship.

The role of England in American demonology has been a special one. As America's most ancient enemy she has been the prime villain of the Old World. As the "mother country" she has been a favored exception to the general rule. The Yankee of old-stock heritage was thus exposed to very complicated conflicts. Against the continent and its emigrants he was proud of his English ancestry; yet he also inherited a historic hostility to the British oppression which had provoked so many American symbols of patriotic pride from the Declaration of Independence to *The Star Spangled Banner*. If frightened by revolutionary radicalism in Europe, or threatened by the upsurge of the masses at home, the conservative old Yankee (like the hyper-Federalists of the Essex Junto in the War of 1812) often yearned for the stability of English institutions and for an aristocracy to keep the "lower orders" in line. Unaware of his own "hyphenated" characteristics as a nostalgic Anglo-American, the Yankee was dangerously vulnerable to hostile suspicions of the foreign ties of immigrants from other countries.

The American tradition had strongly supported hospitality to immigration because it was part of the glory of the New World to be "an asylum for all mankind." Melville voiced this generous hope with his characteristic eloquence in the middle of the nineteenth century, after immigrants from Ireland and Germany had begun to flood the United States: "We are not a narrow tribe of men, with a bigoted Hebrew nationality—whose blood has been debased in the attempt to ennoble it, by maintaining an exclusive succession among ourselves. No: our blood is as the flood of the Amazon, made up of a thousand noble currents all pouring into one." This claim to the world was part of his vision of an "Earth's Paradise" in the New World. "Not a Paradise then, or now," he admitted; "but to be made so, at God's good pleasure, and in the fullness and mellowness of time." The children's children would witness the federation of peoples on the Western Hemisphere, the curse of Babel would be revoked, and all would speak "the language of Britain."[4]

But in his own day the signs of a curdling of the "melting pot" had already appeared. In the 1830s New Englanders like Samuel F. B. Morse (who had enjoyed the aesthetic and educative pageantry of Rome) sounded the alarm of a Catholic "conspiracy" to destroy American Protestantism and liberties. Lyman Beecher toured the East for money to proselytize the West before it fell into the hands of the dreaded Papists in league with the Holy Alliance. By the middle 1850s there was extensive middle-class support among all Protestants for a crusade against the Catholic enemy. Inspired by religious bigotry and sensational propaganda, many Americans indulged themselves in a nativist passion for a national housecleaning which would wipe out every taint of foreign influence. For a brief time the Know-Nothing Party, which channeled these inflamed feelings, enjoyed political success in gaining office in New England, the border states, and the South. Their efforts to put political disabilities on Catholics and immigrants were stifled by the growing entanglement of the Party in the slavery crisis, which split it hopelessly apart.[5]

After the Civil War, a new national mood of confidence sup-

[4] This selection from *Redburn* can be found in Philip Rahv, ed., *The Discovery of Europe, the Story of American Experience in the Old World* (Boston, Houghton Mifflin, 1947), pp. 137–138.

[5] See Ray Allen Billington, *The Protestant Crusade 1800–1860: A Study of the Origins of American Nativism* (New York, Rinehart, 1938), pp. 280, 390, 416. (Reprinted 1952).

ported the old-fashioned hospitality to immigrants. The enormous expansion of the economy, stimulated by the war, gave businessmen an economic interest in having a constant stream of immigrants flow into the factories. The public domain was not yet exhausted, and the country enjoyed a happy freedom from crises in foreign affairs. If Americans were condescending to the new arrivals from foreign shores and critical of their habits, they did not doubt their ultimate assimilation as loyal countrymen. But in the 1880s and 90s the problems of class conflict in America produced a host of alarmists who saw in the presence of the immigrant the source of national troubles. Europe, according to sanctified American myth, was a center of corruption; the conflicts of class which had marked its history were now appearing on American grounds; therefore the immigrant must be the carrier of the dreaded contagion. By this specious syllogism businessmen, social reformers, and fearful citizens convinced themselves that the line between the New World and the Old must be heavily redrawn. In this way it was hoped that the evils of cheap competition, poverty, class bitterness, radicalism, crime, immorality, and popery would be kept in the Old World where they belonged. Hostility to the immigrant was at first strongest in the urban areas of the Northeast and the older Middle West, but by the end of the 90s the West and the South had joined the other sections, and now both businessmen and workers were anxious to restrict immigration.[6]

A new element was added to the "melting pot" which provided a convenient rationalization for anti-immigrant feeling. By the end of the century the tide of immigration was heavily flowing from southern and eastern Europe. Slavs, Jews, Magyars, and Italians had broken the "old sweet Anglo-Saxon spell." In the strangeness of these new arrivals old Americans saw a threat to national cohesion and identity. The New World was being contaminated by the "social dregs of Europe" which "enfeebled" and "degraded" the nation; the old theory of America as the asylum of the op-

[6] See John Higham, *Strangers in the Land: Patterns of American Nativism 1860–1925* (New Brunswick, Rutgers University Press, 1955), pp. 24, 74.

pressed was patently "ridiculous."[7] Editors searched the language of vituperation to describe the "refuse," "scum," and "cancerous fungus" they saw with mounting horror in the swirling currents of the melting pot. Formerly seen as refugees from Europe's diseases the immigrants were now feared as dreaded carriers of her worst contagions, concentrated in a particular area of the Old World.

The power of this image of the foreign peril derived from deep-rooted feelings of fear, anxiety, and nostalgia for the dream of a New World uncorrupted by Old World evils. It made no difference that most immigrants were docile and conservative peasants; a handful of anarchists represented them all in the new mythology. Poor, ignorant, and helpless, with a pathetic patience and hopefulness, the immigrant tried to make himself at home in this strange new American world, and it was the essence of his tragedy, as Oscar Handlin has shown, that the very institutions which he developed to further this process—his mutual aid societies, schools, newspapers, theatrical stock companies, and patriotic organizations—only marked him out more clearly as alien in the eyes of old Americans. They cruelly compounded his difficulties by a desperate search for national homogeneity based on an Americanism rooted in racial affinities and denied by definition to the new immigrants. The United States, many of them said, was "an organic body, a nation with bones and muscles, compactly joined," and its national blood ran only in the veins of the "free people of Northern Europe."[8] The new immigrants from southern and eastern Europe could not become assimilated to a standard which predated their coming. The logic was clear: immigration should be stopped and tests should be applied to limit the immigrant's power to vote.

[7] Quoted from the *Chicago Times*, April 30, 1887, *Public Opinion*, 3 (1887), 49.

[8] Edwin Percy Whipple, "American Principles," *Outlooks on Society, Literature and Politics* (Boston, Ticknor, 1888), pp. 132, 145. The best modern analysis of the immigrant's problems is Oscar Handlin, *The Uprooted* (Boston, Little, Brown, 1951); for a perceptive analysis at the time see Kate Holladay Claghorn, "The Changing Character of Immigration," *Public Opinion*, 30 (February 14, 1901), 205.

The cult of a racial mythology of Anglo-Saxonism helped justify hostility to the immigrant while it undercut the old-fashioned antagonism to Britain. New England Brahmin leaders of this movement gave up the traditional enmity to England and indulged an Anglophilia which would have horrified John Quincy Adams. Henry Cabot Lodge, spokesman for the Immigration Restriction League, solemnly studied The Distribution of Ability in the United States in 1891, measured by the lives of persons appearing in an encyclopaedia of American biographies, and concluded that English ancestry was the common factor. The Brahmin had lost his old mood of defiance of John Bull. Shortly after the Civil War James Russell Lowell in a famous essay had expressed his irritation at the Englishman's assumption that everything good in America was of English origin; in reality Americans were worth nothing except so far as they had "disinfected" themselves of Anglicism. By 1880, as American Minister to England, he had concluded that the differences between Yankees and Englishmen were "mostly superficial."[9]

The linkage of Anglophilia and immigrant-phobia was naïvely dramatized in two novels of the day. John Hay's The Bread-Winners (1884) has for its hero a retired professional soldier of English ancestry "at home in field and court." He fights a losing battle against the immigrant hordes of striking workers and their corrupt bosses, who are poisoned by a Jacobin lust to desolate all civilized order and displace their betters. He is pathetically compelled to accept as his meager political reward the chairmanship of the library board in his New York town, while the major plums of office fall to the leaders of the debased mob. Raw democracy and alien anarchism on an immigrant base have reduced the Anglo-Saxon gentry to a marginal existence. Richard Grant White, a New York journalist, vented a similar spleen in The Fate of

[9] For Lodge see Edward N. Saveth, *American Historians and European Immigrants 1875–1925* (New York, Columbia University Press, 1948), pp. 51–62. For Lowell see Barbara Miller Solomon, *Ancestors and Immigrants: A Changing New England Tradition* (Cambridge, Harvard University Press, 1956), pp. 56–57, 60–61.

Mansfield Humphreys, published in the same year as Hay's story. Its hero of old New England stock (like the author himself) sees authentic America as made up of Yankees and Virginians who made a society in the English spirit, while providentially removed from corrupt European influence. Praising Whittier and Long- fellow, the hero mourns for a lost America, overwhelmed by Europe's lower classes, vulgar parvenues rising out of immigrant backgrounds, rampant commercialism, universal suffrage, mass mediocrity, and boss rule. He seeks the hand of an English girl, but her family humiliatingly rejects him for being below her rank. In traditional American versions of this theme the hero would, as one of nature's noblemen, assert his superiority to the English class system, but Mansfield Humphreys is rescued by a rival English suitor who magnanimously brings the estranged couple together. Because neither one can stand living in New York, the most "un-American" place because of its immigrant population, the hero takes his bride back to England "with no diminished love for the memory of the vanishing New England of his youth" to find, "happily for himself, a new home in the old home of his fathers."[10] White, who had traveled hardly at all in America, never been to Europe, and visited England but once, took refuge from the shocks of the Gilded Age in a romantic dream of England that Hawthorne, Melville, and James had warned their countrymen against. In a society without an ac- cepted aristocracy frustrated conservatives could challenge the crudities of democratic capitalism only by indulging in a nostalgia for the home of their ancestors. " 'As a pilgrim father that missed th' first boats,' " said Mr. Dooley, the philosopher of the Archey Road tavern, " 'I must raise me claryon voice again' th' invasion iv this fair land be th' paupers an' annychists iv effete Europe. Ye bet I must—because I'm here first.' "[11]

[10] Richard Grant White, *The Fate of Mansfield Humphreys* (Boston, Houghton Mifflin, 1888), pp. 367–368. Cf. John Hay, *The Bread-Winners, a Social Study* (New York, Harper, 1884), published anonymously.

[11] Finley Peter Dunne, *Observations by Mr. Dooley* (New York, Harper, 1906), p. 50.

Many Americans soothed their fears of losing status by joining various old-American or pro-English societies to which they laid claim by devout researches in genealogy. Social snobbery found a new outlet in Anglophilia. Henry B. Fuller satirized the situation in "The Pilgrim Sons," the story of an American couple seeking a higher social life in England, their credentials based upon the wife's grandmother's second cousin having been a lord. Times had changed from the days of Edith Wharton's parents and friends, who thought it vulgar and snobbish for Americans to seek entrance into good society in Europe, instead of confining themselves to the little American colonies abroad, and "only their most irreproachable members!" In Fuller's story the wife is drawn by her aspirations to hover in the circle of the Mayflowers, an eminent American family which has resolved its tribal disputes by joining forces to resettle in England. If an "entente cordiale" between the two divisions of the "Anglo-Saxon" race was destined, then the wife was determined that she and her husband would "string the earlier cables" rather than merely be members of "the throng of foot-passengers that later will tramp over the completed structure."[12] As the early Pilgrims had renounced the religious ritual of England for the freedom of America, so had the Pilgrims' sons renounced the social ritual of democratic America for the aristocratic gentility of English life. Supported by such glittering trans-Atlantic marriages as those represented by Lady Randolph Churchill, Mrs. Joseph Chamberlain, the Duchess of Manchester, and the Duchess of Marlborough, the American social invasion of London (noted one observer in 1904) had turned into "an American army of occupation, hopelessly dominant, unescapably pervasive."[13]

The theory of American racial and cultural affinity to England was widely propounded by scholars in the fields of literature,

[12] "The Pilgrim Sons," *The Discovery of Europe*, p. 406. Cf. Edith Wharton, *A Backward Glance* (New York, Appleton-Century, 1934), p. 62.

[13] Anglo-American, "The American Colony in London," *Harper's Weekly*, **48** (July 30, 1904), 1176.

history, the social sciences, and religion. In the colleges the study of Anglo-Saxon and of American literature as an offshoot of the English stem had great prestige. Cambridge and Boston looked to England with all the reverence and humility with which provincial American writers of the West and the Middle West, like Bret Harte, Hamlin Garland, and William Dean Howells, looked to New England. Among historians the Anglo-Saxon myth served as a major hypothesis by tracing the origins of New England democracy to Teutonic folkmoots and finding the power and virtue of American institutions in the ancient blessings of Anglo-Saxon vigor and morality. It was no accident that John Fiske, popularizer of the Anglo-Saxon historical school, became president of the Immigration Restriction League in 1894, nor that John W. Burgess, political scientist of Anglo-Saxonism, should have stood before the German Emperor and his court in 1907, as Theodore Roosevelt Professor at the University of Berlin, to praise the beneficence of the old immigration, "confined to comers of the Teutonic races," and to warn of the danger of the new immigrant "rabble" from the racially inferior areas of Europe.[14] Other social scientists served the same mythology. Francis A. Walker, president of the American Economic Association, published his alarm in the 1890s at the declining Yankee birth rate, allegedly due to the adverse effect of competition from "beaten men of beaten races." Religious leaders added their sanction to the new cult of racial superiority, preached in bombastic rhetoric by Josiah Strong, whose *Our Country* (1885), widely propagated by the American Home Missionary Society, laid all American evils at the door of the immigrant and celebrated the American example in faith and politics as the best illustration of the Anglo-Saxon spirit with its

[14] "Uncle Sam!" (Appendix), *Reminiscences of an American Scholar: The Beginnings of Columbia University* (New York, Columbia University Press, 1934), p. 397. For the historians see Saveth, *op. cit.* and for literary men see Howard Mumford Jones, *The Theory of American Literature* (Ithaca, New York, Cornell University Press, 1948), pp. 79–109. Older historians, like Prescott, Bancroft, and Motley, had also cultivated the myth of Teutonic germs of liberty, as David Levin has noted in *History as Romantic Art* (Stanford, Stanford University Press, 1959), pp. 78–87.

"peculiarly aggressive traits calculated to impress its institutions upon mankind."[15]

In American culture, from Philip Freneau to Walt Whitman, it has been a classic anti-European strategy to sing the glories of the rugged West as a symbol for nationalism, individualism, and democracy in a region where the last surviving echoes of Europe are supposedly lost in the crash of forests falling to the pioneer's axe. But in the 1890s this venerable mythology was suffused with an "Anglo-Saxon" coloration. Western writers themselves, like Joaquin Miller, Bret Harte, and Ambrose Bierce, who had gorged themselves on Burns, Byron, and Scott, had traveled to England in the 1870s to pay their pious respects to the culture of their literary homeland. "In learning and letters, in art and science of government," wrote Bierce, "America is but a faint and stammering echo of England."[16] Even Frederick Jackson Turner's famous frontier hypothesis of American development, delivered in 1893 at a meeting of the American Historical Association, contained implicitly the common racist assumptions. It implied that the magic of the frontier in making Americans had worked only on immigrants from Germany, Scandinavia, or the British Isles, for otherwise the failure of French and Spanish settlers to become backwoods democrats would contradict his assumption of a beneficent molding by the American forest. The Western historian Hubert Howe Bancroft made these premises naïvely explicit in 1890 by foreseeing the destiny of history in the concentration of culture on the Pacific seaboard, "the terminal of the great Aryan march," which was supposed to be as superior to the Atlantic coast as America was to Europe.[17]

---

[15] *Our Country* (New York, American Home Missionary Society, 1885), p. 15.

[16] Quoted by Louis B. Wright, *Culture on the Moving Frontier* (Bloomington, University of Indiana Press, 1955), p. 157. It is not so surprising, as Mr. Wright points out, that the collection of Henry E. Huntington, in Pasadena, California, should have been especially strong in Anglo-American literature and painting.

[17] For Turner and Bancroft see the perceptive piece by Gilman M. Ostrander, "Turner and the Germ Theory," *Agricultural History,* 32 (no. 4, 1958), 258–261.

Turner's hypothesis also recorded the felt tremors of the coming change in America's position in world politics. Its poetic eloquence propagated waves of nostalgia for an era that had ended with the closing of the frontier, just as the United States was about to enter upon a new stage of imperialism, blurring the image of an innocent noncolonial power so different from guilty imperialist Europe. President Roosevelt would win enormous popularity by straddling the nostalgic image and the contemporary reality: he hobnobbed with both cowboys and kings. As a result of the war with Spain in 1898, the United States became an imperial power and discovered in Britain a sympathetic partner in world politics. The old division of spheres was breaking down.

Few Americans realized what was happening and few of them planned what happened. The war itself was quite consistent with American tradition. To liberate Cuba from Old World despotism was a cause to stir ancient feelings in the New World. It had the happy usefulness of allowing Americans to close ranks after the bitter campaign of 1896. Bryan, spokesman for silver and the aggrieved farmers, had lost to McKinley, champion of gold and the business community. Silver-tongued oratory warned of the "cross of gold," and the Populists made much of the ancient Western suspicion that the effete East was subservient to English influence. Their vociferous folklorists, like "Coin" Harvey and Ignatius Donnelly, were convinced, in their more hallucinated moments, that the advocates of the gold standard were part of a vast conspiracy of English Jews, determined to use Wall Street as an instrument of capitalistic aggrandizement. To the Populist mind the British lion was as frightful a menace as the immigrant hordes from the Old World. After the defeat of Bryan and the Democrats, southern and western Populists became as ardent for a free Cuba as they had been for free silver. Conflict over monetary policy in 1896 had been a symbol of class and sectional division; hatred of Spain was now the symbol of a common jingoistic passion to assert Americanism against "this cruel and inefficient piece of medievalism" on the very doorstep of the United States. In this burst of antagonism to European monarchy Populists and

Democrats could forget their frustrations, Republicans their fears. "There are no sections, no classes, no parties, no factions now," exulted the Philadelphia *Ledger*.[18] Yet what John Hay called "this splendid little war," so ideologically innocent, was soon to plunge the nation into a great debate on imperialism, and when it was over time-worn traditions had been enthusiastically discarded by men seized with a new vision of the United States as a world power.

The Anglo-Saxon cult now flourished as a rationalization of the new imperial stance, openly encouraged by the English, who were looking for allies against Germany. A small group of Americans found in this opportunity to become an imperial power a fulfillment of hopes they had long nurtured. One of the most influential was Alfred Thayer Mahan, naval officer and president of the Newport War College. Mahan spoke authoritatively to a wider public on the strategic importance of a big navy for a power anxious to compete in "the race of life." He foresaw in 1890 the importance to America of the Caribbean and Pacific areas and made a plea for "a cordial recognition of the similarity of character and ideas" between the United States and England.[19]

These new ideas were soon circulated in high places. Exactly one month before the McKinley administration established its blockade of Cuban ports, Richard Olney addressed a Harvard audience on "The International Isolation of the United States." Three years earlier, as Secretary of State under Cleveland, he had belligerently shaken the Monroe Doctrine in the face of the British during their controversy with Venezuela over the boundary line of British Guiana. Then he had gloried in the "isolated position" of the United States which made it "master of the situation and practically invulnerable as against any or all other powers." Now he was anxious to point an entirely different moral to the American

[18] Quoted from the *Philadelphia Ledger*, April 28, 1898, *Public Opinion*, 24 (1898), 517. Cf. "The War with Spain and After," *Atlantic Monthly*, 81 (June, 1898), 725. For the Populists see Richard Hofstadter, *The Age of Reform, from Bryan to F.D.R.* (New York, Knopf, 1955), pp. 74–79, 86–90.

[19] "The United States Looking Outward," *Atlantic Monthly*, 66 (December, 1890), 824.

story. We had become crippled by blind reverence for Washington's Farewell Address and the base fear that through contact with other nations we might get "contaminated and deteriorate."[20] The time had come to end national self-congratulation on our passive role as an example to all mankind and to take up the burdens of our powerful position. We needed new markets for industrial expansion and we needed to make a friend of England, potentially our most dangerous foe. There was a "patriotism of race" as well as of country. Standing together, Americans and Englishmen could be the peacemakers of the world. In July, 1898, patriots of the "race" on both sides of the ocean formed an Anglo-American League, and the popular magazines of the day broke out in a rash of articles about the profound affinities and marvelous prospects of the Anglo-Saxons.

These new currents stirred in Washington as well. In the previous year, when McKinley had congratulated Queen Victoria on her Diamond Jubilee, John Hay, anonymous author of *The Bread-Winners*, went to London as American Ambassador. "As long as I stay here," he wrote a friend, "no action shall be taken contrary to my conviction that the one indispensable feature of our foreign policy should be a friendly understanding with England."[21] Hay discovered that the American government could count on British sympathy for the Administration's Cuban policy and for American expansionism. The English diplomatic mind was not moved

[20] Cf. *Atlantic Monthly*, 81 (May, 1898), p. 584 and Olney to Thomas F. Bayard, July 20, 1895, Ruhl J. Bartlett, ed., *The Record of American Diplomacy: Documents and Readings in the History of American Foreign Relations* (New York, Knopf, 1947), p. 345. For "hands-across-the-sea" sentiments in English and American magazines see Joseph E. Chamberlain, "A Dream of Anglo-Saxondom," *Galaxy*, 24 (December, 1877), 788–791; James Bryce, "The Essential Unity of Britain and America," *Atlantic Monthly*, 82 (July, 1898), 22–29; James K. Hosmer, "The American Evolution," *ibid.*, 29–36; Sidney Lanier, "The Proper Basis of English Culture," *ibid.* (August, 1898), 165–174; A. V. Dicey, "England and America," *ibid.* (October, 1898), 441–445.

[21] Letter to Henry White, September 24, 1899, William Roscoe Thayer, *The Life and Letters of John Hay*, II (Boston, Houghton Mifflin, 1915), 221. For Anglo-American relations in this period see H. C. Allen, *Great Britain and the United States, a History of Anglo-American Relations (1783–1952)* (London, Odhams, 1954), pp. 549–629.

by sentiment. If the United States became the dominant power in the Pacific and Caribbean areas, Great Britain would be freer to meet the challenges it faced from European powers. Thus it is not surprising that issues of dispute with Britain over the Isthmus of Panama, the Venezuelan debt controversy, and the Alaskan boundary, were decided to American satisfaction. When the Boers sought American mediation of their quarrel with Great Britain, the Administration could repay the British in kind for the policy of benevolent neutrality they had followed during the Spanish-American War. The tradition of nonentanglement still survived as stoutly as ever, but an atmosphere of Anglo-American understanding grew up on both sides.

The growth of an informal entente cordiale with England challenged not only the old isolationist mood but its venerable corollary, anticolonialism. America's imperial ventures blurred one of the most deeply etched lines in the portrait of a distinctively different Old World. With the annexation of Hawaii in the wake of Dewey's victory at Manila, and the acquisition of the Philippines, Guam, and Puerto Rico by the treaty of peace with Spain, the United States took up the burdens of empire. For the first time in American diplomatic history expansion had resulted in the addition of territory without promise of future citizenship and statehood. This dramatic departure from American traditions passed the Senate by a margin of only one vote. In the country at large there was also deep division over the issue, and there was soon formed an Anti-Imperialist League, which had the support of such prominent Americans as Andrew Carnegie, William Graham Sumner, Mark Twain, William Dean Howells, and William James.

Self-conscious imperialists who saw the new territories in strategic and economic terms were few; popular arguments for expansion appealled instead to nationalistic pride and ambition. National unity, victory over "the medieval diplomacy of Europe," and the incurring of new duties "which appeal to the imagination rather than to the private greed of men" were the precious gains of the war.[22] Duty, destiny, obligation, necessity—these were the catchwords of the pro-expansionists, and they covered not a multitude of shrewdly calculated aims but a mass of confused yearnings. The nation was surprised to find itself on the brink of imperialism as the result of its crusade to free the Cubans from Old World despotism, and it went over the edge in a fit of vagueness of mind.

The anti-imperialists were horrified. It seemed as if the Republic, for all its scorn of "the effete monarchies" of the Old World, had, after all, "a sneaking admiration for their system and a sneaking envy of their pitiless exercise of force." For them the meaning of American history—its contrast with Europe—was at stake. Imperialism was contrary to republican Americanism and would end by involving us fatally in the maelstrom of European politics. Bishop John Lancaster Spalding lamented that America seemed to be "drifting away from what Americans have loved and lived for into the evil company of these Old-World nations, drunken with lust for conquest and lust for gold." With bitterness Yale's Professor William Graham Sumner charged that the United States had, in "a petty three months' campaign" against "a poor, decrepit, bankrupt old state like Spain" sold its right to stand "for something unique and grand in the history of mankind" in return for a mess of European pottage.[23] Spain had really conquered the United States. Anti-imperialist orators shrilled that the Republican

[22] See "What War Has Wrought," *Atlantic Monthly* (September, 1898) in *Public Opinion*, 25 (1898), 261–262. For press reaction to the imperial idea see "How the Press Regards 'Imperialism,'" *ibid.* (August 4, 1898), 135. Twenty-eight papers were in favor; sixteen opposed, mainly reflecting a party division. Twenty-one papers, previously opposed, were then wavering. A poll of about 500 papers, undertaken by the *New York Herald* and presented in *Public Opinion*, 25 (December 29, 1898), 810, showed 288 in favor of expansion and 182 opposed. Thirty-eight Republican papers and fifty Democratic papers broke with the majority position of their parties. Independent papers divided 35 pro, 20 con. The West had the largest majority of pro-expansionist papers.

[23] For Sumner see Charles A. and Mary R. Beard, *The American Spirit: A Study of the Idea of Civilization in the United States* (New York, Macmillan, 1942), p. 589; for Spalding see *ibid.*, p. 586. Cf. comment by *Norfolk Landmark*, *Public Opinion*, 25 (December 8, 1898), 709.

spirit of Anglo-Saxon empire had killed the republican spirit of
'76. America had been Europeanized.

Critics of imperialism had the powerful resource of American
tradition. Isolationism and anticolonialism had long been part of
the American dream of a New World dramatically opposed to
the Old. Now many could sympathize with Senator Hoar's anguished lament that the Monroe Doctrine was gone. The imperialists narrowly won the debate in the Senate, but they did not win
over the hearts of the country. When the Boers fought the British,
most Americans felt those conventional stirrings of sympathy for
the underdog that memories of '76 had always provoked. They
had learned from their schoolbooks that one of the greatest events
in modern history was the uprising of the embattled farmers
against the tyrannical redcoats. These Dutch farmers seemed to
be made of similar stuff. John Hay was distraught: there was such
a "mad-dog hatred of England prevalent among newspapers and
politicians" that the Administration had "great trouble" to prevent the Republican convention from "declaring in favor of the
Boers and of the annexation of Canada."[24] Imperialists could charm
the popular mind with appeals to nationalistic pride in expansion,
but their cause was dangerously vulnerable to the powerful charge
of being "un-American." A cartoon in *Puck* during the campaign
of 1904 dramatized the difficulty: In the background on hat racks
are the tricorner, stovepipe, and top hat of Washington, Lincoln,
and Grant, while in the foreground, in contrast to this republican
simplicity, is a mammoth royal crown, inscribed "imperialism"
and advertised as "all the style in Europe." Pointing to it with a
smile of toothy coyness is Theodore Roosevelt, in the stock costume of his colonel's uniform, who confesses: "I rather like that
imported affair."[25]

Despite the racial snobbishness of the Anglo-Saxon theme and
the undemocratic bias of the imperialist argument, these new tend-

[24] Letter to J. W. Foster, June 23, 1900, *The Life and Letters of John
Hay*, II, 234.
[25] Mark Sullivan, *Our Times, the United States 1900–1925* (New York,
Scribner's, 1927), II, 469.

encies had the positive advantage of inspiring a more critical attitude towards the conventional dualistic image of the relationship
between America and Europe. The gain is represented in the
career and outlook of Roosevelt himself, whose vivid personality
remarkably fused a passionate Americanism with a sophisticated
reappraisal of the Old World.

He was not the simple symbol of the Anglo-Saxon cult that
some of his critics have drawn. He was, certainly, one of those
few Americans who had planned the country's embarkment on
an imperialist course. As Assistant Secretary of the Navy he had
seized the opportunity to give Dewey his appointment as Commodore of the American Asiatic Squadron and his orders to begin
offensive operations in the Philippines as soon as war should be
declared. He was quite in agreement with the imperialist views of
Mahan, Lodge, and Brooks Adams, and the Anglo-Saxon cult of
the more aggressive virtues never had a more voluble champion
than this advocate of "the strenuous life." On the other hand he
was justifiably irritated by his friend Finley Peter Dunne's satirical
treatment of the election of 1904 as a triumph for the Anglo-
Saxon cause. "On hearin' the glad news on th' Saturdah followin'
th' iliction," according to Mr. Dooley, who always estimated the
Anglo-Saxon sentiment with a cynical Irish eye, "the king sint
f'r Ambassadure Choate, who came as fast as his hands an' knees
cud carry him."[26] Stung by Dunne's jibes, Roosevelt denied that
he believed in the Anglo-Saxon concept and maintained that his
"whole public life" had been "an emphatic protest against the
Peabodys and Van Rensselaers arrogating to themselves any su-
periorities over the Caseys and Schwartzmeisters." Of patrician
background and mixed ancestry he was contemptuous of servile
and snobbish Anglophiles, as he was of all "hyphenates." "We
Americans are a separate people," he insisted, and he refused to
lend his name publicly to any organization trying to promote a
" 'hands across the sea' alliance, explicit or implicit, with Eng-

[26] *Dissertations by Mr. Dooley* (New York, Harper, 1906), pp. 213–214.

land." Aggressively nationalistic, he branded Henry James "a miserable little snob."[27]

But if Roosevelt was a stout defender of the melting pot, he was just as intent upon having the stew cooked to his own taste. The American ethnic make-up was changing, he felt, to a happy mixture much like his own. The Dutch, the German, the French, the Scotch, the Irish—these strains were readily absorbed as ingredients of the new national character, for they had been present at the time of the Revolution. The English were themselves a mixed race, and American stock had the same composition. Roosevelt's racial views were thus more complex than those of the Anglo-Saxon cult, but they implied a definite connection between his tolerance and his preference for certain ethnic strains among the immigrants. The "new immigration" marked the perimeter of his hospitality—it is not surprising that he joined Lodge in working to restrict immigration. Later, during the crisis of the First World War when he was out of power and out of sorts with his less bellicose countrymen, he expressed his views in the accents of a harsh chauvinism. There was in such anxious times, he felt, no room for divided loyalties in language or in attitudes towards America's enemies. The sentiments and activities of German-Americans and Irish-Americans verged on treason. "The crucible does not do its work unless it turns out those cast into it in one national mould," he thundered; "and that must be the mould established by Washington and his fellows when they made us into a nation."[28] The door was open to the immigrant, provided he conformed to a pre-existing national standard. Now bitterly partisan, Roosevelt promoted nativistic fears about foreigners, rad-

[27] See Elting E. Morison, ed., *Letters of Theodore Roosevelt*, #3368, #5950, #475 (Cambridge, Harvard University Press, 1951–1954), IV, 1041; VIII, 868; I, 390.

[28] "The Children of the Crucible," *The Foes of Our Own Household*, vol. 21 of *The Works of Theodore Roosevelt*, Memorial Edition (New York, Scribner's, 1925), p. 35. Cf. "Biological Analogies in History," *African and European Addresses*, introduction by Lawrence F. Abbott (New York, Putnam's, 1910), p. 176 and *The Winning of the West*, vol. 10 of the Memorial Edition, I, 19–20.

icals, and immigrants with an animus the earlier triumphant Teddy would have condemned.

In the happier days of his prime he was a beloved national hero who spoke for Americanism with remarkable freedom from the ignorance of the provincial. Familiar with Europe from family connections, boyhood travels, and lasting friendships with English intellectuals and men of affairs, he brought to the Presidency a keen sensitivity to the European balance of power and America's relation to it. Loyal to the Monroe Doctrine, which he expanded by his assumption of an American police power over delinquency in the Caribbean area, and a stubborn defender of American interests against British claims in Panama and Alaska, he nevertheless recognized the growing coincidence of Anglo-American interests and the need for good will between the two traditional enemies. Exchanging gifts and friendly sentiments with the King of England in March 1905, Roosevelt was confident that recent Anglo-American cordiality rested on a happy set of circumstances: "The larger interests of the two nations are the same; and the fundamental, underlying traits of their characters are also the same."[29] By personal diplomacy he gave support to England's partnerships with Japan in the Far East and with France in the Mediterranean. As peacemaker of the Morocco crisis and the Russo-Japanese War he brought American influence onto the stage of world politics. If England faltered in preserving the European balance of power, Roosevelt believed, the United States would have to assume the burden. "In fact, we ourselves are becoming, owing to our strength and geographical situation," he prophetically wrote a German diplomat in 1910, "more and more the balance of power of the whole world."[30]

The waning in Roosevelt's mind of the traditional polarity between America and Europe was vividly evident during his ebul-

[29] *Roosevelt Letters,* #3484, IV, 1136.
[30] Quoted by Howard K. Beale, *Theodore Roosevelt and the Rise of America to World Power* (Baltimore, Johns Hopkins University Press, 1956), p. 447. Beale has the best modern account of Roosevelt's foreign policy.

lient tour of Europe in 1910. The ex-president was showered with honors as he carried the gospel of Americanism to Oxford, Cambridge, the Sorbonne, and the University of Berlin. For all his commonplace homilies on the need for a more vigorous nationalism, the manlier virtues, and larger families, he saw Europe with a vision undistorted by the old dualistic spectacles so proudly worn by his anti-imperialist opponents. Like old-fashioned Americans he could not resist lecturing the Europeans, but the lesson was new. In London's Guildhall he urged the British to deal severely with their anticolonial enemies in the Egyptian Nationalist Party. The occasion was remarkable—an American who prided himself on being a "radical democrat" warning the British not to lay down those burdens of empire Americans had long hated the British for assuming!

At the Sorbonne he told his audience that America could develop "by freely drawing upon the treasure-houses of the Old World" and find some profit even in the programs of the Socialists. As a progressive he knew too that social welfare measures of great importance for an industrialized world had been pioneered in Germany and New Zealand. He confessed to an English friend that he had previously adhered to the Anglo-Saxon stereotype of the French as a "people of marked levity"; personal experience gave him instead "a sense of kinship" with French republicans. Roosevelt saw that England and France were democratized, no longer the symbols of Old World despotism that they had been for the Founding Fathers. In his perspective the Western Hemisphere was no longer a unified contrast to Europe, as envisaged by the Monroe Doctrine. Now the differences between South American states and their European cultural homelands were, like the differences between America and England, much less great than those which "separate the 'new' nations one from another, and the 'old' nations one from another."[31]

[31] "Biological Analogies in History," *African and European Addresses*, p. 197. See also "Citizenship in a Republic," *ibid.*, pp. 34, 57. For his advice to the British and kinship with the French see letter to George Otto Trevelyan, October 1, 1911, *Roosevelt Letters*, VII, 350–351, 380–385.

Gone too from Roosevelt's response to Europe was the old fear and contempt of royalty. Conscious of the prestige of the American Presidency, he looked upon kings with tolerant, patronizing affection. They had no such power in the modern world as he had enjoyed, and the social life of royalty reminded him of nothing so much as the circumscribed etiquette of "officers and their wives in one of our western army posts in the old days." He was neither awed nor made defiant. "I thoroughly liked and respected almost all the various kings and queens I met," he confessed. He was much impressed by the King of Italy ("I told him I wished we had a few men like him in the Senate!"), and he was delighted with the royal family of Norway; they were "dears" he would love to have as neighbors near Sagamore Hill.[32] A patrician American, with a taste for sport and literature, he was a strange blend of aristocrat and bourgeois that fascinated the European nobility. If Roosevelt walked with kings without losing the common touch, he had lost the old American touchiness in the presence of royalty.

Two of Roosevelt's intellectual friends, Herbert Croly and Henry Adams, saw even more clearly how the drift of their times was carrying old conventions out to sea. They were both eccentric personalities with a detached love for politics to which they brought a remarkable farsightedness. Despite its gnarled prose, Croly's *The Promise of American Life* became one of the great texts of the Progressive movement. It was a massive assault on Jeffersonian Americanism. Americans had indulged in for too long, Croly complained, an easy optimism, fatalism, and conservatism about the mission of the United States. Inevitable progress was a stultifying myth. The time had come to jettison an old-fashioned individualism, which only promoted the undisciplined accumulation of wealth, and fashion a new democratic nationalism, committed to the use of governmental power with Hamiltonian efficiency. In foreign affairs the spirit of the Monroe Doctrine was dangerously archaic, implying a fundamental antagonism to Europe which was strategically unrealistic. Those who wanted to

---

[32] Letter to Trevelyan, *ibid.*, pp. 366, 360–361, 385.

make peace must be prepared to fight for it and to find partners for the battle. Colonial expansion was a healthy manifestation of national growth and necessary for the political education of Asiatic peoples. "The emancipated and nationalized European states of today," Croly argued, "so far from being essentially antagonistic to the American democratic nation, are constantly tending towards a condition which invites closer and more fruitful association with the United States; and any national doctrine which proclaims a rooted antagonism lies almost at right angles athwart the road of American democratic national achievement."[33]

Croly's most heretical and telling thrusts were directed against the traditional American fondness for a dualistic image of the American people's relation to Europe:

The New World and the new American idea had released them from the bonds in which less fortunate Europeans were entangled. Those bonds were not to be considered as the terms under which excellent individual and social purposes were necessarily to be achieved. They were bad habits, which the dead past had imposed upon the inhabitants of the Old World, and from which Americans could be emancipated by virtue of their abundant faith in human nature and the boundless natural opportunities of the new continent.

The American reformer in his protest against European "feudalism" undervalued necessary social forms and intellectual standards.

It should have been a protest against a sterile and demoralizing Americanism—the Americanism of national irresponsibility and indiscriminate individualism. The bondage from which Americans needed, and still need, emancipation is not from Europe, but from the evasions, the incoherence, the impatience, and the easy-going conformity of their own intellectual and moral traditions.[34]

In his emancipation from the old antithesis between America

---

[33] *The Promise of American Life* (New York, Macmillan, 1911), p. 297. For links between Croly's imperialism and the other Progressives see William E. Leuchtenburg, "Progressivism and Imperialism: The Progressive Movement and American Foreign Policy, 1898–1916," *Mississippi Valley Historical Review*, **39** (December, 1952), 483–504.

[34] *Ibid.*, 424–426.

and Europe Croly was far in advance of most Americans. But Theodore Roosevelt provided Croly with the rough semblance of an American example. Sometime on his European tour, while bagging the big game of the African jungles and European royal society, the ex-president enthusiastically read *The Promise of American Life*. ". . . I think you understand," he told Croly, "as no other literary man does, the kind of thing I am striving for in politics."[35]

Henry Adams was too ironical to take the boisterous Roosevelt with Croly's solemnity, but the historian, for all his romanticizing of the medieval ages, had a shrewd and prescient eye for international realities of power. "We want our Atlantic system," Adams wrote John Hay in 1905, "which extends from the Rocky Mountains, on the west, to the Elbe on the east, and develops nine tenths of the energy of the world,—to control France and Germany as far as it goes." Three months later he concluded from Roosevelt's peacemaking at Portsmouth: "We have got to support France against Germany, and fortify an Atlantic system beyond attack; for if Germany breaks down England or France, she becomes the centre of a military world, and we are lost."[36] He had anticipated the strategic basis of two world wars.

The ancient dualism survived despite the Anglo-Saxon mythology, the diplomacy of imperialism, the life of the Colonel of the Rough Riders, and the insights of Croly and Adams. The crusade against the immigrant exploited highly conventional images of Europe; the new diplomacy produced no alliances; and a good many Progressives still worshipped at the shrine of Jefferson.

[35] July 30, 1912, *Roosevelt Letters*, #5746, VII, 582.

[36] Letters to John Hay, May 3, 1905, and to Elizabeth Cameron, August 27, 1905, Worthington Chauncey Ford, ed., *Letters of Henry Adams (1892–1918)* (Boston, Houghton Mifflin, 1938), pp. 447–448, 461. The evolution of Adams's views on the Atlantic system is traced in R. P. Blackmur, "The Atlantic Unites," *Hudson Review*, 5 (Summer, 1952), 212–232. One of Adams's most ominous predictions was that if Russia organized China, Western Civilization would fall about 1950. It is curious that the date coincides with the Korean War. But by then Adams's American-organized Atlantic system was in effect.

Tenaciously planted in the American imagination, the old antithesis had been vigorously shaken without being uprooted. It would soon be exposed to air again when a world at war would compel another anxious examination of the American position.

CHAPTER

9

THE PARTNERSHIP OF RIGHT

WHEN WILSON LEFT THE VERSAILLES PEACE CONFERENCE and sailed to America on the *George Washington*, in July, 1919, his action symbolized how far the nation had departed from the legendary advice of the first President's Farewell Address. The people of the United States had entered a European war, fought on foreign soil with European allies, and widely acclaimed the ideal of a universal league of nations. Everyone knows the story's remarkable anticlimax—the rejection of Wilson, the Treaty, and the League. The dramatic collapse of Wilsonian idealism was not merely a matter of partisan politics or popular fickleness; the deeper causes lay in the inner weaknesses of the new internationalism itself. Measured by the standard of the American attitude towards Europe, the Wilsonian adventure was much more faithful to native pieties than has been recognized.

The outbreak of war in Europe stunned Americans. They instinctively reacted with feelings bred by a traditional policy of

157

isolation. On Sunday, October 4, 1914, the President called for national prayer to deliver Europe from the scourge of war. Nothing more clearly revealed, as a journalist of the day pointed out, "our moral detachment, our obliviousness to the fact that the passions which brought forth this war were human, not European passions. We, the virtuous, interceded for the vicious; our prayer was 'deliver *them* from evil.' "[1] Americans were grateful that they had no part in such obvious insanity. "We never appreciated so keenly as now," the Wabash *Plain Dealer* editorialized, "the foresight exercised by our forefathers in emigrating from Europe."[2] Walter Hines Page, an ardent Anglophile and Wilson's Ambassador to England, passed a judgment on continental Europe that was undoubtedly widely shared: "As for the continent of Europe— forget it. We have paid far too much attention to it. . . . An ancient home of man, the home, too, of beautiful things—buildings, pictures, old places, old traditions, dead civilization—it is now bankrupt, its best young men dead, its system of politics and of government a failure, its social structure enslaving and tyrannical —it has little help for us. The American spirit, which is the spirit that concerns itself with making life better for the whole mass of men—that's at home at its best with us."[3]

While England had enjoyed American favor since 1900, Germany had fallen out of the good graces of most Americans. They had strongly favored Germany against France in 1870 because of Napoleon III's intrigue in Mexico and the Unionist sentiments of German-American immigrants. A respect for German intellectual life was induced by a generation of American professors who had earned their doctorates in German universities. These claims on American good will had been gradually eroded by 1914 through Germany's imperial actions in Samoa, China, and Venezuela. Critics of American Anglophobia were inclined, like the popular

[1] Walter E. Weyl, *American World Policies* (New York, Macmillan, 1917), p. 33.

[2] Quoted by Mark Sullivan, *Our Times, the United States 1900–1925*, V (New York, Scribner's, 1933), 32.

[3] Letter to Ralph W. Page, November 15, 1914, Burton J. Hendrick, ed., *The Life and Letters of Walter Hines Page*, I (Garden City, N.Y., Doubleday, Page, 1925), 352.

novelist Owen Wister, to correct distortions of British history at the price of substituting for the schoolbook image of the tyrant King George an equally unfocussed image of Germany as an incurable, "cunning, treacherous wild beast."[4] By 1916 most newspapers had come to sympathize with the Allies, but only a minority took a strongly pro-Ally stand, and even fewer wished to intervene. The aversion to entanglement in European affairs ran deep in the American mind.

It was hard to see any good ground for American involvement because a realistic case for intervention was so seldom made. Americans had enjoyed too long a sense of security built upon their continental size and the flanking oceans. Those who bellowed loudest for intervention after the sinking of the *Lusitania* struck sentimental notes. A Southerner schooled in "Anglo-Saxon" imperialistic prejudices, Walter Page felt a close affinity for the English gentlemen he dealt with as Ambassador, and he dreamed of an Anglo-American partnership to "do for Europe on a large scale essentially what we did for Cuba on a small scale and thereby usher in a new era in human history." Wanting to "hang our Irish agitators and shoot our hyphenates and bring up our children with reverence for English history and in the awe of English literature," he was increasingly embarrassed by the Administration's policy of neutrality.[5] His reports to the President were full of anguish at English criticism of American detachment, as if his country should go to war mainly to keep the good opinion of London. Theodore Roosevelt, who waged a private war on the Administration after the *Lusitania* incident, thundered for intervention on the sentimental basis that it would restore "the strenu-

---

[4] *A Straight Deal or the Ancient Grudge* (New York, Macmillan, 1921), p. 46. For an objective account of American-German relations see Clara E. Schieber, "The Transformation of American Sentiment towards Germany, 1870–1914," *Journal of International Relations*, 12 (July, 1921), 50–74.

[5] Letter to Woodrow Wilson, November 24, 1916, and to Edwin A. Alderman, June 22, 1916, *Life and Letters*, II, 194, 144. For Roosevelt see Russell Buchanan, "Theodore Roosevelt and American Neutrality 1914–1917," *American Historical Review*, 43 (July, 1938), 775–790. For newspaper opinion see H. C. Peterson, *Propaganda for War: The Campaign against American Neutrality, 1914–1917* (Norman, University of Oklahoma Press, 1939), pp. 167, 176.

ous mood" to American life and punish the Central Powers for their bad deeds. As sympathy for the Allies increased, especially in the East, there was talk of an ideological conflict between democracy and autocracy, but the argument was not very convincing to anyone who was hostile to the imperialism of the European powers or the despotism of Czarist Russia.

In the light of the Second World War it is easy to think of the first as presenting an earlier challenge to the security of those nations that are bound together by ties of interest and tradition to an Atlantic world. Thus Henry Adams, by now an old man, wrote in 1917 to an English friend: "Meanwhile, here we are, for the first time in our lives fighting side by side and to my bewilderment I find the great object of my life thus accomplished in the building up of the great community of Atlantic Powers which I hope will at least make a precedent that can never be forgotten."[6] But Adams, Walter Lippmann of the liberal *New Republic*, and an obscure second secretary of the American embassy at Constantinople, Lewis Einstein, were then almost alone in seeing the conflict in terms of protecting an Atlantic world against a European-Asiatic combination. Lippmann's fellow editors, Herbert Croly and Walter Weyl, were in agreement in their criticism of traditional isolationism with its pharisaical contempt for Europe, but all three gave their support to Wilson, who defined the issues of the war in his own more traditional way. Wilson charged the diplomatic issues with a passionate moral intensity. As he gradually moved from neutrality to intervention the President constantly invoked the peculiar virtues of the American's special mission.

[6] Letter to Charles Milnes Gaskell, June 8, 1917, *Letters of Henry Adams (1892-1918)*, Worthington C. Ford, ed. (Boston, Houghton Mifflin, 1938), p. 642. For similar views see Walter Lippmann, "The Defense of the Atlantic World," *New Republic*, 10 (February 17, 1917), 59–61; Lewis Einstein's "The United States and Anglo-German Rivalry" (1913) is discussed in William C. Askew and J. Fred Rippy, "The United States and Europe's Strife, 1908–1913," *Journal of Politics*, 4 (February, 1942), 68–79. Robert Endicott Osgood explores the lack of realism in American foreign policy in *Ideals and Self-Interest in America's Foreign Relations, the Great Transformation of the Twentieth Century* (Berkeley, University of California Press, 1953) with close attention to Wilson, Roosevelt, and Lippmann.

His eloquent defense of neutrality was a matter of political principle, for his background gave him a personal basis of sympathy with the Allies. As a student he had much admired the political writings of Edmund Burke and Walter Bagehot; as a historian he had seen American history as "a free working-out upon a clear field, indeed, of selected forces generated long ago in England and the old European world." Shortly after the turn of the century he paid tribute to the "Anglo-Saxon" and the new position of the United States as a world power which imperialism had brought about. Yet as president he was forced to reckon with what he had feared as a historian—the crossing of our own "old Teutonic habit" of self-government with the immigrants' "feverish humors of the restless Old World."[7] Wilson found that as political leader of a diverse society, whose groups had different feelings about various countries of the Old World, he had to speak for a great nation, not for a tribe of "Anglo-Saxons." In his public addresses as President, he repudiated the imperial idea and characterized the United States as a "mediating Nation," compounded of the blood and traditions of all the nations.

Like Jefferson and John Quincy Adams, Wilson believed that America had a mission in the world that was best expressed in isolation from the conflicts of the world. By means of a venerable tradition, as old as the Puritans and the American Revolution, he reconciled the universality of American purpose with the limitation of American responsibility. America was "a special example" to mankind and it served humanity most by its detachment from the evils of Europe. It was America's privilege to be disengaged from a war for whose causes and objects it had no concern; America's role was to aid in "reconstructing the processes of peace." Earnestly the President sought, through the help of Colonel House, his close adviser, to play the role of mediator, hoping to prevent a war with Germany over violations of American neutral rights on the high seas.

[7] Cf. "The Character of Democracy in the United States," *An Old Master and other Political Essays* (New York, Scribner's, 1893), pp. 118, 126, and "The Significance of History," *Harper's Encyclopaedia of United States History*, John Lossing Benson, ed. (New York, Harper, 1901), p. 1.

Wilson and House in talks with the Allies in February, 1916, worked out a plan to stop the war through American mediation. It entailed the remarkable provision of "probable" American intervention on the side of the Allies if the Germans proved hostile to a negotiated peace, or its terms. But, now more confident of victory, the British refused the proposal and bitterly disappointed Wilson's hopes. The peace plan having been rebuffed, Wilson countered with a public announcement of the ideal of a league of nations, for which the British had earlier sought American backing. But now the project was proposed in the spirit of "a plague on both your houses." After his talks with the principal European powers in February, Colonel House expressed to Wilson his distaste for a war in which "incompetent statesmanship and selfishness" were "at the bottom of it all."[8] When Wilson gave official approval to the idea of a league of nations in May, he affirmed American participation as "partners with the rest" in the "life of the world," but he also dismissed any concern with the causes or origins of the war. The principle of the league, he repeatedly stressed, was not that of an alliance, which the isolationist tradition forbade, but of "a concert of power" instead of "a balance of power." His awareness by May, 1917 of the Allied secret peace treaties deepened his suspicions of Europe.

The new internationalism was thus linked to old isolationist feelings about the iniquity of European alliances, while the relevance to the United States of the European balance of power was obscured by the idealism of Wilson's rhetoric. No more than in the past, Wilson told an English audience in December, 1918, was America "now interested in European politics. But she is interested

[8] February 9, 1916, Charles Seymour, ed., *The Intimate Papers of Colonel House*, I (Boston, Houghton Mifflin, 1926), 164. For the House-Grey memorandum see Arthur S. Link, *Wilson the Diplomatist, a Look at His Major Foreign Policies* (Baltimore, Johns Hopkins University Press, 1957), pp. 46–51. For Wilson's views on American detachment, example, and indifference (to the causes of the war) see Address to the Associated Press, April 20, 1915, to the Foreign-Born at Philadelphia, May 10, 1915, to the Daughters of the American Revolution at Washington, October 11, 1915, and to the League to Enforce Peace at Washington, May 27, 1916, Ray Stannard Baker and William E. Dodd, eds., *The Public Papers of Woodrow Wilson: The New Democracy*, I (New York, Harper, 1926), 302–307, 318–322, 375–381; II, 184–188.

in the partnership of right between America and Europe."[9] The new bridge between the New World and the Old was not, then, constructed out of the solid steel of mutual interest and respect; it was spun with the insubstantial stuff of abstract moral principle.

The sting to American sensibilities inflicted by Wilson's intervention in Europe was drawn by the way this departure from tradition was justified. To protect American commercial rights as a neutral nation Wilson had been forced to break with Germany; because a position of armed neutrality seemed only likely to draw America into war without even the rights of a belligerent, he agonizingly committed the nation to conflict. But the horrors of war could only be justified ultimately by the opportunity to make a liberal peace. Confident that the Allies were increasingly dependent militarily and economically upon the United States, he was determined to control the terms of the settlement. Thus his Fourteen Points became the basis of the Versailles conference, accepted in principle by victor and vanquished alike. This diplomatic triumph made American commitment to Europe, including the redrawing of its frontiers, justifiable as the extension of "the spirit of '76" to "the great stage of the world itself."[10] America was engaged in Europe only for the most exceptional reason— the realization of its disinterested mission. As Colonel House told Wilson, urging him to link the proposed league with the Treaty, "the only excuse we could give for meddling in European or world affairs was a league of nations through which we hope to prevent wars. If that was not to be, then we would not care to mix again in their difficulties."[11]

Wilson was careful to call the United States an "associated power" rather than an ally, and the spirit of this relationship was revealed in the American determination to hold the reins of control over European relief. The Allies wanted an inter-Allied board with decisions according to majority vote, but Herbert Hoover,

[9] For the "partnership of right" see his address at Free Trade Hall, Manchester, December 30, 1918; for "a concert of power" see his address to the Senate on Terms of Peace, January 22, 1917, *War and Peace*, I, 353; *The New Democracy*, II, 410, 414.

[10] Address at Mount Vernon, July 4, 1918, *War and Peace*, I, 235.

[11] Diary, March 24, 1919, *Intimate Papers*, IV, 390.

Wilson's Food Administrator, successfully fought the proposal, becoming himself Director-General of Relief. "If we maintain our independence," he wrote Wilson in 1918, "we can confer favors instead of complying with agreements and we can use our resources to make economic exchanges which will maintain justice all round."[12] In a memorandum to his American staff he warned against any reliance on "the second class minds and jealousies of the present inter-Allied bodies" or "the pinheads of bureaucratic Europe."[13] American relief work, backed by credits, purchases, and private charities, was an admirable piece of constructive state-craft for devastated Europe, and Hoover was justly proud of the achievement. But, like the Connecticut Yankee in King Arthur's Court, the American position was not as disinterested as Hoover believed.

As his own memoranda make clear, Hoover wanted independent powers of control because of American guarantees of high prices to domestic farmers, the fierce resolve to contain the spread of Bolshevism, and the desire to get proper appreciation and return for American services.[14] One of his agents in Hungary, though told to keep out of central European politics, even planned a revolution which was briefly successful against Bela Kun's Communist rule. This remarkable episode, candidly recounted in a national magazine, provoked the editor to admiration: "He moved through those many century-old magnificences more a real dictator than any man in their history, but because his reign was benevolent and his American purpose absolutely unselfish and disinterested they submitted to him."[15] Typically, Americans did not recognize their concerns as "interests"; only Europeans had such stakes. Not surprisingly, Hoover wrote Wilson in April,

[12] October 24, 1918, Suda Lorena Bane and Ralph Haswell Lutz, eds., *Organization of American Relief in Europe 1918–1919* (Stanford, Stanford University Press, 1943), p. 27.

[13] November 15, 1918, *ibid.*, p. 50.

[14] See cable to Joseph C. Cotton, November 7, 1918, *ibid.*, pp. 32–33; *The Memoirs of Herbert Hoover: Years of Adventure 1874–1920* (New York, Macmillan, 1952), p. 289.

[15] See T. T. C. Gregory, "Stemming the Red Tide," *World's Work*, 41 (April, 1921), 609. The story was told in three installments from April to June.

1919, that he hoped for an "early end" to "our whole relationship to these political combinations in Europe, which grew up before and during the war" and for American retirement from Europe "lock, stock and barrel" if the Allies refused to adopt peace on the basis of the Fourteen Points.[16]

The shaky basis of Allied unity was also evident in the handling of the Russian problem. Americans had at first enthusiastically welcomed the Russian Revolution, as if "the spirit of '76" had risen again to give the glow of true democracy to the Allied cause. Wilson himself had saluted it as a sign of the fundamentally democratic temper of the Russians, who had been groaning for centuries under a despotism alien to their habits. This thorough misjudgment was soon followed, especially when the Bolsheviks seized power, by traditional American suspicion of radical movements. Elihu Root, the noted Republican whom Wilson sent on a mission to Russia in 1917, voiced the smug condescension that presaged bad future relations in his description of the Provisional Government as "an infant class in the art of being free containing one hundred and seventy million people" who needed "to be supplied with kindergarten material."[17] Edgar Sisson, representing the American Committee on Public Information in Russia, gullibly published a set of forged documents, purporting to show that the Bolsheviks were paid agents of the Germans, and the public soon mistakenly concluded that such an undemocratic revolution could never last. Wilson and his supporters, as George Kennan has shown, had hoped for both the stability of the democratic Provisional Government and the persistence of Russian war efforts against Germany, but these aims could not be realistically harmonized. The Bolsheviks solidified their power by contracting out of the war. When Americans had to face the defeat of their expectations, they found a familiar scapegoat by accusing their European allies of cynicism.

[16] April 11, 1919, *Organization of American Relief*, p. 400.

[17] Root to Secretary of State, June 17, 1917, quoted by George F. Kennan, *Russia Leaves the War*, vol. I of *Soviet-American Relations, 1917–1920* (Princeton, Princeton University Press, 1958), p. 21. For Wilson's welcoming of the Russian Revolution see his Declaration of War against Germany, *War and Peace*, I, 12–13.

For their part neither the French nor the Italian leaders had any taste for Wilson's liberal war aims, and the President had no stomach for the Allied military interventions in Archangel and Siberia, which he reluctantly supported. Inspired by the French and commanded by the British, the Archangel venture was doomed by the quixotic intention of building up an eastern front against Germany. Wilson had repeatedly resisted Allied pressure for the Siberian expedition, but he yielded finally and went on to form his own plans without consulting the Allies. He aimed to give aid to the Czech Corps, whom he mistakenly assumed to be threatened there by captured German and Austrian soldiers. The British and French conducted their own independent action; increasingly committed to helping the White Russians, who were seeking the overthrow of the Bolsheviks, they entangled themselves in the Russian Civil War. Nothing was achieved but bad feeling among all parties.

At the Peace Conference Russia was conspicuously absent and the Allies were at loggerheads. Wilson, who wanted Russian participation, was opposed by the French, while the British urged him to postpone withdrawal of his forces from Siberia. The Big Four finally settled on Hoover's naïve plan for using food relief as a political weapon in negotiations with the Soviets, and it was rejected as such. Nearly half of American agricultural aid to Europe between August, 1919, and July, 1923, did go to Soviet Russia, but this sign of good will was compromised by the bungling interventions in Archangel and Siberia. The public soon began to clamor for getting the boys back home from such a confused mission. Protest meetings were held in Michigan, which had a regiment frozen in at Archangel, and a local paper said that people felt "the League of Nations means internationalism, and that, they suspect, is plain Bolshevism."[18] Although the great ma-

---

[18] See "Nation-wide Press Poll on the League of Nations," *Literary Digest*, **61** (April 5, 1919), 120; Thomas A. Bailey, *America Faces Russia: Russian-American Relations from Early Times to Our Day* (Ithaca, New York, Cornell University Press, 1950), pp. 241–247. The poll showed that 718 favored the League, 181 opposed it, and 478 conditionally supported it. For my account of the Allied relations with the Soviets during the war and the peace conference I have relied on the penetrating analysis in George F.

jority of newspapers in April, 1919, favored the League idea, the size of the group which supported it with many reservations was ominously large in every section except the traditionally Democratic South. Nemesis was preparing revenge.

When it was evident that Wilson could not play a lone hand at Paris and sweep the board, kibitzers at home began to think of the United States as a virtuous innocent victimized by a wily, guilty Europe caught dealing from the bottom of the deck.[19] No group was quicker to see the situation in this light than the insurgent progressive Republicans of the Middle West. Before the war five of them, led by "Fighting Bob" La Follette of Wisconsin, had joined a small band of Senators to filibuster Wilson's Armed Ship Bill, designed to carry out his policy of armed neutrality. When war came, their worst fears were realized. Courageous, dedicated, and doctrinaire, La Follette best expressed the convictions and prejudices of Midwestern Progressivism. He backed neutral mediation of the war, "peace without victory," and the Fourteen Points, but he feared that Wilson's methods made war inevitable. Inspired by a simple faith in popular democracy, La Follette was an ardent foe of military preparedness, conscription, and executive ascendancy in foreign affairs. His experience as Governor and Senator had taught him to suspect and hate the monopolistic ambitions of capitalists, and his regional background nurtured a traditional hostility to the imperialism of Europe. Characteristically, he was sure that he could see the sinister hand of "financial imperialism" behind the war in Europe, a place "cursed with a contagious . . . deadly plague," and he suspected that the machinations of "Wall Street," the symbolic enemy of farmers,

---

Kennan, *Russia and the West under Lenin and Stalin* (Boston, Little, Brown, 1961), pp. 64–150.

[19] Ray Stannard Baker, head of the Press Department at the Conference, wrote in his notebook: "It is noble in the prophet to assert that he has no selfish or material interests . . . but when the prophet sits down with the poker players, each of whom wants the jack-pot, the aura fades." He developed this self-righteous view of Wilson's role in the widely publicized authorized history, *Woodrow Wilson and World Settlement* (1922). Wilson himself urged Baker to call it *America Meets Europe at Paris*. See his autobiography, *American Chronicle* (New York: Charles Scribner's 1945), pp. 422, 495.

had drummed up the growing sympathy for the Allies.[20] He feared, above all, that American entrance into the war would blight democratic reform at home. The raging storm of chauvinism set loose by the Great Crusade, making him a martyr to the cause of civil liberty in wartime, his loyalty shamefully impugned by the press and Senate, did much to strengthen and justify this conviction.

La Follette hoped for the best from Wilson's trip to Europe, but he was typically hypersensitive to the compromises in the Treaty of Versailles. As a champion of the "People" against the "Interests," he saw them as a sorry sellout to the secret treaties of the Allies, who wanted a league "to stand guard over the swag."[21] During the Senate debate on the Treaty he displayed large maps with British territorial gains vividly painted on them and scornfully pointed a righteous finger at the continuing existence of the British Empire. His demands for an acceptable treaty were as "progressive" as they were unrealistic—the right of revolution on the American model for Egypt, India, Ireland, and Korea, the end of conscription, reduction of armaments, and provision for a popular referendum on war. La Follette's Progressivism cherished the ancient conviction that America could serve the world best by remaining aloof to pursue its own democratic ideals.

In the light of the mid-twentieth century La Follette's position seems as old-fashioned as it was idealistic, and historians have saluted Wilson as a prophet. But he went out to meet the future with a deep piety for the past. His Administration failed to explain the war to the people in terms of the relation of the European balance of power to American interests, and he defended the League itself as an escape from the balance of power and from the necessity for alliances. The public language of Wilson's diplomacy was too much keyed to rights, morality, and ideology, and the intoxicating atmosphere of a crusade unbalanced the American mind with emotional images of "hyphenates," "Reds," and European "power politics."

[20] Quoted by Bella Case and Fola La Follette, *Robert M. La Follette,* I (New York, Macmillan, 1953), 577, 649.

[21] *Ibid.,* II, 981–982.

Sparks of isolationist feeling were soon igniting a blaze. Immigrant groups with ties to Europe had various reasons for finding the Treaty unfair to the aspirations of their peoples abroad, and their enemies at home were often the Eastern, old Americans who were most strongly pro-Ally. Progressives with regional and ideological suspicions of the defenders of the peace settlement had constituents with immigrant grievances which led them in the same direction. Republicans, who had widely supported the League idea before Wilson's return to America, were irritated at Wilson's partisanship in staffing his peace commission and in calling for a Democratic Congress at the next election. Once in power as the majority party, the Republicans made Henry Cabot Lodge, a bitter enemy of the President, chairman of the Senate Foreign Relations Committee, and Lodge masterfully devised a strategy to bring together all the forces of opposition. The end of the new internationalism, broadly supported throughout the country before Wilson's return, was in the making.

In retrospect the defeat of the Treaty and the League is easily caricatured as a melodramatic conflict between shortsighted isolationists and farsighted internationalists. But the Wilsonian internationalists had shared many isolationist assumptions; and Lodge himself was not a thoroughgoing isolationist. A leading advocate of a "large policy" for the United States at the time of the Spanish-American War, Lodge was strongly pro-Ally in the neutrality period and was quite willing to accept an Anglo-Franco-American alliance as the best guarantee of future peace. Though Lodge differed from Wilson by advocating a harsh peace for Germany and by condemning the League because it might prevent American restriction of European immigration, both men agreed to the plan of an Anglo-American alliance with France to prevent future German aggression. This realistic proposal was tragically swamped in the fight over the League. As party leader, Lodge found a formula for unity in a set of reservations to the Wilsonian settlement, minimizing American obligations and maximizing American sovereign rights. Having earlier accepted some amendments to the original settlement, Wilson adamantly instructed his supporters to reject Lodge's reservations. Lodge astutely managed strategy so that the President had to accept Republican reservations or no Treaty at all. Twice Wilson rejected the opportunity of compromise and so the Lodge-amended Treaty failed by a margin of seven votes to pass the Senate.[22] The new internationalism was dead.

The situation of "the time-innocent American confronted with the evils of history" is, as Ferner Nuhn has noted, "one of the standard situations of our cultural drama."[23] From Royall Tyler's *The Contrast* to Henry James's *The American*, or Mark Twain's *The Connecticut Yankee*, the theme has fascinated the native imagination. It is irresistible to think of Wilson in this context, and Nuhn himself draws an extensive parallel between Wilson in Europe and Maggie Verver in James's *The Golden Bowl*. He implies that Wilson tried to redeem the Old World, to mend the flaw in the crystal of the Golden Bowl with his American idealism, but settled instead for preserving the appearances. But "The Paris Education of Woodrow Wilson," as Charles Seymour has aptly called it, was more complex. The President had been to Europe only once before, on a short vacation in Italy, and he arrived at Paris with very little knowledge of the scene on which he was to seek an American triumph, like Christopher Newman himself. Through private negotiations with the Allied leaders (which at once qualified his commitment to "open covenants openly arrived at"), he was forced to take seriously European demands for reparations and security, the limits of the national self-determination principle as applied to the intricate patterns of Eastern and Central Europe, and the primary responsibility of the large powers in making the peace. If he had come to terms with the European realities, he had not changed, any more than had Newman himself, his temperament or his principles. On his return to America he failed to provide the public with an understanding of the realistic basis of

[22] For Wilson, Lodge, and the Treaty fight see John A. Garraty, *Henry Cabot Lodge, a Biography* (New York, Knopf, 1953), pp. 344–350 and Link, *op. cit.*, pp. 127–156.

[23] *The Wind Blew from the East: A Study in the Orientation of American Culture* (New York, Harper, 1942), p. 78. For his view of Wilson see pp. 77–78, 160, 259–260.

his compromises and clung instead to the conviction that the League would justify and remedy all the limitations of the peace.[24]

Wilson hoped that the election of 1920 would be "a great and solemn referendum" on the vital issue of internationalism. But already Republican orators were preparing to picture the President as a gullible participant in a rigged poker game with pieces of Europe as chips. At the Republican national convention of 1920 Chauncey M. Depuw provoked hilarious applause by his tale of Wilson, "a babe confident of himself," being expertly fleeced by "those great gamblers in international politics."[25] Soon the intellectuals would be coming to the same conclusion, as wittily presented by John Maynard Keynes in *The Economic Consequences of the Peace,* serialized in the *New Republic.* But who had actually deceived whom? Wilson had committed the United States to readjustment of European affairs in the faith that he spoke for a united people. When he returned to America he found how quickly his wartime support had become unstable, while the tough Europeans who had tied his hands at Versailles increasingly represented the war-inflamed spirit of their own peoples. When America rejected the Treaty and the League, Europeans might well be puzzled to understand how anyone could believe that the Old World had deceived the New. The Fourteen Points suited America well, and, necessarily compromised, they had defined the standards of the peace. But Europe's legitimate security interests were to be protected by a League, and America had rejected it out of fear of compromising its own interests. Americans might hug to their breasts the image of themselves as virtuous innocents, wronged by a wicked Old World, but a recording angel would have to smile.

In 1923 Woodrow Wilson, shattered by his doomed tour of

[24] For balanced assessments of Wilson's European "education" see Charles Seymour, "The Paris Education of Woodrow Wilson," *Virginia Quarterly Review,* 32 (Autumn, 1956), 578–593; William L. Langer, "Woodrow Wilson: His Education in World Affairs," *Confluence,* 5 (October, 1956), 183–194.

[25] Quoted by Mark Sullivan, *Our Times,* VI, 124–125. For a detailed account of the breakdown of Wilson's support see Selig Adler, *The Isolationist Impulse: Its Twentieth Century Reaction* (New York, Abelard-Schuman, 1957), pp. 54–117.

the country on behalf of the League, still had the faith to salvage from the wreck of his hopes the innocent belief that the world had been "made safe for democracy." Like most Americans, he could see in the collapse of the old monarchical order in central Europe a clear gain for a democratic world. "There need now be no fear," he confidently proclaimed, "that any such mad design as that entertained by the insolent and ignorant Hohenzollerns and their counselors may prevail against it."[26] But Wilson did know what later generations were to learn by cruel experience, that the world was not yet "safe against irrational revolution." Faced by its fury, later Americans would find to their surprise that it was from Europe's faltering republics, not from its traditionally hated monarchies, that movements would arise in the 1920s and 30s to threaten much more gravely a much more democratic order than had been the case in Wilson's time.

*   *   *

The aftermath of Wilson's diplomacy is the story of the burnt child who shuns the fire. The impulse to save Europe had been tainted with an American impatience and suspicion. European resistance to American reformation seemed pigheaded. An American officer of Hoover's European Relief staff in one of the Succession States of the Austro-Hungarian Monarchy, disintegrated by the war, complained to an English historian that the Danube ought to be as free as the Mississippi, the people forced to speak one language, and the "cobwebs" of history brushed aside, if the area were ever to enjoy an American-style prosperity.[27] He knew with an American despair that it would never happen. As disillusioned historians began during the Twenties to write the history of the war, minimizing the responsibility of the Central Powers, indicting the Allies, and suspecting Wilson of succumbing to the pressure of bankers, the public began to wonder if there ever had

[26] "The Road Away from Revolution," *Atlantic Monthly*, 132 (August, 1923), 146. See Bertrand de Jouvenel, "Woodrow Wilson," *Confluence*, 5 (January, 1957), 320–331.
[27] Alfred Zimmerman, "America and Europe," *America and Europe and Other Essays* (New York, Oxford University Press, 1929), pp. 8–9.

been any sense in going into the war in the first place. Behind the highest tariff walls of its history the United States, now a creditor nation, demanded the payment of war debts from former Allies, who demanded reparations from their former enemies, who could not pay while America kept out their goods. By extensive American investment abroad, especially in Germany, a specious plausibility was given to this vicious circle. To most Americans it was a simple affair: "They hired the money, didn't they?" President Coolidge's laconic explanation treated the Europeans as if they were dishonest debtors, welching on a gentlemen's bargain.

The American's bitter disappointment with the war and the peace made him hypersensitive to any criticism by foreigners. He took a position of injured innocence against the European ingrates, concealing from himself by his righteous indignation how hypocritical his demands for war debts, his tariffs, and his desertion of the League inevitably made him appear to the Europeans. "But, oh Boy!" fumed an irate American at an English critic of American travelers,

when the *next* European *"squabble"* breaks loose, believe me, *we'll all stay home* and give France and Italy and Greece and the whole she-bang *the glassy eye* and *the marble heart*. When they come whining and begging for men and men and ships and ships and foods and fat and *"give till it hurts,"* we will say, Like Hell, *Shylock holds on to his own!*[28]

Political isolationism became the common cause of ardent liberals and cautious conservatives alike. Touring Europe in 1923, Senator La Follette jotted down in his notebook the sentiments of Midwestern Progressivism: "Democracy is now being crucified in Europe." Communism, Fascism, Monarchism, Allied money lenders—all had frustrated the growth of freedom, American style. The remedy was clear: "The greatest contribution that America can make to Europe and the world is to restore and perfect her democratic institutions and traditions, so that they will stand as a

[28] Letter to editor, *Saturday Review*, **142** (October 16, 1926), 435–436. For the revulsion against the war see Osgood, *op. cit.*, pp. 309–332; Adler, "The War-Guilt Question and American Disillusionment, 1918–1928," *Journal of Modern History*, **23** (March, 1951), 1–28.

beacon lighting the way to all peoples."[29] Like the internationalism of the Democrats, the isolationism of the Republicans was not
defended as a practical instrument of diplomacy; it was hallowed
as a sign of superior national virtue. What was sauce for Wilson
and Jeffersonian Democrats was equally tasty for Hoover, Lodge,
and the Republicans. Hoover, who had served on several committees of the peace delegation and as Wilson's Food Administrator
had "dealt with the gaunt realities which prowled outside," came
out of the war and peace with the conviction, which would last
him a lifetime, that "irreconcilable conflicts in concepts and historic experience between the New World and the Old World"
made it impossible for America to make lasting peace in Europe
and imperative to keep out of future wars. The conventional picture of Europe as a dark and bloody ground trod by men of cunning wiles, deaf to every noble American cry, was etched forever
on his imagination. Wilson may have failed, "but the President
was too great a man to employ European methods," Hoover felt,
"and American idealism was wholly unfitted to such a scene." He
set his face like flint against the insidious temptations of Europe:
"American Society with a capital S, and many of our Intellectuals
with a capital I, have made a sort of fetish of their spiritual home
in Europe. They fail to recognize that ours is a setting three centuries distant."[30] The differences between America and Europe
were established as of 1630 and artificially frozen forever.

Wilson and La Follette saw America as an example of social
change for the world; the conservatives saw it as a safe harbor
in a dangerously unstable world. America, boasted Senator Henry
Cabot Lodge in 1924, had built itself up with no help from Europe, while American isolation helped Europe because the United
States served as a "bulwark" of the civilized world. But basic to
both expressions of national self-righteousness was the sense of a
fundamental contrast between America and Europe, a gulf of
nearly metaphysical proportions. "America and Europe are entirely different," Lodge explained; "All the conditions and situa-

[29] *Robert M. La Follette,* II, 1086–1087.
[30] *The Memoirs of Herbert Hoover, Years of Adventure 1874–1920,* pp.
473, 451, 478.

tions are different. The people of the United States live in a new country, that is I mean new to western civilization." By this national mythology, which he shared with Wilson, he condemned the League as an alien product made by Europe for Europe: "Let the League, which was made in Europe and belongs to Europe, go there and prosper. We wish it well, but let us . . . go on in our own way. . . ."[31]

American diplomatic policy during the 20s was never officially "isolationist," but its prejudice against Europe made all its political actions on the international stage isolationist in temper. Symbols of internationalism were given a widespread lip service in prestige newspapers throughout the decade, but it is more significant that favorable judgments of the outside world, as expressed, for example, even in the editorial pages of *The New York Times,* were at their lowest ebb.[32] Though President Harding had promised American membership in a World Court, when the opportunity came, the Senate accepted it only reluctantly on the crucial condition that the United States be able to countermand any advisory opinion touching any issue in which it claimed an interest. The United States would be happy to join provided this reservation were accepted unanimously without reservation by all other members. When the Europeans requested clarification of this condition of membership, President Coolidge placated the isolationists by refusing to explain exactly what it meant.

As the European nations built up their armaments in the search for a security which a League crippled by American rejection could not provide, the Americans pressed for disarmament conferences, convinced with President Hoover that the basic cause of war was the European penchant for militarism. A pact to outlaw war by mutual declaration, instead of an alliance for security, exactly suited the American temper of moralistic judgment on the Europeans without practical commitment to anything that might

[31] "Foreign Relations of the United States, 1921–24," *Foreign Affairs,* 2 (June 15, 1924), 539.

[32] Ithiel de Sola Pool, *Symbols of Internationalism,* Hoover Institute Studies, Series C, Symbol Studies no. 3 (Stanford, Stanford University Press, 1951), pp. 20–21. See also Pool, *The 'Prestige Papers',* Series C, no. 2 (1952), p. 45.

entangle the United States with them. It was, therefore, not at all surprising that Senator William E. Borah of Idaho—chairman of the Senate Committee on Foreign Affairs, leader of the "Irreconcilables" against the League, supporter of disarmament conferences, and opponent of proposals to join the World Court and to cancel war debts—could pilot the Kellogg-Briand Peace Pact of 1928 through the Senate without a single reservation and only one negative vote.[33] The diplomatic internationalism of the Twenties was profoundly shaped by attitudes towards Europe which had always animated the isolationist tradition. In this respect Wilson and Lodge, Hoover and La Follette, Coolidge and Borah, all stood on common ground. The Great Crusade to save Europe from itself had ended with mutual estrangement and a deep desire to save America from Europe.

[33] For Borah's career see the sympathetic biography by Claudius O. Johnson, *Borah of Idaho* (New York, Longmans, Green, 1936). Borah did not filibuster the Armed Ship Bill, but in voting for the war resloution he stipulated no alliances or obligations as the conditions of his support. Despite his chairmanship of the Senate Foreign Relations Committee, he never made a trip abroad. He did urge withdrawal of our troops from, and recognition of, Russia. For a detailed account of the Kellogg Pact see Adler, *op. cit.*, pp. 228–238. As early as 1932 Frank H. Simonds made a brilliant critique, in the modern "realist" vein, of the diplomacy of the 1920s. See his neglected *Can America Stay at Home?* (New York, Harper, 1932).

10

WHERE THE TWENTIETH
CENTURY WAS

IN THE NINETEEN TWENTIES the idolatry of business, "the tyranny
of the majority," and the spread of mass culture in America
tended to dramatize the differences between the Old World and
the New. Transatlantic prophets of the "Americanization" of the
world were heard as early as 1902, but during this decade European intellectuals began to see in America the dread face of the future: standardization, crowd culture, and regimentation. Georges
Duhamel in 1931 summed up with bitter brilliance a European
image of America in *America the Menace: Scenes from the Life of
the Future*. Just as Americans had created a symbolic Old World
to represent the evils of the past in contrast to the hopeful promise of a New World emancipated from feudal darkness, so did
the Europeans begin to create a symbolic image of America to
represent the feared future of technology and mass society.[1] In

[1] See "Inquiry among European Writers into the Spirit of America,"

America cultural life became polarized. While "one-hundred-per-cent Americans" self-righteously rejected Europe, many sensitive and disaffected American rebels were magnetically drawn to a European world that seemed to offer liberation, inspiration, and redemption.

The isolationism of the Twenties was only a matter of politics. Europe had new importance for Americans as an investment, a mission field, a market, and a playground. American business firms, production methods, machinery, tools, and tourists, became so significant a part of American life in Europe that Sinclair Lewis made the American invasion the subject of a popular novel.[2] But domestic politics were permeated by the anti-European bias that marked American diplomacy. Protected from diplomatic entanglement with Europe, the official guardians of America turned to the danger within. During the closing days of Wilson's administration the Department of Justice, alarmed by the Red Scare growing out of the Russian Revolution, launched a drive against radicals, aliens, socialists, and communists; and the Ku Klux Klan, rabid enemy of Negroes, Jews, Catholics, and immigrants, swelled its ranks to five million. Discriminatory immigration legislation aimed at keeping out Southern and Eastern Europeans expressed the widespread disenchantment with the traditional melting pot theory of American nationality. Fundamentalists rallied to protect American school children from the teachings of Darwin, who traced man's origin to "Old World monkeys" as Bryan complained, and the execution on dubious evidence of Sacco and Van-

---

Transition, 13 (Summer, 1928), 248–277; Cushing Strout, "America, the Menace of the Future: A European Fantasy," *Virginia Quarterly Review*, 33 (Autumn, 1957), 569–581. W. T. Stead as early as 1902 used the title *The Americanization of the World, or the Trend of the Twentieth Century*.

[2] See Francis Miller and Helen Hill, *The Giant of the Western World* (New York, Morrow, 1930), part 2, pp. 53–144; Eric Fischer, *The Passing of the European Age, a Study of the Transfer of Western Civilization and Its Renewal in Other Continents* (Cambridge, Harvard University Press, 1948), pp. 78–97. For figures on Americans abroad as residents or travelers in the period between the wars see Richard H. Heindel, *The American Impact on Great Britain 1898–1914* (Philadelphia, University of Pennsylvania Press, 1940), pp. 35, 43. In 1928 an estimated 27,000 Americans were residents of Great Britain, France, and Italy.

zetti, alien anarchists, gave America its own Dreyfus case. The Volstead Act, which had inaugurated Prohibition in 1919, seemed in retrospect a harbinger of a general campaign of repression.

The decade of the Twenties was a time which, as Henry Adams had said of post-Appomattox America, the sensitive could not contemplate without a shudder. (His elegantly disillusioned autobiography, *The Education of Henry Adams*, now found its readers.) "The business of America is business," opined Coolidge. Henry Ford, apostle of mass production, was a popular hero, and the rise of advertising stimulated the needs which made mass consumption possible. The cult of business was a secular religion, and even Christ was presented by Bruce Barton in *The Man Nobody Knows* as a great executive and salesman who had taken twelve men from the bottom ranks and forged them into an efficient organization. It was a time when the critical and imaginative underwent an inner emigration, easily translated into exile. Europe beckoned as an inevitable refuge from the philistinism, vulgarity, and restrictions of the United States.

The European orientation of American intellectuals had been rapidly developing on the eve of the war. While an older generation of conventional political and literary opinions would support the Allies with sentimental fervor, a younger generation of radical sympathies would respond to Europe as a form of protest against orthodox America. Their strategy was made clear in the reflections of Randolph Bourne on his 1913–14 tour of Europe after his graduation from Columbia University. Bourne, bitter and eloquent opponent of American intervention in the war, scorned Anglo-Saxon sentimentality, puritanism, and practicality. On his tour he was irritated by the snobbery and "fatuous cheerfulness" of the English, who reminded him too much of his own country, and intoxicated by the irony, vivacity, and equality of the French, who could "think emotions and feel ideas." He responded eagerly to Rome as the center of a "new renaissance of the twentieth century" and found in its political ferment a democratic feeling absent from the Anglo-American two-party system. In Switzerland, Germany, and Scandinavia he was exhilarated by the engineering projects, public architecture, and city planning that demonstrated in contrast to the "ragtag chaos" of American cities a capacity to plan for "large social ends." During the war, as both Roosevelt and Wilson trumpeted for Americanization of the immigrants, Bourne dreamed of a "trans-national America" in which the non-Anglo-Saxon elements would keep their integrity and give to the United States a rich cosmopolitanism. As a contributing editor of *The New Republic, The Seven Arts,* and *The Dial,* Bourne's brilliant, impressionistic sketches foreshadowed the mood of the younger generation after the war.[3]

No one mourned Bourne's early death in 1918 more eloquently than Van Wyck Brooks, who saw in him "the flying wedge of the younger generation." Brooks himself in *America's Coming-of-Age* and *Letters and Leadership,* both written before the end of the war, set the tone of criticism for a generation by his anguished sense of the impoverishment of American spiritual life. Puritan and Pioneer had combined, he felt, to produce a fatal cleavage between "highbrow" and "lowbrow." By ignoring the scientific interests of Benjamin Franklin and the aesthetic vision of Jonathan Edwards—two of his major symbols—Brooks located his artificial dualism in the very seed bed of the Republic. Throughout his rhetorical appeal for an American artistic revival, he played the American scene off against the alleged European advantages of a more organic society, a livelier warfare of ideas, a richer interchange between "Court" and "pit," a more cumulative sense of the past, and a deeper sense of experience itself, rather than its practical fruits. In the memoirs of his old age Brooks confessed that it took him twenty years or more to "live down" a "frequently acute homesickness for the European scene" that afflicted him in 1920.[4]

[3] See Bourne, "Impressions of Europe 1913–1914," *The History of a Literary Radical and other Papers,* introduction by Van Wyck Brooks (New York, S. A. Russell, 1956), pp. 75–101 and "Trans-National America," *ibid.,* pp. 260–284.

[4] See Brooks, *Days of the Phoenix: The Nineteen Twenties I Remember* (New York, Dutton, 1957), p. 3. For Brooks's critical essays see *Three Essays on America* (New York, Dutton, 1934), Parts I and IV of "America's Coming-of-Age" and Parts III-VI of "Letters and Leadership."

During the Twenties H. L. Mencken became the witty scourge of American life from the point of view of a romanticized European-style aristocracy. He scorned both the "booboisie" of democracy and the crude plutocracy of capitalism. On the eve of the war, Mencken and his collaborators George Jean Nathan and Willard Huntington Wright had paid their lyrical respects to the pleasures of the Old World in *Europe after 8:15*. Rebuking the typical American traveler as a "deacon on the loose," who saw Europe only through the distortion of his own temporarily released inhibitions, they praised the innocent gaiety of Vienna, free of "the engines of repression" so powerful in "puritanical" America; the "tolerant geniality" of Munich and Berlin, so different from the commercialized bawdiness of New York; and the romantic youthfulness of Paris, "primitive in innocent and unbribed pleasure," despite the inroads of Americanization with its obscene souvenirs, high prices, ice cream, and cocktails. Whatever was noxious in Europe was blamed on Americanization. In Mencken's *American Mercury* foreign residence was defended as a haven of refuge for snobs of "the better class" who could there enjoy privacy, leisure, good music, superior schools, and servants to black their boots.[5]

Though the American pragmatists carried on a vigorous tradition of native criticism, finding hope in the democratic promise of the nation's future, John Dewey's defense of American intervention in the war had tarnished the movement's brightness for some of the young intellectuals. They were worried, like the European critics of America, about Dewey's emphasis on technique and technology, rather than on aspiration and art. Dewey was confident that the technological character of American life was its most promising feature and would finally break down the standardization attributed to it. He admitted the gross defects of his society but traced them to commercialism, capitalism, and "the prevalence of the old European tradition, with its disregard

---

[5] See Mencken, Nathan, and Wright, *Europe after 8:15* (New York, John Lane, 1914), pp. 38, 67, 96, 134, 207, and 221; Lawrence J. Thomson, "Why I Live Abroad," *American Mercury*, 5 (May, 1925), 109–115.

for the body, material things and practical concerns."[6] While Dewey invoked the old stereotype of a "feudal Europe" as the source of evil, the younger generation looked to a nonfeudal Europe for art and freedom.

Expatriates of the Twenties had the examples of the earlier exiles of Gertrude Stein, Ezra Pound, T. S. Eliot, and George Santayana. The sibylic Miss Stein had, like Henry James, found America "a rich and well nourished home but not a place to work."[7] After 1903 she was proud to call America her country and Paris her home town. There she could find the stimulus and isolation of a "second civilization" where she could work out her aesthetic of an abstracted, private, present knowing.

To Ezra Pound (a "village explainer," as Gertrude Stein called him) the American situation was desperate: "Anemia of guts on one side and anemia of education on the other." Dismissed from Wabash College in 1907 for his kindness to a stranded show girl, Pound fled to London, Paris, and eventually Rapallo to maintain a tortuous quarrel with an America whose only successful artists, he felt, had been James and Whistler, the rest, except for the prophetic Whitman, being victims of drowning in the "thin milk" and "pap" of America with its "fizz, swish, gabble of verbiage." His fellow poet William Carlos Williams only survived there, Pound told him, because he had the advantage of arriving with "a fresh flood of Europe" in his veins from his immigrant ancestors.[8]

[6] "'America'—By Formula," *New Republic*, 60 (September 18, 1929), 119.

[7] "Why Do Americans Live in Europe?" *Transition*, 14 (Fall, 1928), 97. See her essays "An American and France," *What Are Masterpieces?* (Los Angeles, Conference Press, 1940), pp. 61–70; *Paris France* (New York, Scribner's, 1940). "I proved you could be an American anywhere in the world," she was fond of saying. See John Malcolm Brinnin, "Gertrude Stein in Paris," *Atlantic Monthly*, 204 (September, 1959), 37. B. L. Reid points out that she did not read or speak French well and chose foreign residence "as a chance for the perfect condition of artistic isolation." See his *Art by Subtraction: A Dissenting Opinion of Gertrude Stein* (Norman, University of Oklahoma Press, 1958), p. 149.

[8] See his letters to Margaret C. Anderson, January, 1918, and to William Carlos Williams, November, 1917, and September 11, 1920, D. D. Paige, ed., *The Letters of Ezra Pound 1907–1941* (New York, Harcourt, Brace, 1950), pp. 128, 158. For Pound's view of James, Whistler, and Whitman see *Patria Mia* (Chicago, R. F. Seymour, 1950), pp. 64–65. Pound saw the

When Pound later conceived of his "Bel Esprit" project to finance an American poet in Europe, he naturally thought at once of T. S. Eliot, who had left St. Louis for Harvard and gone from there to settle in London by the outbreak of the war. Eliot's hegira was a search for a sustaining literary tradition, while his revulsion against the desiccated refinement of American genteel culture and his sense of the hollowness of contemporary life articulated feelings that spoke eloquently to "the lost generation." By the late Twenties he had announced his commitment to classicism, royalism, and Anglo-Catholicism, marking his distance from the American scene in unmistakable letters. His sophisticated self-conscious conservatism had much in common with the deliberately cultivated Latin angle of vision of the philosopher-poet George Santayana. If Eliot's stance was more that of the convert —a matter of fiat, rather than of history—both men had similar targets. Their most barbed shafts were aimed at American gentility, Protestantism, and democracy. Though born in Spain of Spanish parents, Santayana easily adjusted to New England student life and the Harvard aestheticism of the 80s and 90s. When he walked out of his professorship in 1912 for Europe, he was already established in the philosophical materialism, worldly hedonism, and poetic Catholicism which made such trenchant foils for the dominant characteristics of the American mind.[9] Like the other exiles, he prepared sensitive Americans to look across the Atlantic for light.

The expatriate generation of the Twenties shared the delight in European leisure and friendliness to art experienced by earlier American discoverers of the Old World, but these rebels, children of middle-class, small-town and Middle-West America, were attracted by contemporary intellectual life abroad and the free-

---

First World War as a chance for a "more lasting 'human' relationship with England, with other Allies." See "What America Has to Live Down, VI," *New Age*, 23 (September 19, 1918), 329.

[9] See Maurice F. Brown, "Santayana's American Roots," *New England Quarterly*, 33 (June, 1960), pp. 147–163. Ferner Nuhn points out that Eliot, like Henry Adams, idealized a past which would have to be present to realize his demands. See "Orpheus in Hell: T. S. Eliot," *The Wind Blew from the East* (New York, Harper, 1942), p. 253.

dom from "the American conspiracy against the individual."[10]
The contrast between their feelings and an older generation's
piety toward Europe is illustrated by William C. Brownell's
French Traits, written in the late nineteenth century by a distinguished champion of conservative literary opinion. He praised the
organic community, the social types, and the conventions of
French life in contrast to the "characterless individualism" of
America, which had only its zest, energy, and hope to warrant
affection.[11] For the post-war generation America was bereft of
idealism, and it turned to Europe as a haven of art and individualism from the social conformities of their own country.

Harold E. Stearns, an editor of "little magazines," made himself
the spokesman for the "Young Intellectuals." A student of Santayana's, Stearns hoped his teacher would not come back to
America to discover how grimly changed the country had become
since 1912: "Perhaps, through the pathos of distance, there may
remain some to write of us in a friendly spirit, remembering, before they were broken or scarred, our youth and our promise."
Commenting on the exodus to Europe in 1920, Stearns felt that
American institutions had become instruments for the enforce-
ment of eighteenth-century ideals of government, nineteenth-
century ideals of morals and culture, and "the stone age in
business." The young were leaving America for Europe because
the interests of youth were there—art and revolution: "It is youth
rushing to live with youth of its own kind." To the question
"what can a young man do?" he had an answer—"get out!" After
editing *Civilization in the United States*, a symposium which
mourned its absence, he took the boat for France. From this vantage point he sent back letters from abroad protesting against
America's moralistic attitude towards Europe and praising a civilization where individualism, gaiety, and simplicity still survived.

[10] Kay Boyle, "Why Do Americans Live in Europe?" *Transition*, **14**
(Fall, 1928), 103.

[11] *French Traits: An Essay in Comparative Criticism* (New York, Scribner's, 1925), p. 384. For the American Academy, the conservative "cus-
todians of culture," see Henry F. May, *The End of American Innocence,
a Study of the First Years of Our Own Time 1912–1917* (New York,
Knopf, 1959), pp. 76–79, 366, 388–389.

For his readers he glibly painted a picture of himself at a *café* in Paris, cigarette in mouth, wineglass in hand, contemplating going to a nude ball or buying a book on flagellation, while he read in American newspapers of tobacco being barred from Utah, rum ships confiscated in New York, the "shimmy" outlawed and plays banned. After eight years abroad, he summed up the case against the United States: "You are in prison, even if you don't happen to have spirit enough to be in jail."[12]

The serious exiles were too busy working to indulge themselves in an expatriate pose. They went to Paris with no romantic piety for Old-World monuments and no snobbish desires for servants, but instead to find out what was most alive in the modern world. "Twentieth-century Paris was to the intellectual pioneer," as Harold Rosenberg has said, "what nineteenth-century America had been to the economic one." Paris was the center for the artistically adventurous of every country—Picasso, Juan Gris, Modigliani, Brancusi, Mondrian, Lipchitz, Kandinsky, Diaghillef, Klee, Copland, Gershwin, Calder, Duchamp, Hemingway, and, of course, Joyce, Stein, and Pound. What struck the expatriates was Pound's observation that "the contemporary grasp of contemporary things" had "occurred in 'exhausted Europe.'" Gertrude Stein simply said: "Paris was where the twentieth century was." If the exiles shared any literary orientation, it was, as Malcolm Cowley wrote from Dijon in 1921, a feeling for "form, simplification, strangeness," and France was the birthplace of their creed.[13]

[12] For all the Stearns comments quoted see "Distance Lends Enchantment," *The Freeman*, 29 (December 29, 1920), 381; "What Can a Young Man Do?" *ibid.*, 1 (August 4, 1920), 490; "Apologia of an Expatriate," *Scribner's*, 85 (March, 1929), 340. For similar views see his "Wicked Europe," *Freeman*, 6 (December 13, 1922), 326; "So This is Paris!" *ibid.*, 5 (July 5, 1922), 398–399. Sterns fell into the snobbery of admiring in France what he disliked in America, wanting France to be "local, provincial, narrow-minded, split-up, heterogeneous . . ." See his autobiography, *The Street I Know* (New York, Lee Furman, 1935), p. 231.

[13] See Harold Rosenberg, "On the Fall of Paris," *Partisan Review*, 7 (November-December, 1940), 440; Pound, "The Editor," *The Exile*, 4 (Autumn, 1928), 115; Stein, *Paris France* (New York, Scribner's, 1940), p. 11; Cowley, *Exile's Return: A Literary Odyssey of the 1920's* (rev. ed., New York, Viking, 1951), 100, 102. See also Warren I. Susman, "A Second Country: the Expatriate Image," The University of Texas *Studies in Litera-*

American intellectuals had three American rallying grounds where the artists of many countries could discover each other—the salon at No. 27, *rue de Fleurus*, where Gertrude Stein held court as queen bee of the expatriate swarm, Pound's studio, established with superb timing in 1920 at *rue Notre-Dame-des-Champs*, or Sylvia Beach's American bookshop, Shakespeare and Company, at No. 12, *rue de l'Odéon* on the Left Bank, where they could meet Joyce, Sherwood Anderson, Hemingway, and great French writers like Valéry, Romains, and Duhamel. At Shakespeare and Company (where the walls were hung with pictures of America's classic writers) the ardently dedicated proprietress successfully led a small American conspiracy to publish Joyce's great work, *Ulysses*, which would influence so many important American writers. (In America censors brought Margaret Anderson's *Little Review* to trial for printing its Rabelaisian pages.) This vital literary circuit between America and Europe was kept humming by the little magazines which sprang up in Paris, Dijon, Italy, and Germany under American editors committed to avant-garde writing and painting on both sides of the Atlantic, and by the small American publishing houses in Paris: Robert McAlmon's Contact Editions (which first published Hemingway and financed some of the work of Gertrude Stein), William Bird's Three Mountains Press, and Harry Crosby's Black Sun Press.

If Pound, Stein, and Joyce were revered as masters, young Americans who had learned from them could also experience the life-giving pleasure of seeing their work in print. A notable issue of *Transition* bound together under a cover by Picasso a symposium of European writers on America, the work of Joyce and Stein, stories by Kay Boyle and Katherine Anne Porter, and poems by Archibald MacLeish and William Carlos Williams. The editors of *Secession* took playful possession of the scene by "electing" Malcolm Cowley mayor of Montpellier and announcing E. E. Cummings and Matthew Josephson as rival candidates

---

ture and Language, 3 (Summer, 1961), 171–183. Vital statistics on the expatriates can be found in Frederick J. Hoffman, *The Twenties, American Writing in the Postwar Decade* (New York, Viking, 1955), pp. 25–30.

for the mayoralty of Paris, "the present literary capital of America."[14]

From their European vantage points the expatriates could make fun of the embattled stance of the American intellectuals who had stayed home. Malcolm Cowley mocked the young intellectual whose syllogism was "America is bad; America is puritan; therefore puritanism is bad," and who dreamed of "Sunday baseball in Pittsburgh (or better, Sunday cricket); open urinals and racetrack gambling; the works of Freud and Boccaccio and D. H. Lawrence sold at newsstands openly."[15] The exiles enjoyed Paris as Americans who did not despair of their country. "It has a casual grace," wrote McAlmon, and "American openness allowed to be open publicly rather than under cover; and it has no viciousness that will spring out upon one at unexpected moments, and under the cover of refinement." He was confident that the younger generation would educate America: "It, like artists in the Quarter, will come through if it means to." He and his friends commemorated Bastille Day for three days with a memorable drunk, but the carousing side of expatriate life was innocent and playful, "like prom week on a university campus, except that we all belonged to the same fraternity."[16]

Far from seeking to ape the Europeans, the expatriates discovered with Joseph Freeman (who had left for Europe at the height of the Red Scare): "The more American we felt culturally, the more we felt at home in Europe, the more we enjoyed ourselves." Instead of being forced from freedom into isolation, they had "fled from isolation to freedom. . . . True, we were outsiders in Europe," Freeman admitted, "but that was just what we wanted to be, privileged aliens who were not responsible to the society in which we lived, Americans in Paris."[17] Even the master exile,

[14] "Notes," *Secession*, 2 (July, 1922), inside cover. The issue of *Transition* mentioned was 13 (Summer, 1928).

[15] "Young Mr. Elkins," *Broom*, 4 (December, 1922), 55.

[16] Robert McAlmon, "Truer Than Most Accounts," *The Exile*, 2 (Autumn, 1927), 84–86; *Being Geniuses Together: An Autobiography* (London, Secker and Warburg, 1938), 280.

[17] *American Testament: A Narrative of Rebels and Romantics* (New York, Farrar and Rinehart, 1936), pp. 182–183.

Ezra Pound, cautioned Americans to remember that the advantages of Europe existed "only for the patient searcher, for the man willing to pick out small fragments and relics with the greatest possible care." He was passionately convinced that America was a land without enlightenment, but he found England impossibly stuffy and was irritated by the heavy hand of the French bureaucracy. "We have to improve," he announced in his role as sage, "and in very few instances can we do so by consulting European conditions."[18]

To their surprise, and often delight, some of the expatriates discovered European intellectuals who were absorbed in fascination with the most non-European and contemporary features of American life, from billposters, movies, and ads to athletics, skyscrapers, and Negro jazz. When Harold Loeb met French and Italian "futurists" in Rome, the young American editor of an expatriate magazine was startled to hear "praise of skyscrapers in the city of fountains, of jazz in the home of opera, of advertising in the country where Dante had done a superlative job on hell— all in vociferous broken English."[19] Matthew Josephson, who wrote and edited for several expatriate magazines, hotly challenged the indictment of America drawn up in Harold Stearns's *Civilization in the United States*. From the detached perspective of European ground he urged his countrymen to look at "our home products sympathetically, to judge if they are not sprouting with an authentic beauty that justifies their outlandish departures from the past or from previous European traditions."[20] For Loeb and Josephson Europe was a place to refocus the glass of art on American life.

The exodus to Europe, so clearly a challenge to the world of Babbitt, Main Street, and Elmer Gantry, inevitably produced a defensive reaction from defenders of the American *status quo*. Hemingway spoofed the common stereotype of the expatriate in *The Sun Also Rises*:

[18] "The Editor," *The Exile*, 3 (Spring, 1928), 107, 23.
[19] *The Way It Was* (New York, Criterion Books, 1959), p. 67.
[20] "The Great American Billposter," *Broom*, 3 (November, 1922), p. 305. See also his "Made in America," *Broom*, 2 (June, 1922), p. 266–270.

"You're an expatriate. You've lost touch with the soil. You get precious. Fake European standards have ruined you. You drink yourself to death. You become obsessed by sex. You spend all your time talking, not working. You are an expatriate, see? You hang around cafés."

"It sounds like a swell life," I said. "When do I work?"

"You don't work. One group claims women support you. Another group claims you're impotent."[21]

Booth Tarkington, popular novelist of the middle class, sought to turn the tables in *The Plutocrat* by making his crude, gregarious businessman hero the idol of a sophisticated European lady, who admires the "great barbarian" because money and power are what America has to offer. Only the plutocrat Tinker can understand the Roman Forum because Americans with their love of health, plumbing, power, wealth, and bigness are the Romans of the modern world. Lacking the irony of James or Twain in dealing with similar themes, Tarkington makes his villain a snobbish playwright who has to borrow money from the plutocrat and find a living working for the movies. Not surprisingly, the novel was serialized in *The Saturday Evening Post*, which throughout the decade kept a hostile middle-brow eye on the expatriates. One of its cartoons, illustrating a critical article on the exodus called "Uneasy Chameleons," pictured a group of expatriates giving last-minute warnings and dire prophecies to a European taking the boat to America. The Americans are labeled as snobs, rich idlers, professional drunkards, unsuccessful artists, divorcers, poseurs, and failures.[22]

The guardians of middle-brow culture in their warfare with the intellectuals missed the point of the whole emigration. They blindly ignored the fact that in stories like Hemingway's "Mr. and Mrs. Eliot" or F. Scott Fitzgerald's "One Trip Abroad" the expatriates themselves had condemned Americans who went to

[21] *The Sun Also Rises* (New York, Scribner's, 1926), p. 118.

[22] See Gilbert Seldes, "Uneasy Chameleons," *The Saturday Evening Post*, 199 (Janary 1, 1929), p. 21. Cf. Tarkington, *The Plutocrat* (New York, Grosset and Dunlap, 1927). On Americans as Romans see p. 462; also An Expatriate, "Why Return Home After Twenty Years Abroad?" *The Saturday Evening Post*, 202 (June 28, 1930), pp. 32 ff.

Europe in a futile effort to conceal their own sterility by a super-ficial scraping at the surface of Old World civilization. The con-servative critics kept invoking the outworn symbol of an old, picturesque, effete Europe in contrast to a youthful dynamic America, an antithesis which the rebels had neatly reversed.[23]

Three major novelists of the Twenties—Dos Passos, Heming-way, and Lewis—illustrate how ingeniously the rebels had reversed the conventional belief in the contrast between America and Eu-rope. John Dos Passos in his early novels (*Streets of Night, One Man's Initiation,* and *Three Soldiers*) turned away from the "gar-ish lockstep travesty of civilization" in America to the indi-vidualism of the Renaissance, the energy of eighteenth-century Venice, or the revolutionary dreams of his anarchist and Com-munist French friends. After the war he went to Spain to become charmed by the gaiety, pride, and "strong anarchistic reliance on the individual man" in the life of the Spanish peasants, in contrast to the "joyless enforced labor" of industrial America. In the mod-ern radical literature of Spain he found the "manure rich and diverse and promiscuous that might fertilize the "sickly plants in our own culture" into bursting "sappy and green through the steel and cement and inhibitions of our lives."[24]

Spain was also the touchstone for Ernest Hemingway, whose *The Sun Also Rises* became the classic study of the "Lost Gen-eration" in Europe. His characters, Jake Barnes and Bill Grundy,

[23] For the reversal of the image see Daniel J. Boorstin, "America and the Image of Europe," *America and the Image of Europe: Reflections on American Thought* (New York, Meridian, 1960), pp. 19–39. For expatriate criticism of shallow expatriates see F. Scott Fitzgerald, "One Trip Abroad," *The Saturday Evening Post*, 203 (October 11, 1930), pp. 6 ff.; Ernest Hem-ingway, "Mr. and Mrs. Eliot," *The Short Stories of Ernest Hemingway* (New York, Random House, 1938), pp. 259–262.

[24] *Rosinante to the Road Again* (New York, Doran, 1922), pp. 52–53, 175. For his use of the historical past as a contrast to contemporary garish-ness see *Streets of Night* (New York, Doran, 1923), pp. 185, 241, 278; *Three Soldiers* (1921), Modern Library Ed. (New York, Random House, 1932), pp. 214, 373. In *First Encounter (One Man's Initiation)* (New York, Philosophical Library, 1945) America is seen as having betrayed its freedom from "that gangrened ghost of the past that is killing Europe to-day" by becoming a military nation and ignoring the revolutionary hope of radical-ism. See p. 142.

poke fun at the American world of Coolidge, Prohibition, the Klan, the Scopes Trial, and the craze for Freud, while they relish the delights of the wine bags of the generous festive Basques, the pastoral peace of trout fishing near Burguete, and the disciplined courage and craft of the bullfighter Romero at Pamplona. In the Spanish ritual of the bullfight, to which he paid lengthy and loving tribute in *Death in the Afternoon*, Hemingway found that ordered response to the actuality of death, which Americans enshrouded in abstractions, platitudes, or evasion. In his brief sketch "Banal Story" he drew an ironic picture of a romance-seeking American writer reading an advertising booklet for *The Forum* magazine, with its earnest middlebrow optimism about impersonal problems and "homespun" tales, while in the real world outside a bullfighter dies of pneumonia and the whole populace of Triana turns out in reverent tribute for his funeral. "It had been a good country and we had made a bloody mess of it," he wrote of America in 1935, "and I would go, now, somewhere else as we had always gone. You could always come back."[25]

This same image of a vital, earthy Europe to redeem Americans, lost in their artificial world of industrialism, commercialism, and mass culture, animates Sinclair Lewis's *Dodsworth*, his version of the Jamesian theme of the American businessman and the American woman abroad. In part a caustic attack on the romantic illusions of the industrialist's wife, who seeks to achieve a more passionate life by "running away to a more complex and graceful civilization," the novel also makes the experience of Europe necessary to the hero's growth. From a European scholar Dodsworth learns the value of learning and personal dignity in "a Fordized world" while through the good offices of women schooled in European attitudes he discovers the curative sanity of Europe's closeness to the soil and the elements. Like the other rebels of the Twenties Lewis fought a caricatured "puritanism," but he had a powerful nostalgia for a sentimentalized pioneer tradition which America had lost and needed to regain. Sam Dodsworth can re-

[25] *The Green Hills of Africa* (New York, Scribner's, 1935), p. 285. For "Banal Story" see *The Short Stories of Ernest Hemingway*, pp. 458–460.

cover it only through "the good vulgarity of earth" which is "the strength of Europe."[26] When he returns to America, with brave plans for building skyscrapers and motorized caravans, Dodsworth has been fitted by European experience for the American pioneering tradition. Europe has liberated the Pioneer by slaying the Puritan Babbitt—an extraordinary piece of symbolic fantasy for a "realistic" novelist.

"You are all a lost generation," Gertrude Stein told Hemingway.[27] But in retrospect it is an odd description, as Sylvia Beach has remarked, when so many, like Hemingway himself, "so quickly found themselves."[28] It seems even odder when it is remembered that most of the talent that has enriched American literature spent an apprenticeship abroad. The special distinction of this emigration to Europe was the commerce created between America and a contemporary Europe, unlike the visits of earlier passionate pilgrims to the legendary shrines of tradition. In this respect these American artists achieved a sense of collaboration with their European counterparts that American politics was not to discover until after a second world war had transformed both the Old and the New World.

Towards the end of the decade most of the expatriates began coming home. "We live in a continual storm," wrote Matthew

[26] Daniel J. Boorstin points out that Lewis in his Nobel Prize speech of December 12, 1930, voiced the conventional demand for a non-European American literature, "worthy of her vastness," but in *Arrowsmith, Elmer Gantry,* and *Dodsworth* he kept falling back on the idea that America had to be refreshed "by the waters which ran along the left bank of the Seine." "America and the Image of Europe," *op. cit.,* p. 27. He merges these two myths in *Dodsworth* through the character Nande Azeredo, an internationalized working girl, described as an ideal wife for a pioneer. She frees Dodsworth of his inhibitions: the Pioneer—"half Portuguese, half Russian, and altogether French"—slays the Puritan on European ground. See *Dodsworth* (New York, Harcourt, Brace, 1929), pp. 322–325.

[27] But Kathleen Cannell has said that Gertrude Stein told her the famous phrase was meant to describe the young French Dadaists, not the American expatriates. See "The 20's, by One Who Was There," *Christian Science Monitor,* Western Ed. (February 9, 1962), 5.

[28] *Les Années Vingt: Les Ecrivains Américains à Paris et leurs Amis 1920–1930,* Exposition, March 11–April 25, 1959, Centre Culturel Américain, Paris, p. 12. This catalog, prepared by Sylvia Beach, is a mine of information on the period. See also her charming memoir, *Shakespeare and Company* (New York, Harcourt, Brace, 1959).

Josephson in a fruitless plea for Ezra Pound to return home; "we make our peace, as we can, and lie down to sleep beside the volcano."[29] It was increasingly clear that Europe would follow the path of modern mass society, while the ground of the Old World was shifting treacherously underfoot with the growth of terrorist political movements, giving "an abiding sense of the threatened failure of old Europe as a last resort of leisure, individualism, personal freedom—as a place of escape."[30] Even Harold Stearns, who returned in 1932, realized that he was, after all, an American who had a literature, a language, and a country with a present and future.[31]

The contrast between America and Europe now seemed to have recaptured its traditional meaning. Returning to America in 1934 after ten years in Europe, Ludwig Lewisohn, literary critic and novelist, rejoiced in the "bladelike burnish" of the face of the New World, despite the gash of the depression, in contrast to an Old World distraught with despair, cynicism, and fanaticism: "Now more than ever in this immediate retrospect Northern and Central Europe seemed a land perpetually swathed in gray, wrapped in a downy atmosphere, faintly tinted at best, shadowy and with uncertain outlines." The bent of simple Americans towards political isolationism from contemporary Europe seemed to him to reflect "their undefined and not quite definable conviction that, though stricken by comparable difficulties and defeats, we must find another, we must find our own way out."[32]

[29] "Open Letter to Mr. Ezra Pound, and the other 'Exiles,' " *Transition*, 13 (Summer, 1928), 101.

[30] Matthew Josephson, *Portrait of the Artist as American* (New York, Harcourt, Brace, 1930), p. 297. Cf. Martha Gruening "American Expatriates," *Nation*, 136 (June 7, 1933), 638–640.

[31] *Rediscovering America* (New York, Liveright, 1934), p. 220.

[32] "An American Comes Home," in William H. Cordell and Kathryn Coe Cordell, eds., *American Points of View 1934–1935* (New York, Doubleday, Doran, 1936), pp. 144, 149. See also Eugene Bagger, "Uprooted Americans," *Harper's*, 159 (September, 1929), 474–484; "Expatriates in Time," *Harper's*, 167 (August, 1933), 363–374; Joseph Hergersheimer, "Good-by, Europe," *The Saturday Evening Post*, 205 (January 7, 1933), 3 ff. The theme of a dying Europe is also presented in Waldo Frank's turgid, romanticized lament for the end of the medieval synthesis, *The Rediscovery of America: An Introduction to a Philosophy of American Life* (New York, Scribner's, 1929).

A few would discover the expatriate experience in the nineteen thirties, but the big migration was over. They added nothing new to the story. Thomas Wolfe, whose search for a final, fortunate, happy place for the artist had led him unsuccessfully to Paris in the 1920s, found the bright face of fame in his ancestral Germany, which became for him a fabled land of enchantment. He returned, however, from a visit in 1936 with a painful sense of the curse that had fallen on his "second country" under the atavistic horrors of the Nazi regime, and he nurtured a growing belief in the old American dream, which became the credo of his last work, *You Can't Go Home Again:* "America was young, America was still the New World of mankind's hope, America was not like this old and worn-out Europe which seethed and festered with a thousand deep and uncorrected ancient maladies."[33]

For Henry Miller there was no such familiar reconciliation, though his alienation was of classic dimensions, a decade out of step. In 1930 he abandoned job, wife, and child for France, made a literary career (and an under-the-counter reputation) out of his exile from an America he savagely attacked as an "Air-Conditioned Nightmare" of industrialism, materialism, vulgarity, prudishness, ugliness, conformity, and "progress." Europe for him was both culture and vitality, spoiled only by Americanization, and in America the only places he found congenial were those, like New Orleans and Charleston, which reminded him of Europe. Exuberant, garrulous, optimistic, and humorous, in good American style, he was most American in his perpetual reference to a contrast between America and Europe. An admirer of Thoreau, Emerson, and Whitman, he dreamed like them of a "new race of man to be born on this continent, hope for a new heaven and a new earth."[34] Miller's massive disenchantment with America ultimately rested

[33] *You Can't Go Home Again* (Garden City, New York, Sun Dial, 1942), p. 730.

[34] Quoted by Annette Kar Baxter, *Henry Miller: Expatriate* (Pittsburgh, University of Pittsburgh Press, 1961), p. 118. She fully and sympathetically documents and analyzes Miller's involvement with the America-Europe contrast. Samuel Putnam found his expatriate experience of the late 1920s best memorialized in Miller's *Tropic of Cancer*. See *Paris Was Our Mistress: Memoirs of a Lost and Found Generation* (New York, Viking, 1947).

on a romantic faith in "the brave new world it might have become" if Americans had only had the courage to turn their backs on Europe. For his country's failure to become an authentic New World, he perversely rejected it for the Old World. The Second World War drove him back to America, where in the isolation of the Big Sur he could carry on with fierce dedication his increasingly monotonous and anachronistic quarrel with an America that had failed his dream.

By then the American confrontation with the Depression and the war had set in motion a process which was destined to make obsolete the antithetical terms by which the differences between America and Europe had for so long been described. The search for vitality and freedom in the Old World was over. Europe had been as always a stimulus for art; it could no longer be a port of refuge.

11

THE HELL-BROTH OF EUROPE
AND THE AMERICAN HEMISPHERE

THE CRISIS OF THE GREAT DEPRESSION, bringing in its wake the bleak tidings of mass unemployment and business failures, posed at first a formidable challenge to the old American confidence in superiority over Europe. As totalitarians of the Right and Left on the Continent battened on disaster, the "New Deal" in its own pragmatic style improvised what was hailed by liberals as an American solution to the problem, castigated by conservatives as a Europeanization of America, and scorned by radicals as the last gasp of a system doomed to be succeeded by the new order of Soviet Russia, land of the future. Confirmed in its detachment from Europe by the need for reform at home and the threat of war abroad, the public mind was, however, reluctantly forced by the threat of Fascism to recognize its need for European allies. Reform at home would also bring America closer to the welfare states of western Europe, while the war would greatly accelerate the "Americanization" of the Old World. History was digging a grave for the idea of a perpetual polarity between America and Europe even before the corpse had been pronounced dead.

Despite the dimensions of the depression Herbert Hoover clung stoutly to the American "conservative" faith that "American individualism" was a uniquely non-European system only temporarily distressed: Europe itself was to blame for the Depression. While the crisis worsened, Hoover strove energetically to contain it, but his fidelity to rigid principles of "Americanism" drastically inhibited his capacity to succeed. He would not use the agency of the federal government to establish a power plant at Muscle Shoals, to influence production, prices, and purchasing power, or to undertake a relief program. When the policies of his more flexible successor, Franklin D. Roosevelt, did these things, Hoover condemned them as un-American departures from old-fashioned liberalism, heresies which converted the ideals of the United States into European collectivism: Not only was Europe the source of American troubles, but American efforts to deal with them under the New Deal were tainted with European attitudes and techniques. The spell of the old antithesis between the New World and the Old had completely enchanted the American "conservatives," holding them fast in a dream of the unsullied virtue of their own American system, menaced by the innovations of the New Dealers.

The reformers retaliated by preaching the pragmatic adjustments of the Roosevelt Administration as an essentially American way of dealing with the disaster without succumbing to European totalitarianism of the Right or Left. The major defense of the New Deal from this point of view was Gilbert Seldes's *Mainland* (1936). It made a biting attack on American intellectuals of the 1920s for their subservience to European models and acclaimed the New Deal for its pluralistic, pragmatic approach which sharply contrasted with the European ideological style of Fascism or Communism. Seldes buttressed his Americanist position with uncritical acceptance of Frederick Jackson Turner's frontier hypothesis of American development and identified the true source of Americanism with the Mississippi Valley and the Pacific Coast, rather than the civilization of the Atlantic and the Hudson, too much indebted to Europe.[1] The new President had begun on a nationalistic note by repudiating his earlier stand for the League of Nations and by torpedoing the World Economic Conference in London. While the Hoover Administration had been moving in foreign affairs toward closer cooperation with the League, the New Deal began with a determination to give top priority to setting the American house in order with a minimum of involvement in European affairs.

Ironically, the "American way" of the New Deal, by developing national standards for minimum wages and maximum hours, public planning in the area of the Tennessee Valley, a steeply graduated income tax, and a social security program, moved closer towards the welfare policies of progressive countries in Western Europe, where socialist parties were much more powerful and conservatives lacked the American business community's fear and suspicion of the state. Yet American liberals who felt the New Deal was not moving far or fast enough had some justification for scornfully asking: "What was there in the New Deal as revealed in act that had not been ordinary practice in advanced European countries for anywhere from ten to thirty years?"[2] Despite his "pump-priming" measures of public spending, Roosevelt never fully understood or consistently practiced the deficit-spending theory of depression economics worked out by the English economist John Maynard Keynes, and after six years of the New Deal there were still eight or nine million people out of work.

The severity of the American economic crisis moved many intellectuals to fix their fascinated gaze on revolutionary Russia. Matthew Josephson's *Portrait of the Artist as American* (1930) romantically linked the expatriate theme of the alienation of the artist in America with the vision of Soviet Russia as the new society of the future by prophesying the coming of a collectivized

---

[1] *Mainland* (New York, Scribner's, 1936), p. 7.
[2] Nathaniel Peffer, "Why Liberalism Is Bankrupt," in William H. Cordell and Kathryn Coe Cordell, eds., *American Points of View 1934-1935* (Garden City, New York, Doubleday, Doran, 1936), p. 22.

regime which might be "nobly led" by artists who had learned to control modern machinery.[3] While Europe was now condemned as the failure of a bourgeois civilization, the hopes of radicals were shaped by the dream of a New World in Russia. The Bohemian rebel John Reed, poet, journalist, and advocate of the proletariat, had already shown the way in 1917 by committing himself to the Bolshevist cause on Russian soil, where he later received an honored burial by the Kremlin wall. For American radicals he was a legendary symbol of revolutionary dedication. Their American feelings responded sympathetically to the reconstruction of a Russia caught up in a period of pioneering, industrial development, and social reform. Soviet life seemed closer to American experience than traditional Europe did, which now looked by contrast (in Edmund Wilson's phrase) like "a pack of little quarrelsome states, maintaining artificial barriers and suffering from morbid distempers."[4] American radicals were stirred by Soviet enthusiasm for machinery and science as well as the prestige given for political reasons to literature and intellectuals. "It was a new culture," exulted Lincoln Steffens, who had been the most influential muckraking journalist of the Progressive era, "an economic, scientific, not a moral, culture." With an American enthusiasm for practicality Steffens announced on his return from Russia in 1919, "I have been over into the future, and it works."[5] With its

[3] *Portrait of the Artist as American* (New York, Harcourt, Brace, 1930), p. 307.
[4] *Travels in Two Democracies* (New York, Harcourt, Brace, 1936), p. 319. Similar views are expressed by Joseph Freeman, *American Testament: A Narrative of Rebels and Romantics* (New York, Farrar and Rinehart, 1936), p. 185; Harold Stearns, *Rediscovering America* (New York, Liveright, 1934), p. 220; and Lincoln Steffens, *The Autobiography of Lincoln Steffens* (New York, Harcourt, Brace, 1931), pp. 851–852.
[5] *Autobiography*, pp. 796, 799. For his pro-Communism see Dimitri S. von Mohrenschildt, "Lincoln Steffens and the Russian Bolshevik Revolution," *Russian Review*, 5 (Autumn, 1945), 31–41. For the idea of Socialism as a science of revolution see Max Eastman, "Reflections on the Failure of Socialism," *U. S. News and World Report*, 38 (April 1, 1955), 56–61. For a pro-Communist biography of John Reed see Granville Hicks, *John Reed: The Making of a Revolutionary* (New York, Macmillan, 1936). For American sympathetic observers of the Russian Revolution see Mohrenschildt, "The Early American Observers of the Russian Revolution, 1917–

"scientific" Marxist-Leninist theory, its organizational fervor, and its working model in a remote and idealized far corner of the earth Soviet Communism held many intellectuals spellbound. Like an opiate it dulled the sensitivity of its sympathizers to its ruthless terror, its idolization of dictators, and its corruption of art.

In criticizing their own country radicals attacked the standardizing impact of mass production, the debasement of literature by propaganda, the idolatry of political hero worship, and the sacrifice of individual liberty to reasons of state; but in Soviet Russia, by a strange alchemy which produced an intellectually dishonest double standard, all these evils were transmuted into virtues, justified by "the great experiment." Joseph Freeman, a young Bohemian in New York and an expatriate in Europe, went to Russia in 1926, becoming a translator in the Comintern. There he praised the machinery worship he had scorned in America, justified the slavish deification of Stalin, in whom he saw the "scientific temper" applied to society, accepted censorship of the theater as part of the struggle against "reactionary" forces, defended a system of justice which convicted prisoners he knew to be falsely accused of being German agents, and applauded a Russian audience for its generous response to poetry he recognized as mediocre. Even the distinguished literary critic Edmund Wilson, who kept a sympathetic but remarkably honest eye on Soviet defects and virtues during his travels in 1935, felt that in Russia he was "at the moral top of the world."[6] Joseph B. Matthews, who came to Communism by way of the Christian social gospel, pacifism, and the Socialist Party, explained the heady confidence Communist sympathizers found in their cause: "I was on the side of history where I could look across and view with sincere pity the floundering

1921," *Russian Review*, 3 (Autumn, 1943), 64–74; "American Intelligentsia and Russia of the N. E. P.," *Russian Review*, 6 (Spring, 1947), 59–66. The appeal of Soviet Russia for American intellectuals is illuminated in Granville Hicks' personal memoir, "Communism and the American Intellectuals," in Irving De Witt Talmadge, ed., *Whose Revolution?* (New York, Howell, Soskin, 1941), pp. 78–115.

6 *Travels in Two Democracies*, p. 321. For Freeman's use of the double standard (in contrast to Wilson) see *American Testament*, pp. 474, 490, 547, 550, 581, 583, 603, 626.

liberals and the obstructing capitalists. History would crush them like a juggernaut."[7]

The misery of the Great Depression in America, the "popular front" Communist policy after 1935 of seeking allies with socialists and liberals, and the anti-Nazi stand of Soviet Russia in the Spanish Civil War made it easy for liberal magazines, like the *Nation* and *New Republic*, to minimize the elimination of the kulaks, the bloody purges, the Moscow Trials, the slave labor camps, and the policy of cultural censorship. Hemingway's *For Whom the Bell Tolls* (1940) had a recognizable liberal hero in its Midwestern professor who finds in the Loyalist government of Republican Spain the American cause of "Life, Liberty, and the Pursuit of Happiness." In this political variant of the international novel, Robert Jordan, the story's hero—indifferent to Marxist dialectics —is initiated as an innocent American idealist into the cynical political realities of the war, and comes to accept Soviet discipline as a temporary strategic necessity in the fight against the Fascists.[8]

The second American Writers Congress, held in New York in 1937 and presided over by Archibald MacLeish, clearly expressed the Popular Front ethos of collaboration with Communists, idealization of the Soviet Union, and solidarity with liberals everywhere in support of the Spanish Republicans. It was one of the writer's social obligations, Eugene Holmes explained, "to come at all times to the defense of the Soviet Union." For American intellectuals there was an exciting sense of participation in action on an international scale, a feeling that, as George Seldes wrote from Spain, "for the first time in our history . . . all the intellectuals of the world are united. They are on our side—the side of the Spanish Republic today, the side of the people's front in France tomorrow, and eventually for us, in our war against fascism in

[7] *Odyssey of a Fellow Traveller* (New York, Mount Vernon, 1938), p. 91. At this stage of his career Matthews was critical of those who violated due process and resorted to misrepresentation and hate in opposing Communist activity; later he became one of Senator McCarthy's hatchet men. The *Odyssey* could be quoted against them both.

[8] *For Whom the Bell Tolls* (New York, Scribner's, 1940), pp. 229–230, 248, 305. See David Sanders, "Ernest Hemingway's Spanish Civil War Experience," *American Quarterly*, 12 (Summer, 1960), 133–143.

America."[9] To climax the proceedings in New York parts of the film *The Spanish Earth* were shown (Hemingway, MacLeish, and Lillian Hellman later collaborated on the written and spoken dialogue for it), and some of America's best poets read aloud the Spanish Loyalist poems they had translated.

The political naïveté of this American response to European realities was not the monopoly of intellectuals, who were motivated by genuine idealism and a healthy desire to break out of their provincialism. A notable example of official innocence abroad was Joseph E. Davies, Ambassador to the Soviet Union in 1937–1938, who arrived in time to be completely gulled by the Communist explanations of the purge trial of political prisoners. Blandly sure that human nature was everywhere the same, Davies thought he saw homey American qualities in Soviet officials, youth organizations, the Soviet Constitutional Convention, and the Russian people. His credulous account of his experience, published as *Mission to Moscow*, found a receptive public in 1941 when Russia had become an American ally.[10]

Intelligent radicals inevitably experienced their moment of truth about the illusions they had created about the Russian model under Stalin. By 1937 the disenchanted had the forum of the *Partisan Review* to expose the oppressions of the Soviet regime and the self-deceptions of the fellow travelers, though liberals paid little attention until much later. Just before the signing of the Nazi-Soviet Pact in 1939 many anti-Stalinist radicals (including Edmund Wilson and John Dos Passos) joined the Committee for Cultural Freedom in condemning Soviet totalitarian practices, but over 300 American intellectuals still clung to their mythology by indignantly signing a counterpetition.[11] After the Pact only

[9] See Holmes, "A Writer's Social Obligations," in Henry Hart, ed., *The Writer in a Changing World* (London, Lawrence and Wishart, 1937), p. 176; Seldes quoted by Hart, *ibid.*, p. 204.

[10] See Richard H. Ullman, "The Davies Mission and United States–Soviet Relations, 1937–1941," *World Affairs*, 9 (January, 1957), 220–239.

[11] See for the popular front period Irving Howe and Lewis Coser, *The American Communist Party: A Critical History (1919–1957)* (Boston, Beacon, 1957), chaps. 7–8; also Daniel Bell, "The Background and Development of Marxian Socialism in the United States," in Donald Egbert and

the most stubbornly deluded or deeply alienated could close their eyes to the decline and fall of "the god that failed." The rebels (including former expatriates like Josephson, Freeman, and Cowley) who had looked to Soviet Russia for the vigor, purpose, morality, and liberation once traditionally identified with the New World were doomed to disappointment.

For American Communists the policy of isolation or intervention in foreign affairs was a mere tactic, determined by the shifting position of Moscow; for most Americans isolationism was an article of fundamental faith. American Institute of Opinion polls taken from 1935 to 1939 showed that heavy majorities believed that the United States should never have gone into the First World War and that everything possible should be done to preserve neutrality in the future. By 1939 a majority of those polled sympathized with England and France, but two thirds of those polled in October, 1939, would not favor measures of support at the risk of war.[12] The American suspicion of Europe, intensified by the course of events since 1919, was deep-rooted and pervasive, shared by liberals, conservatives, and anti-Stalinist radicals alike.

This rejection of entanglement with European politics was, paradoxically, quite compatible with sentimental attachment to the home country on the part of immigrants who had been stimulated by the nationalistic passions of the European states and wounded by the ethnic struggles of the American melting pot. Too anxiously watched, it had always tended to boil over with a loud hiss of nativistic steam in times of crisis. Old Americans of English background were part of the same pattern. At the Coro-

---

Stow Persons, eds., *Socialism and American Life*, I (Princeton, Princeton University Press, 1952), 346–365. The former expatriates Matthew Josephson and Malcolm Cowley were part of the popular front ethos until after the Nazi-Soviet pact.

[12] See "Gallup and Fortune Polls," *Public Opinion Quarterly*, 4 (March, 1940), 83–115; Francis Sill Wickware, "What We Think about Foreign Affairs," *Harper's*, 179 (September, 1939), 397–406. For the isolationism of anti-Stalinist radicals see "War Is the Issue!" *Partisan Review*, 6 (Fall, 1939), 125–127. The AIPO poll of October 22, 1939, showed 34 percent for aid to England and France even at the risk of war. With the risk-of-war factor not mentioned, the figure for proponents of aid, short of intervention, jumped to 62 percent. See *POQ*, p. 112.

nation of King George VI in 1938 an astonished observer noted that middle-class American tourists from Main Street led the shouting and applause, singing " 'God Save the King' with more ardour, loyalty, and devotion than probably they had ever sung the 'Star-Spangled Banner.' "[13] Ethnic passions especially tended to exacerbate isolationist convictions in German, Italian, or Irish immigrant groups who wanted no part of American intervention with England against Italy and Germany. The vicious demagoguery of "the radio priest" Father Charles E. Coughlin concocted a rank brew of Populist economics, the Catholic social gospel, and Fascist propaganda, which appealed to some Irish-American and German-American haters of England and the Jews. By 1938 he had an estimated five and a half million listeners, concentrated most heavily in the North Central states. Some sections of the country were especially intense in their isolationism: the provincial, traditionally Republican, northern tier of New England states; the urban sectors of the Anglophobic Irish Catholics; the northern Middlewestern zone from Ohio to Idaho, with its heavy concentration of rural areas, German and Scandinavian immigrant communities, and the Progressive Republican tradition of agrarian hostility to Wall Street and England. Least isolationist of all was the South with its Anglo-American white population, traditionally oriented towards England, free trade, and the Democratic Party.[14]

[13] William Zukerman, "Americans and the Call of Europe," *Quarterly Review*, 270 (January, 1938), 51. For immigrant isolationism see Selig Adler, *The Isolationist Impulse: Its Twentieth-Century Reaction* (New York, Abelard-Schuman, 1957), pp. 291–295. For Coughlinite isolationism see Morris Janowitz, "Black Legions on the March," in Daniel Aaron, ed., *America in Crisis: Fourteen Crucial Episodes in American History* (New York, Knopf, 1952), pp. 312–317.

[14] See Ralph H. Smuckler, "The Region of Isolationism," *American Political Science Review*, 47 (June, 1953), pp. 386–401; Ray Allen Billington, "The Origins of Middle Western Isolationism," *Political Science Quarterly*, 60 (March, 1945), 44–64; William G. Carleton, "Isolationism and the Middle West," *Mississippi Valley Historical Review*, 33 (December, 1946), 377–390; Leroy N. Rieselbach, "The Basis of Isolationist Behavior," *Public Opinion Quarterly*, 24 (Winter, 1960), 645–657; Samuel Lubell, "Who Votes Isolationist and Why," *Harper's*, 202 (April, 1951), 29–36. Smuckler defines an isolationist area measured by House votes 1933–1950; Billington explains the ideological and political basis of Middle Western isolationism; Carleton shows that the Middle West did not really

The melodramatic investigations into the influence of muni-tionmakers and bankers on foreign policy, conducted in 1934 by Senator Gerald P. Nye, a Progressive Republican from the most isolationist state in the Union, convinced Americans that they should meet the problems of the present by measures ideally de-signed to have kept them out of the last war. Having defeated a proposal to join the World Court, a nearly unanimous Congress passed the Neutrality Laws of 1935–1937, imposing an inflexible arms embargo and forbidding Americans to extend loans or credits to belligerents, and refusing to protect American rights of travel on their ships. In this period even an expatriate like Ernest Hem-ingway could voice common opinion in an essay that won a prize for the best article for 1935: "But of the hell broth that is brewing in Europe we have no need to drink. Europe has always fought: the intervals of peace are only armistices. We were fools to be sucked in once in a European war, and we should never be sucked in again."[15] The public could find support for its prejudices in Walter Millis's *The Road to War*, published that same year, which followed the fashion of greatly exaggerating the economic inter-ests at work leading to intervention in 1917.

The Spanish Civil War, bringing the major European powers into conflict, jolted Hemingway and many intellectuals into in-volvement, but it never really broke the isolationist mood of the country. Liberals, socialists, and Communists rallied in sympathy with the Republican Loyalist government against the Fascist-sup-ported Rebels, and about two thousand Americans joined bri-gades to fight for the democratic cause abroad. It was a familiar

---

become an atypical center of isolationism until 1939–1941; Rieselbach, ana-lyzing 76 Congressional districts outside the Far West and the Deep South on Congressional votes on selected issues in the periods 1939–1941, 1949–1952, stresses the complex of Republicanism, ruralism, and the ethnic affilia-tion—in that order—as determinants; Lubell stresses ethnic sensitivity and parochialism of German, Irish, and Scandinavian groups in too monistic a fashion. I have treated isolationism as a changing pattern, involving past and present, and supported by many factors (ideology, party, area, and ethnic ties).

[15] "Notes on the Next War," in *American Points of View 1934–1935*, p. 8. For the "revisionist" movement, which supported isolationism, see Adler, *op. cit.*, pp. 256–260.

dilemma for those Progressives who had always been passionate, crusading democrats and also fervent isolationists. Senator Borah blasted the murder of civilians in the bombings of Guernica, and Senator Nye led a protest of twenty-one Congressmen against the one-sided effect of a special arms embargo applied to Spain, which favored the Rebels and their German and Italian supporters. Fearful of domestic repercussions, especially from American Catholics, the Roosevelt Administration did not lift the Spanish embargo until after general war had broken out in Europe, nor did it give official backing to the efforts of the friends of Spanish democracy to bring Basque refugee children to America. While a majority of those Americans who took emotional sides in the civil war were pro-Loyalist, polls showed that in late 1938 forty percent were still neutral.[16]

Pro-Fascist propaganda exploited the mood of isolationism, but it did not need to create it. Italian-Americans and German-Americans differed from most citizens only in having reasons of "old-country" pride and sympathy for not taking vigorous action to resist fascism in Europe. Popular magazines for the general public, like *Colliers*, *The American Magazine*, and *The Saturday Evening Post*, were much more worried about Communism than Fascism, and they were more sympathetic with Germany than with the Allies, who were constantly blamed for a harsh peace that "explained" the rise of Fascism. The German people were seen through stereotypes that Americans easily understood. Despite the excesses of the Nazis, the Germans were praised for their industry, cleanliness, hospitality, organizational genius, and scientific talent—in short, for their being very like Americans. Thoroughly convinced that American idealism had been betrayed by Europe in 1919, these magazines did little to give their readers any realistic sense of the dynamics of the Nazi totalitarian movement, which deliberately exploited the myth of betrayal and punishment as the causes of German difficulties after World War I. Not until the Spring of 1939 did these magazines markedly shift their sympa-

---

[16] F. J. Taylor, *The United States and the Spanish Civil War, 1936–1939* (New York, Bookman Associates, 1956), p. 137, *passim.*

thies towards the victims of Nazi aggression.[17] The public was more easily moved by sympathy for Finland, which not only paid its war debts but suffered invasion by the Soviets, whose unpopularity (outside of fashionable intellectual circles) remained notable until after America entered the war.

Herbert Hoover, who headed the Finnish War Relief Fund, was the eloquent spokesman for the traditional isolationist position of defending only the Western Hemisphere. An admirer of Wilson's idealism, set in melodramatic opposition to European "sinister demands for power," Hoover scored the Allies for their failure to pay their war debts, warned the public in August, 1939, of the effect of British propaganda in arousing American sympathies before the First World War, and urged Americans to avoid the contagions of European politics: "When we take sides in their controversies, when we talk of using force of any kind, we are playing power politics at the European chess table."[18] European international affairs were summed up in American terms as the rivalry of selfish interests, implicitly opposed to American policies presumably based on disinterested virtue. By this idiom political questions involving European countries were simply repressed in the American consciousness, censored by the national image of "power politics" as a peculiar Old World disease.

The prejudices behind the conservative uses of this ancient dualism of New World and Old were reflected in the editorials of *The Saturday Evening Post,* which clung to isolationism after both *Colliers* and *The American Magazine* had moved away from it. Like Hoover, the *Post* linked its anti-Europeanism with a passionate conservative hostility to the New Deal. "When shall we learn again that Europe is Europe, America is America, and these are two worlds?" it complained in March, 1940. "When shall we believe again that our destiny is unique, parallel to nothing?" Alas, this absoluteness was fast becoming relative by the planting of

[17] See the illuminating study by Roberta S. Sigel, *Opinions on Nazi Germany: A Study of Three Popular American Magazines, 1933–1941,* unpublished Ph.D. thesis, Clark University, 1950.
[18] "Shall We Send Our Youth to War?" *The American Magazine,* 128 (August, 1939), 138.

"Old World seeds" in "soft warm places," like the leisured rich and the intellectuals, producing the poisoned harvest of political unionism, paternalist government, and intervention in foreign affairs. "Every important idea of the New Deal," it falsely charged, "was borrowed from Europe, out of Harold J. Laski's exquisitely revolutionary mind, or from J. Maynard Keynes' brilliantly insolvent economics, and all that beautifully printed literature of an aristocratically decadent British radicalism. . . ."[19] Isolationism was a hex symbol to exorcise all the devils of middle-class American folklore. The *Post* was faithful to this venerable mythology right down to the dropping of the bombs on Pearl Harbor.

Isolationism, based on a contrast between the Western Hemisphere and Europe, was not monopolized by conservative enemies of the New Deal. Many of the New Dealers themselves were heirs of the old Progressive faith in democracy, economic reform, and American moral superiority. Jerome N. Frank of Roosevelt's Department of Agriculture and the Securities and Exchange Commission, using his own version of *The Saturday Evening Post* tactic, accused both right and left wing opponents of the New Deal of deriving their ideas from either dominant or submerged groups in the European order. Frank attacked reliance on extensive foreign trade as hostile to New Deal reforms and peace. "Unless and until Europe rids itself of that English-fomented European disunity," he warned in *Save America First* (1938), "America is helpless in the task of helping Europe or of promoting world order." Liking the British as people, he nevertheless came to the remarkable conclusion that the English government's treatment of the Irish for a hundred years was "only slightly (if at all) better than Germany's treatment of the Jews *for the past five years.*"[20]

Frank's foreign policy was shared by Stuart Chase, popularizer of reform economics, in his breezy *The New Western Front.* America as an integrated, homogeneous, standardized country was happily contrasted to Europe where "the poor devils have never got together since the fall of Rome." Like Frank, he linked Wil-

[19] "That of Our Own," *The Saturday Evening Post*, 212 (March 23, 1940), 26; "The Foreign Malady," *ibid.*, 214 (August 2, 1941), 26.
[20] *Save America First*, 2nd ed. (New York, Harper, 1938), pp. 89, 157.

son's intervention in World War I to the influence of foreign trade pressures and the propaganda of Perfidious Albion, who must not again persuade Americans to "pull the chestnuts of the British Empire, or any other empire, out of the fire." Chase made an unconvincing argument for the underlying similarities of the United States with Latin America:

We are all New World people—pioneers. We all became independent of Old World masters. . . . We are all political democracies in theory, if not always in practice. . . . We are practically a unit in being willing to fight military invasion from the Old World. We are bound together by our geographical isolation—even though Brazil is closer to Africa than to Florida.

Chase was anxious to prevent the New World concept from being taken as an excuse for American "dollar diplomacy" or imperialism south of the border, but his most vigorous polishing of the image of the American-European contrast reflected the traditional narrowing of the New World to the United States. What distinguished the New World fundamentally were the very things Americans could pride themselves on when they looked in the European mirror: no monarchists, no "shirted rabble drilling and shouting for a strong man to save us," no state church, no racism, no "official snoopers," no "festering minorities," no "vested aristocracy," no "fixed classes," no "class-conscious proletariat," no territorial aims, and no *revanche* to appease." As usual, the American reformer, locked in passionate struggle with his domestic enemies, whom he often branded as Fascists, reactionaries, Tories, or "economic royalists," blandly found his society as free as utopia from authoritarianism, class conflict, and racial oppression whenever he fell back on the conventional dualism of America and Europe. At home he was surrounded by political enemies; looking abroad, he felt strangely at peace with his world: "Fortunate above all other, unified above all others, stronger than any others, in a sense we have civilization in our keeping. The responsibility is passing from the Old World to the New."[21]

[21] *The New Western Front*, collab. Marian Tyler (New York, Harcourt, Brace, 1939), pp. 11, 31, 149–150, 185–186, 187.

The most vigorous and respected of the liberal isolationists was Charles A. Beard. His study in 1913 of the economic basis of the making of the Constitution (read as a muckraking portrait of the Founding Fathers as Funding Fathers) had been one of the most controversial and influential books of the Progressive era. A dedicated supporter of Wilson's intervention in 1917, Beard had anxiously followed the historical literature of "revisionism" on the coming of the war, though his own contributions to it were notably restrained, especially by contrast with Harry Elmer Barnes, a friend and former colleague at Columbia University. He chided Barnes in 1926 for forgetting that a triumphant German military party might have soon challenged Washington. Americans were well advised to prevent the rise of any European power to a dominant position. This tactic called for cold-blooded calculation, not a sensationalizing of history into a melodrama of heroes and villains.[22] Yet a debate with fellow historian Carleton J. Hayes in 1930 flashed a few signals of the isolationist direction Beard was to take. Preparing a draft of a study by the American Historical Association on the teaching of history and the social studies in the schools, Beard had written: "We can import nothing fundamental from Europe. Having rounded out the Continent, Americans have turned in upon themselves and are taking time to wonder about the next great tasks ahead. While a few critics go abroad for inspiration the great body of thinkers still agree with Emerson that we must stand fast where we are and work out our destiny on lines already marked out."[23]

This passage provoked a sharp challenge from Hayes, who thought of America as culturally a part of Western Civilization. "But, after all," he objected, "we Americans of the Twentieth Century are just as much heirs of the Greeks and the Romans and of Shakespeare as anybody living in Scandinavia or Germany or Scotland at the present moment. In that sense we are Europeans

[22] "Heroes and Villains of the World War," *Current History*, 24 (August, 1926), 730–735.
[23] "Investigation of History and Other Social Studies in the Schools," transcript of meeting of a Committee of the American Historical Association, October 16, 1930, Turner Papers, Huntington Library, p. 10.

and we can't escape it." Beard conceded finally that "it ought to be clearly emphasized that our cultural relation [is] to Europe and the sense of unity and general ideas with Europe"; but he was basically moved by a faith in the promise of American life, which left him "boggled up" with the sense of its possibilities and a "deep and personal desire to see this civilization richer than it is . . ."[24]

After the melodramatic charges of Senator Nye's committee had convinced him that loans and credits to the Allies, as a prop against a domestic crash, had forced Wilson into war, the old idea of an unbridgeable gulf between America and Europe shaped Beard's writings. At first he entrusted his passionate hopes for America to the New Deal's attack on the Great Depression. The promise of American life was "the economy of abundance," a goal in keeping with his view of the American tradition as "hard, economic and realistic" in contrast to the "feudal and theological heritage" of Europe.[25] But Beard feared that history would repeat itself: Roosevelt would indulge a messianic temptation to play a large role in international politics, yield to the pressure of economic interests, unite a divided party, and postpone his domestic reform program by pouring out "American blood and treasure" to "the advantage of British and French imperialism."[26] Six years before Pearl Harbor he had set the stage for his post-war appearance as the leading proponent of the conspiratorial myth, promoted by isolationists as retroactive justification of their position, that Roosevelt had invited attack in the Pacific.

Drawing on the past to support his present hopes and fears, Beard's historical writing became increasingly a tendentious and sardonically phrased plea for a policy of continentalism. He appeared before the House Committee on Naval Affairs to speak

[24] *Ibid.*, pp. 11–12.
[25] "That Promise of American Life," *New Republic*, 81 (February 6, 1935), 352. For his reaction to the Nye Committee see "Emerging Issues in America," *Current History*, 41 (November, 1934), 203–209; "On Keeping Out of War," *ibid.*, 43 (March, 1936), 625–632.
[26] "Our Choice in Foreign Policy," *Events*, 1 (March, 1937), 164. For his prophecy of war in the Pacific see "National Politics and War," *Scribner's*, 97 (February, 1935), 65–70.

against the building up of a big navy; he testified in the Senate Foreign Relations Committee against the Lend-Lease program; and he was consulted for advice by such prominent isolationists as Colonel Charles A. Lindbergh. In the pages of the *Congressional Record* Beard's testimony and writings appeared as weapons in the hands of isolationist senators and representatives, who found potent ammunition for their cause by quoting the passionate urging of one of America's foremost historians to "stay out to the last ditch, and preserve one stronghold of order and sanity, even against the gates of hell." Representative Blackney of Michigan leaned on Beard to oppose changing the Neutrality Legislation to a cash-and-carry rule for arms in 1939 and in the conventional isolationist idiom spoke of Europe as a "sordid story of broken pacts, reversed policies, secret treaties, and hidden treacheries."[27]

The last three volumes of Beard's masterwork, *The Rise of American Civilization*, were vibrant with his sense of crisis and his vision of a unique society, whose pursuit of the dream of progress was menaced by imperialistic adventurers, acquisitive capitalists, and foreign critics. In the last of these, *The American Spirit: A Study of the Idea of Civilization in the United States*, Europe is portrayed as a malignant chorus to the New World Symphony of American life. European spokesmen merely confused Americans with ideas—Freudian, Catholic, and Marxist—derived from reactionary, hierarchical societies, doomed to be forever beyond the pale of progress. "The prolonged censure of American civilization by foreign critics," he complained, "acted as an aggressive, divisive force, introducing intellectual disorder and embittering factional and racial disputes in the United States. . . . Often it diverted American talents and affections from concentration on tasks clearly within the scope of American capacities and opportunities, clearly delimited by the necessities of American life." Convinced that America had "a unique history" and was "stamped by national characteristics differentiating it ineradicably from European civilizations," he was led by his devout continen-

[27] *Congressional Record*, 76th Cong., 2nd sess., 85:1 (October 31, 1939), 1140. See also *ibid.*, 77th Cong., 1st sess., 87:2 (February 22, 1941), 1273.

talism to scold the internationalists for "resorting to a materialism just as bald as that of the Communist Manifesto" in stressing the common forces of technology and industrialization which assimilated the American economy to other nations.[28]

As an isolationist Beard found himself in the uncongenial company of conservative American nativists and chauvinists. He had resigned from his teaching post at Columbia University in 1917 on an issue of academic freedom for colleagues who did not share his support of Wilson. He had done graduate work at Oxford, advised the Japanese on the reconstruction of Tokyo after the great earthquake of 1923, and made a trip to Yugoslavia to study its governmental problems. Always a generous friend to European refugees from Fascism, he was also noted in the historical profession for his alert interest in the ideas of modern European philosophers of history. Yet his devotion to an insulated "promise of American life," protected from the rusts and stains of European history, brought him as an uneasy guest into the company of xenophobes who celebrated the American way of life with provincial smugness and reactionary rancor.

The conflict of both liberal and conservative isolationists with the Administration flared into spectacular conflagration in the debate over the Lend-Lease Bill in 1941. As a former Assistant Secretary of the Navy with a personal love for the sea, President Roosevelt had a keen sense of geopolitical strategy, and he knew that American security had depended historically on factors well outside the Western Hemisphere. "The buffer," he told a group of businessmen confidentially in May, 1940, "has been the British Fleet and the French Army."[29] After the fall of France and the *Luftwaffe's* onslaught on Great Britain in the summer of 1940, the Administration, worried about lack of Congressional support, moved on executive authority alone to transfer fifty overage destroyers to the British in return for leases on naval and air bases

[28] *The American Spirit: A Study of the Idea of Civilization in the United States*, vol. 4 of The Rise of American Civilization (New York, Macmillan, 1942), pp. 484, 536–538.

[29] Quoted by Stetson Conn and Byron Fairchild, *United States Army in World War II: The Western Hemisphere, the Framework of Hemisphere Defense* (Washington, Department of the Army, 1960), p. 34.

in Newfoundland and the Caribbean. Following the election of 1940, in which both Willkie and Roosevelt promised aid to Britain and no participation in "foreign wars," Harry Hopkins was sent abroad as the President's personal representative to Winston Churchill, and the defeated candidate Willkie brought encouragement to the Prime Minister from the President in the form of a stanza from Longfellow—humanity, "with all the hopes of future years," was "hanging breathless" on Britain's fate. The Lend-Lease Bill, bringing tangible aid to the British "Ship of State," represented the Administration's major public commitment to the position that the first line of American defense lay outside the Western Hemisphere.

Opponents of the bill in the House and Senate rang all the changes on the old American theme of holding Europe in suspicion and violently twisted the Lion's tail for several months: The British had been our enemy ever since 1776; their imperialism was as bad as Fascism; the Europeans were hopelessly entangled in an un-American system of power politics; they had welched on their war debts; George Washington's Farewell Address was the Ark of the Covenant, violated by a faithless Administration; the "godless Communists" would benefit from the program; American idealism had been "sucked in" under Wilson by propaganda, bankers, munitions makers, and wily Europeans; the Western Hemisphere was impregnable. Every hackneyed theme in the litany of hyper-Americanism was exploited to the full. In outrage Representative Tinkham of Massachusetts placed in the *Congressional Record* a London reporter's vision of the future, entitled "Roosevelt to Reside in England, the King and Queen of England to Live at Mount Vernon, and the United States Congress to Meet in Bermuda." Representative Sweeney of Ohio protested that the British had "taken over the United States without firing a shot" and proposed a new battle hymn for the republic:

> God save America from British rule.
> Stand beside her and guide her
> From the schemers who would make of her a fool.

From Lexington to Yorktown,
From blood-stained Valley Forge,
God save America
From a king named George.

Senator Bulow, in a candid plea for ignorance, admitted that Roosevelt knew a great deal about European affairs, but that was the trouble: "I learned that the boy who knew where the hornet's nest was and kept monkeying around there and thought he knew something about hornets was the boy who got stung, and the boy who did not know anything about hornets never got stung." Senator Brooks of Illinois suggested that the English prove their good faith by turning over their islands and South American securities to the United States in escrow. Senator Nye of North Dakota, who had given so many so much ammunition by his exposure of the munition makers, attacked Great Britain as the "ace aggressor of all time" and "proved" it by twelve pages of fine print in the *Congressional Record*, all devoted to the acquisition of British colonies.[30] Both houses of Congress became chambers of horrors.

Public opinion outside was organized by the William Allen White Committee to Defend America by Aiding the Allies and by the America First Committee.[31] (Ironically, White, one of the two founders of the former was, atypically, a Republican of the old Progressive strain, friendly to both the New Deal and Roosevelt's foreign policy, while R. Douglas Stuart, Jr., one of the two founders of the latter was, atypically, a New Deal Democrat until 1940.) White's organization proposed the destroyer-bases deal to the President, urged support of Lend-Lease, and advocated the convoying of merchant ships to England. The America First organization would go no further than "cash-and-carry" aid to

[30] Tinkham, *Congressional Record*, 77th Cong., 1st sess., 87:11 (March 27, 1941), A1464; Sweeney, *ibid.*, 87:12 (June 19, 1941), A2941; Bulow, *ibid.*, 87:2 (February 21, 1941), 1255; Brooks, *ibid.*, 1251; Nye, *ibid.* (March 4, 1941), 1722–1733.

[31] For the White Committee see Walter Johnson, *The Battle Against Isolation* (Chicago, University of Chicago Press, 1944); for the America First Committee see Wayne S. Cole, *America First: The Battle Against Intervention* (Madison, University of Wisconsin Press, 1953). White drew the line at campaigning for convoying merchant ships to England and resigned.

Great Britain, and it hoped to make peace or war a matter of popular or Congressional referendum. It never supported any practical positive defense measures, and, despite its efforts to keep out subversive elements, it found itself entangled on the fringes with pro-Fascist, anti-Semitic groups and a few German agents. The Klan, the Coughlinites, and the German-American Bund urged support of the Committee, and its most prestigious speaker, Colonel Charles A. Lindbergh, created an embittered controversy by a speech which blamed the British, the Jews, and the Roosevelt Administration for moving the United States towards war. The most parochial and prejudiced strain in the old Republican Progressivism found a hoarse voice in Senator Burton K. Wheeler, La Follette's running mate in 1924. Wheeler's silverite reform outlook, vulnerable to Populist phobias about the British, bankers, munition makers, and Jews, had long been out of sympathy with the New Deal, but it found a home in the America First Committee, which financed his nationwide speaking tour in 1941 on behalf of isolationism.[32] The largest source of support for the Committee came from those who hated the New Deal, and isolationist votes in Congress were more closely correlated with Republicanism than with other factors. The Republican counter to Lend-Lease was Senator Robert A. Taft's proposal for a loan to the British of two billion dollars (instead of a direct grant without strings of vehicles, weapons, food, and fuel), and for no aid to the Soviets. Taft, with a prophetic sense of the way history was going and a stubborn resistance to it, did not want the United States to assume England's traditional burden of maintaining the balance of power in Europe.[33]

A new American relation to the Old World emerged from the debate. The Lend-Lease Bill, after nearly three months of talk, passed both branches with solid majorities. A heavy American weight was belatedly placed on one side of the balance of power to counteract its dangerous tipping in favor of the Axis. The drag of isolationist attitudes was still strong, however, for the Soviet

---

[32] See Hubert Kay, "Boss Isolationist: Burton K. Wheeler," *Life*, 10 (May 19, 1941), 110–119.

[33] *Congressional Record*, 77 Cong., 1st sess., 87:2 (March 7, 1941), 1973.

Union was not formally included in Lend-Lease until November, nearly five months after the German invasion of Russia. The "common-law alliance" with Britain flourished with Hopkins as the intermediary between the two governments and W. Averell Harriman as "Expediter," established in London with the rank of Minister. Exchange of scientific information, pooling of military intelligence, cooperation of security branches, reciprocity of repairing and training services—these remarkable steps of close collaboration, without treaty or declaration of war, were climaxed by joint Anglo-American staff talks for the formulation of grand strategy in the event of American entry into the war.

Roosevelt struggled awkwardly with the limitations of the increasingly irrelevant but persistent "Western Hemisphere" orientation. At the time of the Lend-Lease debate it had become clear that the designation of the area to be included in the Western Hemisphere was an act of arbitrary judgment. Traditionally, as the Geographer of the United States explained to a senator, the Azores and the Cape Verde islands had been excluded and Iceland brought in, despite their position according to the conventional dividing line 20° West of Greenwich. Senator Ellender's effort to amend the Lend-Lease Bill so as specifically to restrict the use of land and naval forces to the Western Hemisphere ran into this difficulty of definition and was abandoned as an explicit limitation on the Bill. The Geographer later pointed out what the Monroe Doctrine had always obscured: there are an infinite number of hemispheres, the conventionally mapped "Western Hemisphere" being merely the one that includes almost the maximum area of ocean in any hemisphere also containing the Americas. A hemisphere unfavorable to isolationist illusions might be drawn which would include nearly all of the Americas, Europe, Africa, and forty percent of Asia.[34]

[34] See the Senate debate, *ibid.* (March 5, 1941), 1810–1811; S. W. Boggs, "The American Hemisphere," in Harold and Margaret Sprout, eds., *Foundations of National Power* (Princeton, Princeton University Press, 1945), pp. 607–614. The hemisphere concept obscured the fact that Buenos Aires, for example, is farther from Madison, Wisconsin, than any capital of Europe. See Eugene Staley, "The Myth of the Continents," *Foreign Affairs,* 19 (April, 1941), 481–494.

Isolationists were hypnotized by the conventional maps, and Roosevelt despaired of breaking the spell. Worried about French military collaboration with the Germans, he contemplated a plan to extend the Monroe Doctrine to include West Africa and the Atlantic islands, especially Dakar and the Azores. In May, 1941, he directed the Army and Navy to prepare joint plans (later abandoned) for an expeditionary force to the Azores. In July the Marines were ordered to Iceland. Secretary of War Stimson urged Roosevelt to tell the public that the true purpose of the Iceland operation was to protect the North Atlantic convoy route to Great Britain, but the President, still fearful of the power of isolationist opinion, carefully explained the step in misleading orthodox terms as being necessary to prevent German occupation of the island, from which she might attack the Western Hemisphere.[35] From July 19 onward, however, the American Navy, under secret orders to shoot on sight or sound of hostile vessels, protected ships going to Iceland and the British isles. In deference to the logic of the "Western Hemisphere" the convoys stopped at a mid-point between America and Europe. By September 11, 1941, that logic was in principle abandoned by the Chiefs of Staff, who advised the President that American security depended upon the existence of the British Empire and the establishment in Europe of a favorable balance of power. These aims could only be secured by military victories "outside this hemisphere" in which the United States participated.[36]

Only the steadily increasing American involvement in the war could teach the hard lesson effectively. The isolationists' fears and hopes were deeply rooted in the American past. Around them images had accumulated of some of the country's greatest heroes and highest ideals. If what had once been a realistic, limited policy was now a shibboleth, if the promise of American life could no longer be fulfilled in continental self-sufficiency, what had history in store for Americans? A proud people had measured themselves by contrast with the Old World, from which most of them had come. The brief experiment of collaboration with Europe in the first World War had been too ill-prepared, too innocently distorted by unreasonable expectations, and too brief to initiate Americans into the graceful outgrowing of isolationism. Who could say what guidelines would exist for Americans once they had made common cause with European allies and left behind them the satisfying contours of a New World in the Western Hemisphere? History has often been kind to Americans. It was uncommonly severe with the isolationists. On the day that extension of the draft passed the House by only one vote, on August 12, 1941, the Atlantic Conference between Roosevelt and Churchill came to an end with an agreement to work together after the war for "the establishment of a wider and permanent system of general security." One month before Pearl Harbor Congress agreed to revise the Neutrality Act to allow American armed merchant vessels to carry cargoes directly to belligerent ports. The British and Americans began to pool their efforts to develop an Atomic Bomb.

This awesome weapon was itself a symbol of the new world in the making. The bomb was the joint product of European scientists, many of them refugees from Fascism, and of American theoretical physicists, "sick and tired of going to Europe as learners," who had in the 1930s put American physics "at the top of the heap."[37] It would bring an end to the war and explode forever any ground for the illusion of a self-sufficient national security.

[37] Testimony of Dr. Isadore I. Rabi, *In the Matter of J. Robert Oppenheimer*, Transcript of Hearing before Personnel Security Board (Washington, Atomic Energy Commission, 1954), pp. 464–465.

12

THE TIES OF AN INDISSOLUBLE HISTORY

By 1941 THE UNITED STATES HAD MOVED with painful reluctance into close collaboration with powers outside the "Western Hemisphere," a political concept which had lost its traditional meaning. But the nature of America's new relation to the European world was still not clear. Three views competed for national support: American dominance through world leadership; American partnership in an Atlantic Community of nations; and general internationalism under a universal security system like the League of Nations. The seeds of the Atlantic idea, nourished by wartime collaboration, would not take firm hold until 1946.

Henry Luce in an editorial called "The American Century," written for *Life* magazine in February, 1941, made a fervent plea for an "American internationalism." The mass-produced products of American popular culture and industry were already worldwide; what was needed now was "a sharing with all peoples of our Bill of Rights, our Declaration of Independence, our Constitution, our magnificent industrial products, our technical skills."[1] Designed to appeal to the progressive elements of the business community, which generally supported the left wing of the Republican Party, the Luce editorial sang the glories of "free enterprise" American-style and dangled the lure of American dominance of world trade. This rhetorical plea for an internationalism on American terms for American advantage tapped much of the same nationalist feelings that had always given the isolationist tradition its powerful force.

The imperialistic overtones of Luce's "The American Century" were absent from the Atlantic Community idea, even though it rested fundamentally on the concept of Anglo-American cooperation, which had once been the favorite nostrum of both British and American imperialists at the turn of the century. The lineage of the Atlantic Community concept goes back to the reflections of Henry Adams on Theodore Roosevelt's policies and of the editors of *The New Republic* on Wilson's. Walter Lippmann, one of its early formulators, was its most influential and eloquent spokesman during the Second World War. In support of his policy he appealed to history to show that Americans had participated ever since 1689 in European wars involving the British, bound by the "compulsion of geography and by the ties of an indissoluble and irreversible history." Lippmann sometimes used bad history to prove a good case by treating the Monroe Doctrine as if it had been an explicit Anglo-American agreement, and he considerably underemphasized the important role of anti-British feeling in American policy until the imperial days of Theodore Roosevelt. But Lippmann's conception was neither imperialist nor sentimental. In *U. S. War Aims* he saw the Atlantic Community as including Pan-America, the British Commonwealth, France and her Latin neighbors, the Low Countries, and Scandinavia. This vast area made up a strategic and historical common region requiring a common defense and a common foreign policy. By this

[1] *The American Century* (New York, Farrar and Rinehart, 1941), pp. 32–33.

interpretation America was integrated into a common set of problems and a common civilization where the similarities were more important than the differences.[2] The long tradition of America as an anti-Europe was attacked in its vitals.

Lippmann's view was also directed against the general internationalism of Wilson's League. It was condemned as impracticable and morally invidious, because it meant holding other countries to standards America itself felt no obligation to observe. Universal collective security was too abstract and legalistic to fit the diversity of history and the limits of effective, felt national responsibility. Lippmann's idea was carried much closer to Wilson's by Clarence Streit, whose "Union Now" movement, formed in July, 1939, sought a nucleus of world government on the American model in a federal union of the United States, Great Britain, and the Commonwealth. Streit had been at the American Peace Commission in Paris in Wilson's day and was later *The New York Times* correspondent in Geneva. Disenchanted by the Versailles Treaty, he had not fought for the League; but his Union Now proposal, which became very popular among college students and professors, was a forerunner of the post-war United Federalists for World Government.[3]

Neither President Roosevelt nor his Secretary of State, Cordell Hull, ever fully broke with the Wilsonian tradition, however much political exigencies forced them to compromise it in deals with Darlan regarding North Africa, recognition of Pétain in France and Franco in Spain, or making peace with Marshal Badoglio in Italy. Roosevelt at first favored a four-power policing of a disarmed post-war world by the United States, Great Britain,

[2] "The British-American Connection," *Washington Post*, February 4, 1941, reprinted in *Congressional Record*, 77th Cong., 1st sess., 87:10 (February 4, 1941), A411–A412; *U.S. War Aims* (Boston, Little, Brown, 1944), *passim.* Cf. the map of "the Atlantic area" in Francis P. Miller, "The Atlantic Area," *Foreign Affairs*, 19 (July, 1941), 727–728. Luce's "American Century" approach was turned into an Anglo-American alliance for free trade and joint economic action in "An American Proposal," *Fortune*, 25 (May, 1942), Part II, 59–63.

[3] *Union Now: A Proposal for a Federal Union of the Democracies of the North Atlantic* (New York, Harper, 1938), *passim.* For his career see Annex 5, pp. 288–302.

Russia, and China with international responsibility and organization divided into regional blocs, as Churchill had suggested. But Hull and his associates were adamantly opposed. "War anywhere was considered to be an infectious disease against which there was no immunity in isolation," as Russell H. Bastert has described the position, "and which therefore must be totally eliminated. The only way was to have the world vaccinated with the serum of collective security, which would immunize the world against aggression."[4] Hull's views prevailed at the Moscow Conference of 1943, and he rejoiced that when the provisions of the Four-Nation Declaration went into effect "there would no longer be any need 'for spheres of influence, for alliances, for balance of power or any other of the special arrangements through which, in the unhappy past, the nations strove to safeguard their security or to promote their interests.' "[5] The Fulbright Resolution in the House and the Connally Resolution in the Senate, passed that same year, committed the legislative branch to joining in some kind of general international organization at the end of the war.

Wilsonian internationalism was also the theme of Wendell Willkie, titular leader of the Republican Party. In his widely read *One World*, a record of his tour, which bypassed Western Europe entirely, he defended the United Nations while expressing conventional hostility to British colonialism and the "machinations of Old World intrigue."[6] General internationalism, because it was abstract and nonpolitical, was compatible with American prejudices against Europe. "The internationalists, too," as William H. McNeill has acutely pointed out, "wanted an international organization mainly in order to be free to cultivate their own garden in peace."[7]

The American strategy of making military victory an end in itself, insulated as far as possible from political decisions, was also

[4] "The Two American Diplomacies," *Yale Review*, 49 (Summer, 1960), 523.

[5] *The Memoirs of Cordell Hull*, II (New York, Macmillan, 1948), 1648.

[6] *One World* (New York, Simon and Schuster, 1943), pp. 161–162.

[7] *America, Britain, and Russia: Their Co-operation and Conflict 1941–1946* (London, Oxford University Press, 1953), p. 31. My account of these years has been much instructed by McNeill's dispassionate and penetrating book.

congenial to the isolationist belief that intervention abroad was only a temporary distasteful expedient that would no longer be necessary when the end of the war had restored the familiar outlines of the normal world. Yet the strategic decision to make Europe the main theater of the war made it inevitable that the fighting of the war would be an allied effort. (The isolationists, as McNeill has remarked, stressed the importance of the Pacific because only Japan had attacked the United States directly.) General Marshall made a major contribution to the new collaborative diplomacy by his powerful arguments for unified theater commands and combined staffs (for allocation of munitions and shipping as well as military operations), which finally convinced a reluctant Churchill. The American Joint Chiefs were willing to accept a British officer as overall commander for European operations in order to preserve the principle of unified command. Operation Overlord, the invasion of Europe by allied forces, was finally placed under the unified command of General Eisenhower, who acted with a tenacious conviction in persuasion and mutual confidence as the only viable instruments for this gigantic amphibious operation. According to a legend which reflects the spirit of coalition in his command, he did not care if an officer called another an s.o.b., provided he did not call him a British s.o.b. Despite its persistent tensions, the Anglo-American collaboration justified McNeill's judgment that it was "the most intimate and effective war-time alliance of history."[8] It was all the easier for Americans to accept when it became clear that American military and industrial power gave the United States an inevitable preponderance in disputes about strategy.

The American soldier, provincially educated, far from his home, and forced to endure the monotony of waiting and the agony of battle, inevitably looked at the war from a narrower point of view. He fought for the survival of himself, his outfit,

[8] *Ibid.*, p. 117. The British opposed the unification of air and ground operations against Germany under a single commander. See Richard M. Leighton, "Allied Unity of Command in the Second World War: A Study in Regional Military Organization," *Political Science Quarterly*, 67 (September, 1952), 399–425.

and his country. He tended to feel more respect for the Russian military effort than the British, and he found Englishmen, when he fought with them in the Middle East, less congenial as individuals than the Russians. The French people he rated even below the Germans. He reflected current American feelings in favoring some kind of general international organization after the war, while looking with a distinctly jaundiced eye on post-war economic aid to his Allies.[9] There was for him no corner of a foreign field forever American.

He naturally distrusted the idealistic generalities that rationalized his particular hell. The G.I. gripes of "Clem" and "Kilroy," carved on latrine walls all over Europe, were mainly directed against the Allies and the Displaced Persons, and military authorities were shocked to discover that over half of the replacements polled in the fall of 1945 admired Hitler's prewar role in Germany, while nearly a quarter conceded Germany's right to rule Europe and persecute the Jews. This crude cynicism usually came from the Army's own displaced persons, the "repple-depple" replacements who had been cut off from close ties with their outfit. Most soldiers judged foreign countries by their military victories, the local purchasing power of G.I. pay, and the availability of girls. If the American invaders came to like the conquered enemy rather than their allies, it was because a cigarette or a chocolate bar could more easily buy a girl or a camera among a demoralized, defeated people anxious to curry favor with occupation forces.[10]

As the wartime conferences among the Allies multiplied, the tensions that divided them came increasingly to the surface. The war debts issue was wisely buried by the considerable effect of Reverse Lend-Lease from Britain on the invasion of Europe and the willingness of the United States to accept military victory and freer trade in the future as recompense; but American suspicions of the Allies had not been entirely lulled by the euphoria of com-

[9] See the tables and polls in Samuel A. Stouffer *et al.*, *The American Soldier*, vols. I and II of *Studies in Social Psychology in World War II* (Princeton, Princeton University Press, 1949), I, 432; II, 574, 575 n. 12, 576, 592.

[10] See Karl Frucht, "Clem Has Been Here," *Commentary*, 1 (March, 1946), 39–45.

radeship in arms. Conservative isolationists had never looked with favor on an alliance with Soviet Russia and liberal interventionists had their doubts about the Tory convictions of Churchill. In the later light of the massive intensity of American anti-Soviet feeling in the Cold War it is hard to remember that suspicion of the British was far more widespread and influential than fear of Russia in late 1944 and early 1945. Popular magazines like *Collier's*, *The Saturday Evening Post*, and *Life* featured articles praising the Soviet people, minimizing the undemocratic features of the political system, and stressing the common aims that Russia shared with the United States for peace and prosperity. *Life* entirely devoted its March 29, 1943, issue to Soviet-American cooperation and described the Russians as "one hell of a people" who "look like Americans, dress like Americans, and think like Americans."[11] Ambassador Davies' pro-Soviet book, *Mission to Moscow*, was condensed in the *Reader's Digest*, made into an even more flattering movie, and recommended by the *Rotarian*. Critical protest against the distortions of Davies' report came from Norman Thomas and other anti-Communist radicals who had never drifted with the tides of national feeling. Their traditional critics, the business executives, had more confidence (according to a *Fortune* poll) in Soviet post-war intentions than any other group.[12]

These illusions about Soviet realities were also reflected in Roosevelt's efforts to reassure Stalin of the good intentions of the West. Just as Wilson had justified his compromises in the Treaty of Versailles by the greater good of the League, so did Roosevelt temper resistance to Soviet demands by his widely shared hopes for post-war collaboration and the effectiveness of the United Nations. He was also hampered in assessing European realities by having a common American animus against Britain as a colonial power. He prodded Churchill about the British policy of imperial preference in trade, control of Hong Kong and India, and predilection for monarchy in Italy. Roosevelt reluctantly accepted on

[11] Quoted by Paul Willen, "Who Collaborated with Russia?" *Antioch Review*, 14 (Fall, 1954), 265.
[12] *Ibid.*, p. 281. Just under 50 percent of the business executives expressed confidence in Soviet post-war intentions.

trial Churchill's deal with Stalin in the spring of 1944 for a temporary division of spheres of influence in Romania and Greece, but he worried about British motives. It was, of course, quite true that Churchill had not become the King's First Minister, as he bluntly said, "to preside over the liquidation of the British Empire"; it was also true that he had a remarkably accurate prescience about the growing dangers of Soviet expansionism.

The American anti-imperial attitude was sometimes justified, but it also could blind the citizens of the New World to the complexities of the European scene. With respect to Italy Churchill's stubborn adherence to the King and Marshal Badoglio, even after the fall of Rome, justifiably provoked Roosevelt to increase his pressure on him, and his new Secretary of State, Stettinius, publicly announced that the United States expected the Italians to form their own democratic government without interference from outside. This conflict was sharpened by the troubles in Greece when Churchill took decisive action to stop Communist-led guerillas from gaining control of the country. There was again a public outcry in America (though not from Roosevelt and Hopkins) against this seeming highhanded action, and Churchill later had the wry satisfaction of pointing out that the American government's own action in 1947 against the Communists in Greece had demonstrated the Prime Minister's foresight in this case.[13]

Tempted by his feeling that Russia, like America, was not a colonial power in the British sense, Roosevelt indulged in a dangerous optimism about his ability to persuade Stalin into a cooperative frame of mind. The President had resisted Churchill's urgent plea for an Anglo-American meeting before the Teheran Conference out of fear that Stalin might think they were conspiring against him. At Yalta the Anglo-American partnership, despite these growing differences, reached final accord on the Polish question and on France's role in the Occupation, but Roose-

[13] *Triumph and Tragedy*, vol. 6 of *The Second World War* (Boston, Houghton Mifflin, 1953), pp. 305–306. For Anglo-American tensions see H. C. Allen, *Great Britain and the United States: A History of Anglo-American Relations (1783–1952)* (London, Odhams, 1954), pp. 819–831, 855–885. Sympathetic to Churchill, Allen provides a useful balance to Sherwood, who is sympathetic to Roosevelt.

velt's bargains with Stalin were made on the basis of an optimistic hope, Churchill's in a mood of growing pessimism. Roosevelt's concessions to Stalin in the Far East were predicated on the idea of restoring most of Russia's losses sustained in the Russo-Japanese War in 1905 in order to purchase her support for the final invasion of Japan, which was expected to be long and bitter. Since Stalin had already in the fall of 1943 intimated to American officials that he would enter the Pacific war within a reasonable time after the defeat of Germany—without any reimbursement whatever—he must have returned from Teheran and Yalta, as George Kennan has said, "muttering to himself about the 'inscrutable Americans,' and assuring his associates that the motives of American policy were 'a mystery wrapped in an enigma.' "[14] History seemed determined to demonstrate the truth of James's dramatic vision of the innocent good-natured American encountering the grim necessities of a more sophisticated European order.

After Roosevelt's death, two months after the Yalta Conference, the rifts in the Grand Alliance cracked wider. President Truman inherited Roosevelt's policy of cooperation with the Soviets and the general American notion that the purpose of war was not the continuation of politics by other means but the simple pursuit of military victory. Churchill was persistently frustrated in his efforts to persuade Truman, Eisenhower, and the American Joint Chiefs of Staff that Anglo-American forces ought to press on to Berlin, liberate Czechoslovakia, and stand fast beyond the designated zones of post-war occupation until the peace had been hammered out in order to deter the momentum of Soviet power. The Prime Minister was further irritated by Eisenhower's communication of his policy directly to Stalin without consultation with his British Deputy or the Combined Chiefs of Staff. From the American point of view the expected need of Russian help in the war against Japan and the organization of the United Nations at San Francisco seemed much more important than Churchill's increasingly anxious efforts to develop a common policy of taking a firm stand

[14] *Russia and the West under Lenin and Stalin* (Boston, Little, Brown, 1961), p. 378.

against the encroachments of Soviet power. By its traditions the American public, its soldiers, and their leaders had been trained to respond to the deep-seated impulse to get out of Europe and go home after military defeat of the enemy.

By May, 1945, the American government was worried about the tensions among the Allies. Lend-Lease shipments were abruptly stopped to both Britain and Russia, and President Truman, refusing Churchill's suggestion for an Anglo-American conference preparatory to a mutual visit with Stalin, sent Harry Hopkins to Moscow. The Soviets had unilaterally recognized the Warsaw government and signed a treaty with it. What happened in Poland would test the soundness of Allied agreements at Yalta. Already ominous news had come of the seizure by the Russians of leaders of the Polish underground, invited for a meeting near Warsaw about the formation of a united Polish government in accordance with the Yalta agreement. The American emissary was, however, still skeptical of Churchill's policy and determined (according to Forrestal's Diary) "that we be not manoeuvered into a position where Great Britain had us lined up with them as a bloc against Russia to implement England's European policy."[15] At the same time Joseph Davies, a notorious flatterer of the Soviet Union, was sent to England to represent the American position to Churchill, a rebuke not lost on the Prime Minister, who was able to drink a grim toast to the irony of history in his memoirs, written at a period of the Cold War when the fervor of American anti-Soviet policy had then put England in the position of a moderator.

In Moscow Harry Hopkins sought to impress upon Joseph Stalin the importance of having free elections in Poland as a symbol,

in the sense that it bore a direct relation to the willingness of the United States to participate in international affairs on a world-

[15] May 20, 1945, quoted by Herbert Feis, *Churchill Roosevelt Stalin: The War They Waged and the Peace They Sought* (Princeton, Princeton University Press, 1957), p. 650. Feis has a scrupulously thorough and fair account of the rifts in the Alliance. The story is well told from Churchill's point of view in *Triumph and Tragedy*. McNeill's *America, Britain, and Russia* is especially illuminating on the fundamentally different political styles of the three powers.

wide basis and that our people must believe that they are joining their power with that of the Soviet Union and Great Britain in the promotion of international peace and the well being of humanity.

But American military power was not then in a position to lend force to this persuasion, and Stalin himself told Hopkins that "whether the United States wished it or not it was a world power and would have to accept world-wide interests."[16] The threat of a return to isolationism was not only useless as a lever, since it would merely leave the sheep to the wolves, but it could not have been credible to Hopkins himself. The Roosevelt Administration had persistently taken steps to insure a bipartisan commitment to internationalism after the war. They were determined not to repeat Wilson's blunders of domestic political strategy, but they failed to appreciate how much conventional distrust of European affairs had entered into the basic concepts of general internationalism for which Hull was the doctrinaire spokesman. At Yalta Churchill had been alarmed by Roosevelt's warning that American forces could not stay in Europe for more than two years after the war, but the President had an accurate sense of the public's impatience to get out of Europe after victory had been won. Less than a year after the defeat of Germany, American forces in Europe were drastically reduced.

The American people could not claim any foresight not granted to their leaders. They criticized England far more often than the Soviet Union in late 1944 and early 1945. The image of the Englishman as class-conscious snob and imperialist, exploited and reinforced by numerous Hollywood films, was as deeply rooted in the American imagination as Huck Finn.[17] (Hollywood has yet to make a film about post-war England; it produced highly romanticized films about modern English life during the war, but soon reverted to older images and scenes when the controversial Labor government came to power.) As the war approached its end, the sense of the importance of foreign policy problems

[16] Cited in Sherwood, *Roosevelt and Hopkins*, pp. 899–900.
[17] See Siegfried Kracauer, "National Types as Hollywood Presents Them," *Public Opinion Quarterly*, 13 (Spring, 1949), 53–72.

steadily declined. In late August, 1945, after V-J Day, pollsters found that only six percent were concerned with foreign affairs as major problems, though heavy majorities favored increased participation in world affairs.[18] Americans had rejected isolationism and placed their confidence in a general internationalism (only two votes were recorded in the Senate against membership in the United Nations), but they had retained their traditional aversion to the political complications of the European world. It was as if they had recognized the involvement of the New World in the world at large without recognizing any change in their relationships with the specific countries of the Old World.

The admiration and affection between the English Prime Minister and the American President had, despite dissension, nevertheless sustained a partnership in world affairs closer than anything ever achieved in American history. The two leaders exchanged over seventeen hundred messages, met together at nine conferences, and shared rooms at the White House, Hyde Park, or Roosevelt's retreat in the Maryland Blue Mountains. In their relationship, as Robert Sherwood has pointed out, "the sacred tradition" that the American statesman is "plain, blunt, down to earth, ingenuous to a fault," while the English statesman is "sly, subtle, devious and eventually triumphant," had become confused. Churchill quickly learned that Roosevelt was "an artful dodger who could not readily be pinned down on specific points," and Roosevelt discovered just "how pertinacious the Prime Minister could be in pursuance of a purpose."[19] More often than not the Englishman, because of the weight of the American military position, was forced to bow to the American, and if Churchill was shrewd and cunning in appraising the political situation in Europe as the war drew to a close, he did not succeed in persuading Roosevelt and Truman to look at the world through his eyes. (An American, later wakened to the realities of the conflict with Russia, might wish he had).

[18] For polls on anti-British feeling and indifference to foreign policy problems at the end of the war see Gabriel A. Almond, *The American People and Foreign Policy* (New York, Praeger, 1960), pp. 96, 76.
[19] *Roosevelt and Hopkins*, p. 364.

In their own countries both men had been bitterly controversial figures, the American attacked for his liberalism by his Republican opponents, the Englishman attacked for his conservatism by his Labor opposition. Across the water they both increasingly enjoyed on the other shore a remarkable reverence, unqualified by partisan animosities. Hopkins was staggered at Churchill's defeat in the general election shortly before the Japanese surrender and saluted him as "a gallant fighter" whose deeds would "go down in Anglo-Saxon history for all time."[20] On the evening of April 12, 1948, when the English statue of Franklin Roosevelt was unveiled in Grosvenor Square, Winston Churchill expressed his conviction that "in Roosevelt's life and by his actions he changed, he altered decisively and permanently, the social axis, the moral axis, of mankind by involving the New World inexorably and irrevocably in the fortunes of the Old."[21]

On the American side Harry Hopkins in August, 1945, foresaw the future in the memoranda he wrote for an unfinished book:

If I were to lay down the most cardinal principle of our foreign policy, it would be that we make absolutely sure that now and forever the United States and Great Britain are going to see eye to eye on major matters of world policy. It is easy to say that. It is hard to do, but it can be done and the effort is worth it.

Though he was still confident that the Soviet Union was only interested in protecting its borders from unfriendly states, he did prophesy that future relations with Russia were going to be "seriously handicapped" by deep-rooted differences "between our fundamental notions of human liberty—freedom of speech, freedom of the press and freedom of worship." He thought it essential too that France be made sure of American friendship and economic support—a policy needed for "all of Western Europe."[22]

The American people would soon be forced to show whether they saw as clearly as Hopkins how the world had changed—that the familiar outlines in the relationship of the New World to the

[20] Letter to General Ismay, July 28, 1945, quoted by Sherwood, *ibid.*, pp. 919–920.
[21] Quoted by Sherwood, *ibid.*, p. 933.
[22] Quoted by Sherwood, *ibid.*, pp. 922, 942.

Old had indeed dissolved. Early in 1946 the Truman Administration introduced the proposal of a $3.75 billion loan to the British in return for ending restrictions on exchange of sterling for other currencies. The scheme was at first discussed and defended as a measure to liberate international trade, but the political undertones were much more significant. The isolationists and conservatives were aroused to play upon American fears of the British Empire, socialism, and the New Deal. These were insidiously linked by raising the specter of the economist Lord Keynes as a sinister mastermind behind the spending policies of Roosevelt and the loan proposal of Truman.[23] Conventional suspicion of British colonial policy, especially voiced by Irish-American spokesmen, mingled with the distrust of free enterprisers for the socialist Labor government of Britain. Politicians with Jewish constituencies were also highly critical of British policy in Palestine. But the attack made by Republican Representative Karl Mundt of South Dakota was the most striking illustration of the pre-Cold-War mood of the Congress. On record as an opponent of Lend-Lease in 1941, he branded the current measure "Russia-baiting dollar diplomacy and monetary imperialism" which would threaten the peace by "dividing the world into rival camps," dashing the generous hopes for the United Nations.[24] His position demonstrated the compatibility of isolationist impulses and prejudices with the general internationalism of the time.

Isolationism had not disappeared with the America First organization in 1941. Seventy-five Representatives and twelve Senators, who had voted against Lend-Lease, also voted against the British loan. Only twenty-seven former isolationists had changed their outlook since 1941 towards aiding Britain.[25] In the upper house Senators Bilbo, Ellender, Langer, and Wheeler staged a near filibuster. An amendment to make permanent the American use of British bases under lease during the war was defeated by only

[23] See Representative Smith, *Congressional Record*, 79th Cong., 2nd sess., 92:7 (July 12, 1946), 8825–8830.

[24] *Ibid.*, p. 8852. Mundt later became a rabid supporter of the indiscriminate and irresponsible anti-Communism of the McCarthy era, exchanging one popular mood for another.

[25] The measure passed in the Senate 46–34 and in the House 219–155.

five votes. Senator Arthur H. Vandenberg of Michigan, who had recently announced his conversion from isolationism, split the Republicans by upholding the Administration, and a Democratic majority passed the measure. Republican opponents in the House outnumbered Republican supporters two to one, but the Democrats mustered their heavy forces after majority leader McCormack had implied that the bill was necessary to counter a Soviet attempt to dominate Europe. He evasively refused to admit that this political motive was fundamental to the purpose of the proposal, but he cited the Soviet Union as a civilization "the opposite of ours . . . challenging our civilization directly and other civilizations indirectly."[26] Outside the halls of Congress the bill found solid support from organizations of businessmen, bankers, farmers, and labor. Before the year ended, the British and American zones in Germany were economically merged.

While the British loan was being debated, free elections were held in Greece under supervision of representatives from America, Britain, and France. As politicians in Congress plucked the chords of anti-British anticolonial sentiments in American hearts, a victorious conservative royalist party in Greece recalled King George II, and the British magnanimously announced the end of their imperial rule in India and Burma. A new world was in the making, confounding old American prejudices and challenging American wills. The contours of the Old World had shifted bewilderingly under the American gaze, which had been forced to confront its special relationship to England. The "ties of an indissoluble history" had survived the tension of wartime collaboration and had earned limited recognition of their continuing vitality.

[26] *Congressional Record*, 79th Cong., 2nd sess., 92:7 (July 12, 1946), 8824.

CHAPTER

13

AN ATLANTIC COMMUNITY

IN 1947 THE AMERICAN GOVERNMENT began to build the structure of the post-war world in a bold style which fashioned itself on the profoundly altered relationship of the New World to the Old. The threat of Soviet imperialism and its American counterresponse dramatized the political collapse of Europe as a self-sufficient system. With bipartisan support and public approval the American tradition of peacetime nonentanglement in European affairs was scrapped. But the emotions upon which that tradition had fed survived to express themselves in recurring angry assaults, often as outrageous as they were outraged, against the new consensus built upon the ruins of the old order, which the Second World War had brought tumbling to the ground. The conflict would continue to shape the course of the new historical relationship which had transformed both the New World and the Old, flattened out their differences, politically and culturally, made them uneasy partners in an Atlantic alliance, and confounded the conventional mythology an earlier history had favored.

The generous but abstract internationalism of the war years, supported by Democrats, Republicans, and the general public, proved to be inadequate as a primary reliance when the fissures in the Grand Alliance were at last clearly visible. Soviet satellite pressures on Greece and Turkey, combined with the candid confession by the British of their inability to sustain the balance of power by themselves, forced the American government to reappraise cherished expectations of the restoration of a normal European world, a world that would not be dependent on American power. President Truman (who had as a boy in thick-lensed glasses spent long hours in the library reading about the Middle East, while his peers played sand-lot baseball) reacted vigorously to the announcement of British withdrawal from former outposts. His proposal of a combination of economic and military aid as requested by Greece and Turkey met a mixed reaction based upon increasingly irrelevant hopes and fears: the governments of these countries were not democratically chaste, the United Nations was by-passed, the intervention would lead to war, British chestnuts were being pulled from the fire. When the Administration had carefully explained the imminence of the danger, the altered balance of power, and the inability of the United Nations to meet the situation, large majorities of both parties in both branches of Congress came to his support under the pressure of the mounting fears of Soviet expansion.

Senator Arthur M. Vandenberg, Republican foreign-policy leader, had requested the broad exposition of a Cold-War context of conflict in order to win public support, though some of the President's advisers, especially George F. Kennan in the State Department, were highly critical of the ideological sweep and military aid emphasis of the doctrine.[1] Since the conservative isolationists of the prewar years had been hostile to the Soviets, they were in the early post-war years hard pressed to find suitable arguments against intervention. Senator Robert A. Taft, for example, the revered leader of the Republican right wing, found himself in

[1] See Joseph M. Jones, *The Fifteen Weeks* (New York, Viking, 1955), pp. 142–143, 155.

league with the left-wing Democrat Henry A. Wallace in protesting that Truman's action would create a bipolar world of "zones of political influence."[2] It was a mark of the post-war change in outlook since the debate over Lend-Lease in 1941 that now the issue of intervention was largely discussed in the context of national or United Nations responsibility for taking action.

The Spring of 1947 exposed the awesome dimensions of the need for American involvement with Europe. The continent was reeling from the devastation of war and a hard winter. It was suffering from crop failures, famines, and fuel shortages; its finances were a shambles; and some of its important Cabinet posts in France and Italy were held by Communists. While Undersecretary of State Dean Acheson was looking ahead to the need for a general European recovery program, his immediate superior, General George C. Marshall, accompanied by John Foster Dulles, was finding out at the Moscow Conference of the Council of Foreign Ministers that agreement with Soviet Russia on the political future of Germany was impossible and that her fate turned upon the general problem of Europe.

The ideas of Acheson, Marshall, and George F. Kennan, head of the State Department's recently created Policy Planning Staff, converged on the need for what columnist Walter Lippmann described as a peacetime Lend-Lease program for Europe as a whole with the needs and distribution estimated by the Europeans themselves. Presented to all of Europe (including Russia and its satellites, which refused to participate), the European Cooperation Act of 1948 (Marshall Plan) authorized American aid to sixteen Western European nations and West Germany on a systematic four-year basis with the purpose of fostering economic and political stability on a continent threatened by "hunger, poverty, desperation, and chaos." This "most unsordid act in history," as Churchill called it, brought Western Europe and America into peacetime partnership for common action. Though spokesmen for the far left and right wings of the American spectrum opposed the new program (an unlikely combination of *The*

[2] Quoted by Jones, *ibid.*, p. 175.

Wall Street Journal with The Progressive Citizens for America), heavy bipartisan majorities were racked up in both houses of Congress.[3]

Western Europe was stimulated into taking the first steps towards unity, which increasingly became an avowed object of American policy. With the Soviet coup in Prague and the blockade of Berlin the Europeans, spurred by Britain's Ernest Bevin, moved to establish a military counterpart to their economic cooperation. In March, 1948, Great Britain, France, the Netherlands, Belgium, and Luxembourg signed the Brussels Pact of collective self-defense. President Truman interpreted the move as a signal for American support, and Senator Vandenberg laid the basis for American participation by a resolution which called for collective arrangements for mutual defense under Article 51 of the United Nations Charter. Definitive recognition of the need for particular alliances, rather than merely for general collective security under Wilsonian principles, came with the formation of the North Atlantic Treaty Alliance of April, 1949, which joined the United States, Canada, and ten European nations in a common defense of "the security of the North Atlantic area."

Despite the revolutionary nature of this twenty-year, peacetime alliance, only two Democrats and eleven Republicans refused to sanction this major departure from venerable American tradition. The voices of the past still summoned spirits from the deep, but they would not come when called. In the Senate hearings traditionalists, Progressives, and reactionaries had combined to attack the alliance, finding common ground in the conventional opposition to Old World power politics from abroad. To the traditionalist the alliance was a challenge, as the United Nations was not, to "uniquely American traditions and principles underlying the New World dream, a practical program, of a New World civilization made secure and ever better despite the Old World's inner decay and decline which America is powerless to cure."[4]

[3] See *ibid.*, pp. 225–256.
[4] Hamilton A. Long, "A Traditionalist's 10 American Principles of a Sound Foreign Policy in this Russo-American Era," *North Atlantic Treaty,*

Progressives (who admired the New Deal and still adhered to the outdated policy of Soviet-American collaboration and primary reliance on the United Nations) and reactionaries (who abhorred both welfare liberalism and internationalism of any kind) had a common penchant for simplistic conspiratorial interpretations of history, which led them to a joint attack on some of the same scapegoats. Wallace (whose Progressive Party had been heavily invaded by Communists in 1948) condemned the pact as a provocative piece of power politics invented by Winston Churchill in the interests of British imperialism and supported by big business and the Catholic Church. He was inclined to justify by sympathetic understanding every move of the Soviets which had alarmed the Administration; while the far right, furiously anti-Communist in principle, was equally sure that "Perfidious Albion," abetted by Acheson cast as an arch-Anglophile, and the greedy "Shylocks" of Wall Street were the sinister architects of the Alliance. Progressives were fearful that their bogies—Britain and Big Business—would entangle America with Fascist elements in Spain or Portugal; reactionaries were fearful that the same diabolic forces would entangle America with socialist states, instead of with "reliable" anti-Communist countries like Spain and Portugal. Spokesmen for certain German-American and Irish-American groups added their Anglophobia, based on ethnic ties and grievances, to the debate.[5] But these prejudices no longer commanded significant power in Congress.

The new alignment with Western Europe was more than a strategic response to Soviet pressures. Though the Administration did not sanction the recently formed Atlantic Union Committee—which praised the pact as a steppingstone to political federation of its partners—Secretary Acheson did stress the liberating idea of an Atlantic Community, joined by common political experience, hospitality to liberal democracy, and cultural affinities, as well as by industrial and strategic mutual interests:

Hearings, Committee on Foreign Relations, Senate, 81st Cong., 1st sess., Part 3, pp. 1258–1259.

[5] For Wallace see *ibid.*, Part 2, pp. 417–479; for reactionaries see *ibid.*, pp. 713–716; for ethnic views see *ibid.*, Part 3, pp. 1094–1102, 1227–1231.

The North Atlantic Treaty, which now formally unites them, is the product of at least three hundred and fifty years of history, perhaps more. There developed on our Atlantic coast a community, which has spread across the continent, connected with Western Europe by common institutions and moral and ethical beliefs. Similarities of this kind are not superficial, but fundamental. They are the strongest kind of ties, because they are based on moral conviction, on acceptance of the same values in life. . . .

It is clear that the North Atlantic pact is not an improvisation. It is the statement of the facts and lessons of history. We have learned our history lesson from two world wars in less than half a century. That experience has taught us that the control of Europe by a single aggressive unfriendly power would constitute an intolerable threat to the national security of the United States.[6]

Despite the major responsibilities which the United States carried as the strongest member of the alliance, the Administration was careful to avoid any hint of domination over lesser powers. The Marshall Plan had deliberately encouraged European assessment of the economic and financial needs of the Atlantic area and, though it envisaged the breaking-down of European barriers of tariffs and cartels, Acheson had successfully argued against making extension of aid conditional on European compliance with American suggestions for closer association. "We must never forget that we are dealing not with abstractions," Acheson told the Senate, "but with people. Our allies in Western Europe are human beings, with human hopes and fears. Because of the constructive and productive efforts which we and they have put forth together in recent months, their hopes today are greater than their fears. We must keep their hopes in the ascendancy."[7] Out of deference to European feelings and a United Nations recommendation he refrained from sending an ambassador to Franco's Spain, nor did he, despite pressure from Senatorial friends of the regime, press for integration of Spain into the NATO system without consider-

[6] "The Meaning of the North Atlantic Pact," *Department of State Bulletin*, 20 (March 27, 1949), 385.

[7] *Military Assistance Program*, Joint Hearings, Committee on Foreign Relations and Committee on Armed Services, Senate, 81st Cong., 1st sess. (August 8, 1949), p. 10.

ation of the attitude of American allies. (In 1950 the President did send an ambassador to Spain when the symbolic gesture of not sending one had clearly produced no changes in General Franco's authoritarian system; the next year, under the impact of the Korean War, bilateral agreements were made with the Spanish ruler for American air and naval bases in Spain.) Acheson understood that the United States had to take the lead in shoring up the West, but he also grasped the more subtle point that

we will continue to be accepted as the leader only if the other countries believe that the pattern of responsibility within which we operate is a responsibility to interests which are broader than our own—that we know today what Thomas Jefferson was talking about when he spoke of the need of paying a decent respect to the opinions of mankind.[8]

A decent respect for the opinions of Great Britain and Western Europe was precisely what the American isolationist tradition was sworn never to indulge. Its voices had been temporarily drowned out by the war and by the new policy of "containment" (in Kennan's authoritative phrase) of Soviet expansion, which gave priority to Western Europe. But these guardians of the native pieties, ever since the routing of left-wing isolationism by the Progressive Party's demoralization through Communist influence, were now massed on the right wing of the Republican party. Embittered by nearly twenty years of wandering in the political wilderness, they found explosive materials for a furious campaign to discredit the New Deal and the new foreign policy in the inflammatory issue of Communist infiltration (dramatized by the case of Alger Hiss), the fall of China to the Communists in 1949, and the public's impatience with the drawn-out agonies of the Korean War. The death of Senator Vandenberg, who had skillfully performed the essential work of mediating the new policies to the Republican Party, provided the irreconcilables with their opportunity. Republican leadership fell to Senator Taft, a foreign aid skeptic, a

[8] "An Estimate of the Present World Situation," *State Department Bulletin*, 25 (July 23, 1951), 128. Acheson's policies are sympathetically traced in McGeorge Bundy, ed., *The Pattern of Responsibility* (Boston, Houghton Mifflin, 1952).

disbeliever in NATO, and an enemy of Truman's intervention in Korea. The stage was set for the pent-up emotions of nostalgia, frustration, and revenge to come surging to the surface.

The "Great Debate" on the Truman-Acheson policy was first launched by Herbert Hoover as the Administration prepared to implement its "forward strategy" of making the Elbe the first line of defense by sending General Eisenhower abroad as Supreme Allied Commander in Europe and strengthening the NATO defense forces with American ground troops. Hoover, in a nationally broadcast address in December, 1950, revived the pre-Pearl Harbor idea of the Western Hemisphere as "the Gibraltar of Western Civilization," which could be defended by sea and air power alone. He was not opposed to a base in Britain, if it gave up "flirting with appeasement of Communist China," but he urged that the Europeans, as a condition for American aid, prove their "spiritual strength and unity" by providing over a hundred combat divisions as "a sure dam against the Red flood."[9] The United States, he felt, did not need any allies, the ones it had were too indulgent of socialist parties, and it should give aid only when that aid was no longer critical. His traditional suspicion of Europe and dedication to the American dream of a self-sufficient New World animated the whole speech.

Senator Taft led the attack in the Senate against the sending of troops to Europe by seeking to put a fixed limit to the number of divisions and to keep the decisions in the hands of Congress. He inclined towards Hoover's emphasis on sea and air power in non-European bases and called for "re-examination" of the policy of aid to Europe. Taft denied that anybody any longer could be meaningfully called an "isolationist," but Acheson witheringly replied that "a re-examinist might be a farmer that goes out every morning and pulls up all his crops to see how they have done during the night."[10] Taft did admit that a Soviet attack on

[9] See "Our National Policies in This Crisis," *Addresses Upon the American Road 1950–1955* (Stanford, Stanford University Press, 1955), pp. 3–10.
[10] "Plowing a Straight Furrow," *State Department Bulletin*, 23 (November 27, 1950), 839. For Taft's views see *Assignment of Ground Forces of the United States to Duty in the European Area*, Hearings, Committee on

Germany or any Atlantic Pact country would bring the United States into war, but he opposed an American commander for NATO, did not consider the loss of Western Europe fatal, and complacently assumed the perpetuity of America's atomic advantage. His traditionalist illusions were betrayed in his citation of the Monroe Doctrine as proof of past American ability to deter European invasion, as if the friendly British fleet had never existed.

The Hoover-Taft objection that American land forces could not stop an all-out Russian attack missed the point. The problem, as the Secretary explained, was to provide insurance against the temptation of an easy take-over, conquest by subversion, disguised aggression through a satellite, the growth of neutralism, and the future waning of America's atomic advantage. Acheson's real difference with his opponents lay in his basic premise: "We are bound to our allies by ties of common interest, and a clear appreciation of these ties is the fundamental basis of the actions we are here discussing."[11] The prestige of General Eisenhower's testimony that European action depended upon America's example of leadership ensured the passage of the proposal, though its critics were successful in making it "the sense of the Senate" that future Congressional authorization would be necessary for more than the current four divisions.

The enemies of the Atlantic Community concept had yet to find a popular rallying-cry. Their role had been to act as a drag on Administration policy, but the pre-Pearl Harbor myth of a self-sufficient Western Hemisphere was not entirely convincing even to Senator Taft, who, groping for new ground, came to favor an alliance with Britain.[12] The right-wing Republicans at last discovered a popular cause and a charismatic hero when President Truman recalled General Douglas MacArthur from his command of the United Nations forces in Korea. Intervention to

---

Foreign Relations and Committee on Armed Services, Senate, 82nd Cong., 1st sess. (February, 1951), 603–666. Former Ambassador Joseph P. Kennedy also supported Hoover's position.

[11] *Assignment of Ground Forces* (February 16, 1951), p. 84.

[12] See his Address at Arden House, in *United States—Western Europe Relationships as Viewed Within the Present World-wide International Environment* (American Assembly, 1951), pp. 188–196.

protect South Korea had been widely supported at first; as the war turned into a costly stalemate, the public mood hardened against the Administration. News of the General's dismissal provoked national shock, and the President and his Secretary were burned in effigy in several communities.

From the Administration's point of view the recall of the General was necessary in order to assert civilian supremacy over the military, to reaffirm the political logic of limited war, which MacArthur had publicly challenged and disobeyed, and to reassure America's anxious allies of American restraint. The General had not only sought support from dissident Republicans for his own strategy by writing the House minority leader; he had also violated Administration policy by sending non-Korean troops into the area near the Manchurian frontier; and he had embarrassed the President's decision to seek a settlement with the Chinese by making a statement insulting to the enemy, threatening extension of the conflict, and proposing terms that precluded any accommodation. The enemies of the Administration at home seized upon the dismissal of a military hero by an unpopular President as the occasion for an angry challenge of the Truman-Acheson foreign policy.

That former isolationists should identify themselves with MacArthur's cause, when his own strategy was to intervene further by blockading the China coast and bombing the interior bases in Manchuria, is a paradox easily explained by the traditional linkage of isolationist attitudes with hostility to Europe. The General himself had been bitterly disappointed throughout the Second World War because his suggestions for a second front in the Pacific had not been followed. At the hearings held on his dismissal he accused the British of shipping strategic materials to China through Hong Kong, ignoring the fact that they engaged in the same kind of normal trade that he permitted Japan under American occupation. He could only explain his failure to predict Chinese intervention in the Korean War by the speculative hypothesis that the British traitors, Burgess and MacLean, must have told the enemy about the strategy of not carrying the conflict to the Manchurian air bases. Finally, he had long been dedicated to a point of view in flat contradiction to the Administration's commitment to the fundamental priority of Europe: "Europe is a dying system. It is worn out and run down, and will become an economic and industrial hegemony of Soviet Russia. . . . The lands touching the Pacific with their billions of inhabitants will determine the course of history for the next ten thousand years."[13] If the Pacific had long been "a Republican ocean," the old "America Firsters" now found it an ideological sanctuary. "No one in it," as Richard H. Rovere and Arthur M. Schlesinger, Jr. have pointed out, "had to abate for a moment his dislike of Roosevelt, Churchill, the New Deal, the British, the Russians or Europe."[14] It is not at all surprising, therefore, that the General was hailed by the Hearst and McCormick press and exploited by Republican isolationists, led by Senator Taft and Herbert Hoover. If there was historical symbolism in the coincidence of MacArthur's triumphant appearance before the joint session of Congress on the anniversary of the day when the embattled farmers at Concord and Lexington fired the shots heard round the world at the redcoats, there was an epiphany in the event as seen by reverent isolationists: "We saw a great hunk of God in the flesh, the voice of God."[15]

The long hearings before the Senate Armed Services and Foreign Relations Committees, which hypnotized the country for a month, not only proved that the Joint Chiefs of Staff supported the President in repudiating MacArthur's military strategy; they also demonstrated that the General's appeal to the old isolationists lay in his determination to fight the war even if it meant "going it alone" and in his suspicion that American policies were "largely influenced, if not indeed in some instances, dictated, from

[13] November 22, 1944, as quoted by Bert Andrews from an interview with MacArthur, in Walter Millis, ed., *The Forrestal Diaries* (New York, Viking, 1951), p. 18. For a thorough critical account of the Truman-MacArthur affairs see John W. Spanier, *The Truman-MacArthur Controversy and the Korean War* (Cambridge, Belknap Press, 1959). For the General's anti-European bias see pp. 93–94, 174–176.

[14] *The General and the President* (New York, Farrar, Straus, and Young, 1951), p. 230.

[15] Rep. Dewey Short, quoted by Rovere and Schlesinger, *ibid.*, p. 16.

abroad."[16] His attitude contrasted sharply with President Truman's acceptance of the necessities of a coalition strategy and his concern for European interests: "Our European allies are nearer to Russia than we are. They are in far greater danger. If we act without regard to the danger that faces them, they may act without regard to the dangers that we face. . . . We cannot go it alone in Asia and go it in company in Europe."[17]

MacArthur's position was quickly exploited by the right wing. After the hearings he increasingly stressed the danger not of any external threat but "rather of insidious forces working from within which have already so drastically altered the character of our . . . American way of life."[18] This conspiratorial theme played directly into the hands of the right-wing Republicans who had spent much of the hearings raking over the Yalta agreements and the fall of China in 1949, seeking to link together in the public mind the names of Hiss, Acheson, Marshall, and Truman, and thus nourishing the growing public fear and suspicion that treason in high places accounted for America's reverses. Those who had forged the links with Western Europe were made prime targets.

On this tactic of feeding and stimulating public anxiety about domestic subversion Senator Joseph McCarthy cynically built his sensational career. There was no clear evidence that Communist penetration of American society and government in the 1930s and 1940s had made any significant impact on American foreign policy; Communist infiltration had largely become by 1950 a dated episode of an earlier age of innocence. But McCarthy was more than equal to these limitations of reality, and he created his own garbled record of the past and image of the present for a credulous public, a frustrated party, and a revengeful crew of unforgiving isolationists. He had first fought for public attention in 1949 by exploiting a document (actually a piece of Communist propaganda) designed to show that American officials had brutally

[16] Speech at Austin, Texas, June 13, 1951. See *Congressional Quarterly*, 7 (1951), 252.

[17] "Why We Need Allies," *State Department Bulletin*, 24 (May 14, 1951), 765.

[18] Address before the Massachusetts Legislature in Boston, July 25, 1951, *The General and the President*, Appendix VII, p. 312.

abused German prisoners of war, a performance calculated to appeal to those German-Americans of his state who had long nursed corrosive doubts about the wisdom of American entrance into World War II. In the troops-to-Europe debate he rejected both the Truman-Acheson and Hoover-Taft positions, making a plea instead for major reliance upon the "two great potential sources of anti-Communist manpower," Western Germany and Spain. The Europe he favored was precisely the one which lay on the periphery of the most deeply rooted area of the Atlantic Community. He kept up a steady barrage of hostile fire upon the State Department, the Foreign Service, the Information Agency, the Voice of America, and British policy, and he climaxed his public career with a sort of shabby consistency by appearing in 1956 at a Washington's Birthday rally in Carnegie Hall, sponsored by the "For America" organization, to unite reactionary isolationists under the banner of General MacArthur.[19] The General had become a symbol for the lost causes of the fanatic right-wing isolationists who had never made their peace with the post-Depression world. On the lunatic fringe Gerald L. K. Smith's Christian Nationalist Front and Merwin K. Hart's National Economic Council—whose members were drawn to both McCarthy and MacArthur—mingled hatred of the New Deal, Europe, Communists, and Jews in furious irrational diatribes against the United Nations, the Marshall Plan, and the Atlantic Pact. The honorable tradition of nonentanglement had fizzled out into a reactionary spasm of bitter demagogic rant.

Despite the nationwide keening over General MacArthur's return from Korea, the enemies of the bipartisan consensus on the

---

[19] For McCarthy's foreign policy views on Europe see "American Foreign Policy" (March 14, 1951), reprinted from the *Congressional Record*, in *Major Speeches and Debates of Senator Joe McCarthy 1950-51*, pp. 187-213. For a detailed refutation of McCarthy's charges, an exposure of his tactics, and an analysis of his support see James Rorty and Moshe Decter, *McCarthy and the Communists* (Boston, Beacon, 1954). McCarthy shifted to isolationism in 1950. The linkage of McCarthy and the isolationists is well established in Selig Adler, *The Isolationist Impulse: Its Twentieth-Century Reaction* (New York, Abelard-Schuman, 1957), pp. 456-464, 468-470. See also Stanley K. Bigman, "The New Internationalism Under Attack," *Public Opinion Quarterly*, 14 (Summer, 1950), 235-261.

new alignment with Europe, who stood on the shores of the New World like so many King Canutes defying the ocean, did not succeed in turning back the tide. The prestige of another general, who symbolized American commitment to Europe, swept the Republicans into power in 1952. General Eisenhower was forced to compromise with both Senators Taft and McCarthy, whose continuing influence would condition the course of the new Administration; and the Secretary of State, John Foster Dulles, rhetorically challenged the "containment" policy with slogans of "liberation" of Soviet-dominated areas and "unleashing" the Chinese Nationalists, but these political manoeuvers concealed without destroying a basic continuity of policy.

Every challenge of the new internationalism had produced a debate in which its defenders had displayed powerful resources of argument, knowledge, and witnesses to educate the public on the rationale of the new programs. The turbulence of controversy in the press and among the politicians obscured the fact that in September, 1953, eighty-one percent of a national poll was convinced that the United States could not "sit out" another war in Europe, and only nine percent voted for halting and reducing American commitments abroad. The Plains states and East Central states of the Middle West still remained the hard Congressional core of "old-guard" Republicanism, and Southern legislators increasingly after 1952 would put up a growing share of the resistance to foreign aid programs; but neither region, class, nor party was a clear index to the friends and enemies of the new departures in foreign policy.[20]

Yet some polls left a margin of doubt that alignment with Western Europe had been realistically accepted in the public mind. Nearly half of the citizens questioned in the 1953 poll placed their confidence in general internationalism of the Wilsonian kind, choosing a strengthened United Nations or world government over the somewhat less utopian proposal of a feder-

[20] See Elmo Roper, "American Attitudes on World Organization," *Public Opinion Quarterly*, **17** (Winter, 1953), 401–442; Samuel Lubell, *Revolt of the Moderates* (New York, Harper, 1956), pp. 98, 100, 274.

ation of the democratic states. The idea of the Atlantic Community, the most important transformation in the American tradition of setting itself as a New World in opposition to the Old, had, nevertheless, survived the traumas of birth.

The American commitment to England and Western Europe, sustained by the collaborative experience of the war, had brought remarkable results. Looking with an American pragmatist's eye on the post-war chaos of Europe and its existentialist philosophy of despair, John Dewey had found it "now more definitively the *old* world than ever before."[21] Under the stimulus of American help and leadership European action proved the American philosopher wrong. The hopes of the Marshall Plan were generously fulfilled by the economic recovery of Europe. The United States, the United Kingdom, and Canada joined seventeen European countries to liberalize European trade and payments through the Organization for European Economic Cooperation. These European states (except for Spain, Switzerland, and Portugal) formed a parliamentary forum, the Council of Europe, to promote cultural relations and civil rights. The French successfully organized the economic integration of coal and steel industries for France, Germany, Italy, and the Benelux countries. In 1958 these same partners of "Little Europe" set in motion a Common Market and, in the following year, a scheme for integrating the production and use of atomic energy. Meanwhile NATO (later expanded to include Greece, Turkey, and West Germany) had established in 1951 a Supreme Allied Command under General Eisenhower, who had been requested by the Europeans themselves to head "balanced, collective forces" with a corps of officers internationally trained to represent the needs of the alliance as a whole. By 1952 NATO had a permanent organization of national ambassadors sitting continuously in Paris to reconcile national viewpoints on economic, military problems with the collective outlook of its staff. Primarily a military security treaty, NATO was formed, never-

[21] Letter to Robert V. Daniels, October 28, 1949, "Letters of John Dewey to Robert V. Daniels, 1946–1950," *Journal of History of Ideas*, 20 (October-December, 1959), 572.

theless, with explicit recognition in its text of the "common heritage and civilization of their peoples, founded on the principles of democracy, individual liberty and the rule of law," and its representatives from the smaller countries persistently kept before the eyes of the larger powers its long-run social and economic purposes as an Atlantic Community.[22]

The historic Old World was dead, but Europe had come alive again to play its part as a partner with America in a common destiny. MacArthur's judgment of Europe as a "dying system" was discredited by the actions of the Americans and Europeans whom his supporters had chosen to regard as political enemies. To confound the widespread prejudice of American conservatives— Hoover was their classic spokesman—that European countries by departing from the gospel of "free enterprise" had fallen into original sin, the socialist welfare states of the United Kingdom, Scandinavia, and the Netherlands provided more stability, more civil liberties, and more immunity to totalitarian subversion and influence from left or right than the more market-oriented countries of France, Italy, and West Germany.[23] The socialist states had themselves significantly qualified the rigidity and orthodoxy of doctrinaire socialism, while the American government, ever since the Progressive era of the Republican Roosevelt, had qualified its market economy by social services and pragmatic regulation. The only significant ideological gulf lay between totalitarian and democratic states. America and most of Western Europe were now together in one camp, engaged in the demanding task of framing a common policy of defense against Soviet expansion.[24] The unity of the "West"—a term which strikingly marked the

[22] For the revival of Europe since the war see Theodore H. White, *Fire in the Ashes: Europe in Mid-Century* (New York, William Sloane, 1953); Arnold J. Zurcher, *The Struggle to Unite Europe 1940-1958* (Washington Square, New York University Press, 1958); Ben T. Moore, *NATO and the Future of Europe* (New York, Harper, 1958).

[23] See Klaus Knorr, "The European Welfare State in the Atlantic System," *World Politics*, 3 (1950–1951), 417–449.

[24] There are, of course, democratic states, like Israel, Switzerland, and Sweden, outside of NATO and undemocratic states, like Portugal and Turkey, within it.

breakdown of old antagonisms—was part aspiration and part achievement. It would have to struggle for a secure foothold in the rugged terrain of modern history, strewn with booby traps, blind alleys, and the bones of lost travelers.

CHAPTER

14

THE PLENIPOTENTIARIES

In 1951 one of America's most distinguished journalists, William L. Shirer, whose work had carried him to the major capitals of Europe ever since 1925, could sum up his travels in *Midcentury Journey* as a requiem for the end of a world he had known: "Europe then was still the center of the world, as it had been since the Renaissance. . . . Now not even the Great Powers in Europe, despite their eminent civilization and the glory of their long history, were strong enough to stand on their own feet."[1] But the European political system had been replaced by an Atlantic system, and in ten years Shirer's picture of a Europe exhausted by war, economic decline, and loss of nerve, would become badly dated. With the stimulus of American aid the European countries had surpassed the United States in monetary stability and gold reserves, while they were narrowing the gap in productivity by their faster rate of industrial growth as a total region. The Old World had become a new world.

[1] *Midcentury Journey: The Western World Through Its Years of Conflict* (New York, Farrar, Straus, and Cudahy, 1952), pp. 251–252. For the revival of post-war Europe in the Fifties see Blair Bolles, *The Big Change in Europe* (New York, Norton, 1958).

The passionate pilgrims of the nineteenth century, who went to Europe to drink at "the pure fountains of wisdom" or revel in "the shadowy grandeurs of the past," as well as the expatriates of the early 1920s, who found abroad a haven of art and individualism, would both have to rub their eyes at the contemporary scene. Europe was no longer the cultural capital of the world. Fascism and the war had uprooted many of Europe's most distinguished intellectuals; and Mann, Einstein, Fermi, Toscanini, and Salvemini—to name only a few—found a hospitable home in America, while American science, scholarship, and art steadily exerted an attraction and a force of their own. In the age of the Fulbright Fellowship and the "Americanization" of Europe, cultural expatriation was an increasingly obsolete American fashion. The exodus had been nationalized, and in American soldiers, government personnel, businessmen, teachers, and ordinary tourists, American writers found new material for the subjects that had attracted Hawthorne, James, Twain, Hemingway, and Lewis.

The contemporary American invasion of Europe was no flight from American problems; it was in pursuit of the responsibilities of power that agents of government, business, and education swarmed over the world. The European absorption, though not largest, was still beyond any precedent. By 1958 nearly 14,000 civilians alone were paid by the government for overseas work, and nearly 3,000 citizens (and over 400,000 foreign nationals) worked for American businesses in Europe. In the academic year 1957–1958 over 200 universities were sending faculty members abroad, while nearly 13,000 students had some foreign experience, usually in Western Europe. Travel to Europe had become, especially by comparison with the Victorian Grand Tour, thoroughly democratized. Housewives made up the largest category; clerks and secretaries considerably outnumbered business executives; and skilled and unskilled labor even topped teachers and students. Although most Americans still preferred home (if they had to live elsewhere, Canada would be their choice), a significant number were now living as Americans-in-Europe.[2]

[2] For government workers, businessmen, teachers, and students see Harlan

The statistics are mute about the quality of understanding in these "overseas Americans" who, unless well educated in their own country's history, were free to enjoy "the quite unsporting and unproductive pastime so commonly indulged in by Americans abroad of comparing the American dream to the foreign reality."[3] Often treated as easy marks for smalltime highway robbery, uneducated American tourists could find ready provocation for an outburst of rude chauvinism. The well-heeled and well-placed Americans in the business and diplomatic echelons inevitably displayed a standard of living, made in America, that could only excite envy, mixed with hostility. Some military authorities even looked with suspicion on civilian employees who preferred to live abroad or speak the local language. "If an American knows the local language," explained the commander of the Air Force's Materiel Command at Chateauroux, France, "he may be injecting wrong ideas into his dealings with the natives."[4] The teen-age dependents of military and political personnel in Europe, most of them in Germany, lived an incapsulated American life, which was transported across the Atlantic like a bottle of Coca-Cola. They reproduced American high schools, soda fountains, cheer leaders, and dating practices with a characteristic indifference to the language and politics of the foreign countries in which they were temporary prisoners. College students abroad, on the other hand, though woefully unprepared historically and linguistically, often agreed on the superiority of European aesthetic taste, the manners of children, and the quality of food, while some developed a xenophilia as distorted by stereotypical thinking as the xenophobia of "one-hundred-percent Americans."

The polar imagery of the American-European relationship

Cleveland, Gerard J. Mangone, and John Charles Adams, *The Overseas Americans* (New York, McGraw-Hill, 1960), pp. 71, table 2; 102–103, table 4; 194, 196, table 6. For tourists see *The American as International Traveller and Host*, Citizen Consultations, U.S. National Commission for UNESCO (December, 1954), pp. 8–10. For second-home preferences see the 1948 Roper poll cited in Otto Klineberg, *Tensions Affecting International Understanding: A Survey of Research*, Social Science Research Council, *Bulletin*, 62 (1950), 134.

[3] *The Overseas Americans*, p. 300.

[4] Art Buchwald in Paris," *New York Herald Tribune*, March 8, 1960.

was, above all, so conventional a part of everyone's intellectual baggage that its attractive symmetry easily substituted for any fresher vision of reality:

The Jeffersonian version: America is young, vigorous, progressive; Europe is old, tired, decadent. The Jamesian version: America is raw, innocent, susceptible; Europe is dark, engaging, profound. The Rooseveltian version: America is practical, experimental, promising; Europe is helpless, reactionary, tragic.[5]

These formulae, exploited on both sides of the Atlantic, often in pride and prejudice, were frequently pressed into the service of polemics over "anti-Americanism," instead of clarifying a dialogue which aimed at the creation of a common American-European community within Western Civilization.

The extraordinary revival of Henry James among American literary critics ever since 1943 testifies to the relevance of the "international theme" in an age of unprecedented involvement with Europe. The European experience of war's destruction, political collaboration, and totalitarian excesses provided new settings for the traditional subject of American innocence abroad. The heroes of these contemporary stories, who are marked by an idealizing of themselves or the countries of their quests, wake up to a disenchantment which either ends in alienation or maturation. The "unsophisticates" of Hollis Alpert's *Some Other Time*, after a brief fascination in Paris with exotic sexuality, black market operations, and girls with collaborationist pasts, return to the American suburbs out of a conventional need for uncomplicated lives and freedom from the wounds of the past and fears of the future. The idealistic, inexperienced American of David Buckley's *Pride of Innocence*, set in demoralized, occupied Germany,

[5] Melvin J. Lasky, "Literature and the Arts," in *America and the Mind of Europe*, introduction by Lewis Galantière (New York, Library Publishers, 1952), p. 89. For teenagers see Jean Libman Block, "*Beaucoup* Dreamy—American Teen-agers Abroad," *Colliers*, **131** (January 24, 1953), 14–17. For xenophilia see Howard V. Perlmutter, "Some Relationships between Xenophilic Attitudes and Authoritarianism among Americans Abroad," *Psychological Reports*, **3** (March, 1957), 79–87; the experience of foreign students is discussed in John A. Garraty and Walter Adams, *From Main Street to the Left Bank: Students and Scholars Abroad* (East Lansing, Michigan State University Press, 1959).

is led by his cult of "experience" into corrupt alliances which end in the death by abortion of a decent German girl. He can only seek to redeem his innocence by suicide, an act which teaches the narrator his own complicity and the inhumanity of the hero's perfectionist zeal. In H. J. Kaplan's *The Plenipotentiaries* the American couple, nonconformist artistic and political pilgrims to Paris, stumble into liaisons with a war-ravaged French painter and his wife only to become unwitting accomplices in the lover's quarrel of partners who are faithful, in their fashion, solely to each other.

James and his tourists were under "the old sweet Anglo-Saxon spell," but now the theme of American innocence confronting European experience is also found in the work of two of America's best Jewish writers—in Saul Bellow's "The Gonzaga Manuscripts" and in Bernard Malamud's terse parables, "Lady of the Lake," "Behold the Key," and "The Last Mohican." Malamud remarkably makes a Jewish adaptation of Jamesian themes in his story of the humanization of a passionless pilgrim, harassed by a refugee beggar with unreasonable demands for charity, who wins his case when his victim has been taught compassion through the magic of Giotto's art and the communal suffering of the Sephardic Jews in the Roman ghetto. But of all the contemporary versions of the international theme William Maxwell's *The Chateau* most masterfully transcends the traditional polarities of invidious comparison. It examines with scrupulous fairness the treacherous but rewarding efforts at communication between an intelligent Francophile American couple and a conservative French family, living together briefly under the shadow of the war and the tensions of the Cold War, separated by all the baffling nuances of their different national characters and histories. It is an artful monument dedicated in an original style and technique to the post-war pilgrims who may, with skill, luck, and patience, make something human, imperfect but equal, out of the possibilities of the European tour.[6]

[6] See Hollis Alpert, *Some Other Time* (New York, Knopf, 1960); David Buckley, *Pride of Innocence* (New York, Henry Holt, 1957); H. J. Kaplan, *The Plenipotentiaries* (London, Martin, Secker, and Warburg, 1950); Saul

What distinguishes the best of these contemporary stories is a new note. Their heroes live in the age of American power; their country has dropped bombs all over Europe; and their political leaders can bring disaster or hope by their actions to those peoples who are no longer primary powers. Despite themselves, these Americans in the Old World are, in Kaplan's phrase, "plenipotentiaries," treated as representative citizens of their country. Drawn to Paris as people who are "outsiders" in America—for political, social, or artistic reasons—Kaplan's Americans discover to their bewilderment that their role in Europe is to be "opulent and vulnerable—even those of us who are poverty-stricken. . . . We have full powers, but we do not always represent what we wish."[7] Malamud's apartment-hunting graduate student in "Behold the Key," who is interminably frustrated by the efforts of Italians to get their small percentage from his venture, is accused of callousness, of driving Italians into the hands of Communists, of buying their votes and culture, of all the sins, actual or imaginary, his country may have committed. Similarly, Bellow's Hispanophile, on a quest for the lost manuscript of a Republican poet he admires for not feeling "responsible for *everything*," is harassed by an English woman who holds him personally responsible for his Congressmen, the Pentagon, the A-bombs, and even the weather. In the end he is mistaken for an Englishman and held responsible for Spanish grievances against Britain. The American cannot escape the European symbolic treatment of him. He remains an ambassador without portfolio in spite of himself.

In the nineteenth century American travelers represented to Europeans a country which, whether admired or disliked, stood in their imaginations as a symbol of democratic liberty. The American traveler in the middle of the twentieth century is forced to see his country in a much more ambivalent relation to European hopes and fears. The Fulbright Fellow may discover abroad

---

Bellow, "The Gonzaga Manuscripts," in *Seize the Day* (New York, Viking, 1956), pp. 161–192; Bernard Malamud, "Behold the Key," in *The Magic Barrel* (New York, Farrar, Straus, and Cudahy, 1958), pp. 57–83; "The Lady of the Lake," *ibid.*, pp. 105–133; "The Last Mohican," *ibid.*, pp. 155–182; William Maxwell, *The Chateau* (New York, Knopf, 1961).

[7] *The Plenipotentiaries*, p. 204.

that the United States means not only fantastic dreams of economic opportunity and Hollywood glamour; it also means nightmares of Babbittry, McCarthyism, the McCarran Act, Little Rock, the Bomb, and Missile Bases. He may make the uncomfortable discovery that the most ardently pro-American Italians (like the industrialist's family described in Herbert Kubly's *American in Italy*) are monarchists, known on the local scene as reactionaries in contrast to the sham "progressivism" of the Communists. "Congressmen still think of the U.S.A. as a young progressive republic with lots of friends," as a character in a recent "international" novel observes, "not as a great modern conservative power with lots of enemies."[8]

In Kubly's book and in Leslie Katz's *Invitation to the Voyage* the American literature of travel triumphs over conventional piety or hostility. Both books measure the distance traveled from *The Innocents Abroad* or the romantic impressionism of Irving and Longfellow. Without sentimentality Kubly is the sympathetic stranger, open to a wide range of people and experience, armed with a strong feeling for social and political realities, who can discover in himself a hidden "Latin, pagan, Catholic, and poor," without forgetting his actuality as an American. Katz's voyager is a contemporary Mark Twain in idiom, breezy, humorous, and in touch with the popular arts and culture; but he is also a sophisticated, urban Jew who speaks French and sees people and landscapes in the aesthetic terms of painting, sculpture, and literature. Like the expatriates of the Twenties, he learns in Europe to respect "material values" ("a breath of fresh air, a quiet room with a tall ceiling, a stroll on a pleasant street in a big city"), which are fast disappearing in an America increasingly absorbed in "spiritual values such as what brand of cigarette do you smoke, the difference between a Ford and a Chevrolet, and how far have you gotten ahead in the world." Katz's alter ego accepts himself wryly as an American: "I was only a tourist, and this my home was the strangest country of all."[9] He returns with a nostalgia for the

8 Gerald Sykes, *The Nice American* (New York, Creative Age, 1951), p. 55.
9 *Invitation to the Voyage* (New York, Harcourt, Brace, 1958), pp. 251–

present and with distaste for the new-style American expatriate he has met, a snobbish, jaded medievalist.

American expatriation to Rome or Paris after the Second World War was a different story from Hemingway's day. "Montparnasse was out of the question," says the hero of Hollis Alpert's *Some Other Time*. "Hemingway and the expatriates of the 'Twenties had made it passé. It even looked passé."[10] The current crop of Bohemian expatriates, condemned to living a role thoroughly exhausted by their elders, generally deserves the tag (misapplied to their forerunners), the Lost Generation. The rank and file of ex-G.I. expatriates in Saint Germain des Près are now drifters, student hangers-on, or deviates, most of them forced into some kind of trade to make ends meet: "They have Right Bank jobs and Left Bank hearts." Nor with the accelerated pace of "Americanization"—drugstores, juke boxes, movies, and supermarkets—was Paris any longer another world—only "a slightly more remote station on the commuting line."[11] Even the temper of *The Paris Review*, established by Americans in 1952, was much more sedate than the eager experimentalism of the 1920s. Only the abstract expressionist painters maintained as a group the originality and stubborn dedication of the earlier exiles to Paris.

Two unusual pilgrims of the post-war period, who had powerful reasons to be drawn to Europe, symbolize the change in the American intellectual's relation to expatriation. Angelo Pellegrini, who had come to America as the son of a peasant at the age of nine and risen to a university professorship, piously returned to Italy in 1949–1950 on a Guggenheim to do a study of the Italian immigrant's contribution to America. He wrote instead a memoir of his discovery of how thoroughly Americanized he had become in his alienation from the attitude of Santayana. Italy's corruption and social misery moved Pellegrini to horror at the thought of

---

253. For Kubly see *American in Italy* (New York, Simon and Schuster, 1955), which says much about various kinds of Americans in Italy and about Italian mythologies of America.

[10] *Some Other Time*, p. 11.

[11] P. E. Schneider, "The Sun Also Sets Americans in Paris," *Encounter*, 13 (October, 1959), 55.

being buried in the Cemetery of the Holy Doors in Florence near the home of his ancestors. (His account makes a sharp contrast with another Guggenheim Fellow and immigrant son, Louis Adamic, who in 1932 left Depression America to visit his peasant family in Carniola, Yugoslavia. He and his American wife were deeply impressed with the dignity of his uncle's death, surrounded with communal ritual, compared to America where "Death is a gangster" in a society of brutal individualism; and Adamic celebrated the "elemental, raw, unspoiled, creative" vitality of the Slavs which had created "New Russia" as "the one hope of multitudes outside her borders."[12]) An even more telling case is James Baldwin, the Negro novelist. Raised in a Harlem ghetto, he fled to Paris in 1948 from "the fury of the color problem." He returned ten years later, having painfully discovered his common ground with Americans, black or white, and their common heritage of Europe. He could not join his literary father Richard Wright in embracing Paris as the "city of refuge," knowing that it was not a refuge for the French, the Algerians, or even the Americans unless they had passports: "It did not seem worthwhile to me to have fled the native fantasy only to embrace a foreign one."[13]

The Old World, though it might still provide Americans (as it did Baldwin) with a necessary sense of the tragic limits of life, was no longer the cultural mecca for intellectuals. The *Partisan Review* summed up the general recognition of the new situation by the American literary *avant-garde* in a symposium held in its pages in 1952. Noting that Van Wyck Brooks, Dos Passos, and Edmund Wilson had all swung round to an affirmative relation to American life, the editors observed:

Europe is no longer regarded as a sanctuary; it no longer assures

[12] *The Native's Return: An American Immigrant Visits Yugoslavia and Discovers His Old Country* (New York, Harper, 1934), pp. 78, 362. Cf. Angelo Pellegrini, *Immigrant's Return* (New York, Macmillan, 1951), pp. 1–4, 201–203.

[13] "Alas Poor Richard," in *Nobody Knows My Name: More Notes of a Native Son* (New York, Dial, 1961), p. 185. See also his "The Discovery of What It Means to Be an American," *ibid.*, pp. 3–12; "A Question of Identity," *Partisan Review*, 21 (July-August, 1954), 402–410.

that rich experience of culture which inspired and justified a criticism of American life. . . . The wheel has come full circle, and now America has become the protector of Western Civilization, at least in a military and economic sense.[14]

This shift of perspective marked the improvement in the position of American intellectuals since the 1920s. Malcolm Cowley's satiric image of the young intellectual of that period, dreaming of Sunday baseball, racetrack gambling, open urinals, and the works of Freud, Boccaccio, and D. H. Lawrence sold openly at newsstands, had lost much of its point. Joyce, Freud, and Lawrence were readily available, often on newsstands, and Nabokov's *Lolita* and Henry Miller's *The Tropic of Cancer*, no longer smuggled from Paris, did a brisk business in respectable hard covers. The monster of literary "puritanism" was almost a dodo.

The political scene had also become friendlier to intellectuals ever since the New Deal had made government an exciting enterprise to which they could make contributions. Its leader had been a friend of Robert E. Sherwood and Archibald MacLeish, and it had experimented with federal support of literary, artistic, and theatrical projects. The McCarthy era with its hostility to "eggheads" squandered this good will, but part of the animus against intellectuals was unpleasant recognition of their importance. In 1952 the articulate urbanity and wit of Adlai Stevenson in the American Presidential campaign held the sympathies of most intellectuals. The defeat of their candidate and the Republican rule of a kindly military hero—who behaved more like a constitutional monarch than an aggressive leader, devoured "Westerns" instead of newspapers, and fought a losing battle with syntax and grammar—only temporarily discouraged the mood of reconciliation. The inauguration in 1961 of a President from Harvard,

[14] "Our Country and Our Culture," *Partisan Review*, **19** (May-June, 1952), 284. Most of the 25 participants agreed with the editors. Some had more confidence in Europe's continued intellectual vitality; nearly all were worried about mass culture and conformity in America. See also *ibid.* (July-August, 1952), 420–450; *ibid.* (September-October, 1952), 562–597. Cf. R. P. Blackmur, "The American Literary Expatriate," in David F. Bowers, ed., *Foreign Influences in American Life* (Princeton, Princeton University Press, 1944), pp. 126–145.

author of two books, voracious reader of history, and seeker of advisers from the academic community, was symbolically graced by the poetic benison of Robert Frost. If the Republicans saw in Mr. Kennedy the return of the prodigal spenders, the intellectuals were more inclined to sense in his Administration an invitation to Intellect to return to the house of Politics. Whatever their disappointments might be, the full circle turning of the wheel of history was not likely to be reversed.

15

NEITHER OMNIPOTENT
NOR OMNISCIENT

DURING THE MIDDLE 1950s both Europe and America suffered a mutual loss of confidence that threatened to shiver apart the NATO alliance. If the isolationist party was dead, it still had a loud band of fellow travelers, wearing masks and shrill with frustration, who were able to affect the tone and temper of the Eisenhower Administration. The coming of nuclear parity between East and West provoked anxious re-examination of alliance strategy, and the new conception of Europe as a partner in the Atlantic civilization was put under dangerous strain. Now more than ever before the American's fond image of his national innocence in contrast to the "power politics" of Europe looked like an archaic relic in the archives of history. Any actual innocence was but a synonym for possible catastrophe. He had to achieve a realistic understanding of both his allies and his enemies across the seas or disastrously bungle the heavy responsibilities of his power.

The Marshall Plan and NATO were the brightest achievements of the containment strategy, but, as Stillman and Pfaff have pointed out, after the Korean War "American policy became a ritual invocation of the European formula—in circumstances where it could not and did not work."[1] Neither in Asia nor the Middle East could history provide the basis for dependable democratic allies. The search for regimes whose only claim to American aid was a vociferous anti-Communism ignored the historical role of neutralism, whether democratic as in India or authoritarian as in the Middle East, as a more viable alternative. As Secretary of State Dulles patched up a network of dubious alliances, conservative Republicans looked with disfavor on aid to European socialist countries. Free enterprise propagandists, with a faith impervious to historical fact, blurred any distinction between socialism and Communism, and the public never understood the role of the European democratic labor movement in carrying the brunt of the European domestic anti-Communist battle. Nor did most Americans appreciate the part that leading socialists from France, Belgium, the Netherlands, and Italy played in the movement for European integration, even though the conservative coalition of Christian Democrats has provided the hard core of parliamentary and public support.[2]

Despite the revolutionary step of NATO itself, the strain of the Cold War put a heavy burden on the growth of mutual respect and confidence between America and Europe. With the withering away of American de-Nazification policies and the vigorous revival of West German prosperity, American leaders began to look to Germany for the military strength their NATO partners could not or would not provide. Fear of Germany and the resurgence of French nationalism aborted the plan for a Euro-

[1] Edmund Stillman and William Pfaff, *The New Politics: America and the End of the Postwar World* (New York, Coward McCann, 1961), p. 32.
[2] See Arnold J. Zurcher, *The Struggle to Unite Europe 1940–1958* (Washington Square, New York University Press, 1958), pp. 191–194; Hajo Holborn, "American Foreign Policy and European Integration," *World Politics*, 6 (October, 1953), 1–30.

pean Defense Community in 1954, after provoking from the American government a tactless threat of "agonizing reappraisal" of commitments to Europe. The situation was saved by Prime Minister Eden's adoption of the Brussels Treaty for Western European Union as a backdoor means of bringing West Germany into the Western alliance. The United States did not consult its allies in 1954–1955 about the defense of Formosa and the Chinese offshore islands, and there were grumblings in popular magazines about the perversity or weakness of allies in Europe who did not see the world in American terms.[3]

The neoisolationists rallied behind Senators Bricker and McCarthy. They raised an alarm about the hypothetical dangers to America from treaties and executive agreements, made under traditional Constitutional procedure, and from the jurisdiction of foreign courts over some of the crimes committed by American troops abroad; while they continued to cheer Senator McCarthy's successful intimidation and sabotage of the government agencies serving America's new overseas responsibilities. As leader of the West, the Administration found itself cabined, cribbed, and confined by right-wing elements in both parties. Eisenhower had been nearly as popular a hero to Europeans as to Americans; but while the Administration bogged down in the frustrations of stalemated conflict and Dulles took on the tone of an arrogant schoolmaster, the Atlantic alliance floundered.

The Suez crisis of 1956 brought into the open the dangerous rifts that were cracking the Atlantic community. Earlier American pressure had induced the British to withdraw their troops from the Canal Zone, and Dulles himself had provoked Nasser by withdrawing the offer of aid for the Aswan Dam. After the Egyptians had seized the Canal Company, threatening the European stake in keeping the waterway free for the shipping of vital oil, Dulles raised the irrelevant issue of colonialism, hinted at an independent American policy, and reneged on his own proposed Users Association, supposed to protect Western interests. In 1954

---

[3] See Capt. W. D. Puleston, "How Long Can U.S. Trust Allies?" *U.S. News and World Report*, 39 (July 22, 1955), Part 1, 102–105; "The Dilemma of France," *Newsweek*, 47 (January 16, 1956), 29–35.

Secretary Dulles had hastily sought Congressional support for an American air and naval strike to defend the French position at Dienbienphu, but he had been unable to win the support of Eden and Churchill; and the President had refused to sanction a unilateral venture that might make the United States look "imperialist." Now, in 1956, the situation was reversed. The British and French, irritated at Dulles's watering down of the Users Association into a collection agency for Nasser, took poorly planned, badly timed, and disingenuous action of their own to support the Israeli invasion of Egypt and their common stake in the Suez Canal, illegally blockaded by Egypt.

The American response was distorted by conventional anticolonial stereotypes. During the later stages of the crisis, actual policy was in the hands of Herbert Hoover, Jr., a true son of his father, apostle of Western Hemisphere isolationism. The Administration smugly chose "to focus attention on the expiring colonialism of Britain and France instead of on the dynamic colonialism of Soviet Russia, then at its most virulent in Hungary."[4] To the shock of its closest allies, who wilted under American censure, the United States put the Suez issue on the UN agenda before dealing with the Soviet brutal crushing of the Hungarian Revolution, proposed oil sanctions against the British and French, and allowed the Egyptians to reoccupy the Gaza Strip and persist in keeping the Israelis out of the Canal, all in the righteous name of "the rule of law." Spokesmen for the Administration, like Vice President Nixon, hailed American emancipation from "colonialism" as if they were living in 1776.[5]

The resolution of the Suez crisis may have looked like internationalism because American policy was in support of the UN,

[4] Theodore Draper, "The Legacy of Suez," *Reporter*, 22 (March 31, 1960), 26. The Suez crisis is critically discussed also by Lionel Gelber, *America in Britain's Place* (New York, Praeger, 1961), pp. 237–265.

[5] The American reader can gain perspective on the Suez crisis if he compares it with the Cuban crisis of late October, 1962. When President Kennedy, responding to the sudden and deceptive Soviet build-up of Cuba into a potentially offensive missile base, unilaterally imposed a military blockade of the island, the European allied governments supported the American position even though they had only been informed rather than consulted about the very risky policy.

not isolation. But the whole episode demonstrated once again how prejudices against Europe, derived from the isolationist tradition, could lend themselves to the moralistic defense of universal collective security principles. Four months after Suez the Administration, turning about, voted in the UN against an eighteen-power resolution in favor of self-determination for Algeria. The anticolonial tradition could not serve as a simple formula for American action.[6]

Dulles's "brink-of-war" diplomacy may, as he claimed, have brought the Chinese to terms in Korea and deterred them from an assault on the offshore islands, but it is certain that his unilateral style frightened America's allies. His pledges of a rollback of Soviet power and liberation of the satellites were shown up as mere slogans when the East German and Hungarian revolts were savagely suppressed without interference. No more than in the nineteenth century did the United States dare to hazard the risks of intervention. His emphasis (later modified) on meeting aggression anywhere by a nuclear threat "to retaliate, instantly, by means, and at places of our choosing" was outmoded almost as soon as it was formulated. With the Soviet development of long-range missiles it became clear that "massive retaliation" was either a bluff or a disaster. This posture, a retroactive criticism of the Korean War strategy of the Democrats, dangerously blotted out the less risky range of alternatives between retreat or holocaust upon which the alliance would have to rely for its security.

Both sides of the Atlantic were dangerously beguiled by nuclear weapons as a form of cheap security. NATO's goals for conventional forces were reduced, while Britain and France (recoiling from the shock of Suez) sought to recover their prestige and influence by building their own nuclear deterrents. In 1957 NATO decided to place intermediate-range ballistic missiles in Great Britain, Italy, and Turkey under the command of SACEUR, while NATO ground troops in West Germany were increasingly outfitted with tactical atomic weapons. The American Congress still

[6] See Robert C. Good, "The United States and the Colonial Debate," in Arnold Wolfers, ed., *Alliance Policy in the Cold War* (Baltimore, Johns Hopkins University Press, 1959), pp. 224–270.

clung to nationalistic control over nuclear warheads and technical information,[7] and it became evident that many Europeans resented dependence upon a purely American decision about the level of force to be used against aggression, but could not afford effective separate deterrents. An insidious question loomed to weaken the mutual confidence of the Atlantic powers: when American cities were vulnerable to Soviet rockets, would the American threat of nuclear retaliation against a massive attack on Western Europe appear credible to either the Soviets or the Europeans? Three solutions—a strengthened arm of conventional forces, a federation of Europe, or a confederacy of the Atlantic community,[8] to provide the mechanism for a common decision without intolerable delay—all pointed to a long road only dimly seen by legislators in the gathering gloom.[9]

Whether the Kennedy Administration, which rejected the "massive retaliation" strategy as a substitute for more flexible

[7] Since 1956 the United States has increasingly shared nuclear secrets with Great Britain because of her progress in acquiring nuclear capability. Missiles and warheads on British soil are subject to a double-veto system of joint control, as they are also in Italy and Turkey. France under de Gaulle has refused to accept missiles under this arrangement. Both the Eisenhower and Kennedy Administrations have proposed a sea-borne missile force under NATO command, provided the allies can work out an agreement for its control and use. If the Europeans really want only closer consultation and participation in nuclear and political strategy, then the answer may lie in a strong civil-military staff under the direction of a revitalized NATO Council, as Alastair Buchan argues in "NATO Awaits the Word from Washington," *Reporter*, 24 (June 8, 1961), 19–22.

[8] There are two encouraging recent steps: The Atlantic Convention of citizen delegates from NATO countries, under the chairmanship of Christian A. Herter, issued a declaration on January 19, 1962, for a strengthened North Atlantic Council, a consultative assembly, a high court, and a council for student exchange and intellectual collaboration. A privately financed Atlantic Institute, under Henry Cabot Lodge, Jr., was also established in January, 1962, to study long-range goals and needs of the Atlantic community.

[9] See Roger Hilsman, "NATO: The Developing Strategic Context," in Klaus Knorr, ed., *NATO and American Security* (Princeton, Princeton University Press, 1959), pp. 11–36; Ben T. Moore, *NATO and the Future of Europe* (New York, Harper, 1958); Henry A. Kissinger, "For an Atlantic Confederacy," *Reporter*, 24 (February 2, 1961), 16–20; Karl W. Deutsch *et al.*, *Political Community and the North Atlantic Area: International Organization in the Light of Historical Experience* (Princeton, Princeton University Press, 1957).

approaches, could heal the crisis of the Atlantic community was an open question. In the early months of the new government, emphasis on the UN, the "Afro-Asian world," and the vote in the Security Council against Portugal on the Angola resolution alarmed many Europeans, including some anticolonialists, about the divisive effect of an independent American policy for undeveloped areas.[10] Only a complex view of the world could sustain the Atlantic community. But as the Kennedy Administration moved toward closer economic cooperation with Europe for growth, stability, aid, and tariffs, right-wing groups, like the John Birch Society, provided asylum for the "terrible simplifiers" who tried to frighten the public into capitalist fundamentalism by fire-and-brimstone sermons against the largely mythical and archaic devil of an internal conspiracy of pro-Communists. That fanatical and obscurantist "anti-Communism" had become the last refuge of the isolationists was proved by the Birchers' dismissal of any *external* Soviet threat and by their obsession with Western Europe as an ultimate scapegoat for the welfare liberalism they so passionately hated. "In my opinion," declared the founder, "the first great basic weakness of the United States, and hence its susceptibility to the disease of collectivism, is simply the age of the *Western European* civilization."[11] The Old World in this fantasy was the apple of Socialist sin that drove the American Adam out of the capitalist paradise. For many Americans the Soviet Union was transformed from a specific country with its own problems of leadership, both internal and international, into a supernaturally clever and wicked Devil, master of a monolithic World Communism, everywhere and always triumphant. Russia was, as David Riesman has observed, a tempting contemporary substitute for Britain as the mythical supersubtle enemy of good-natured, gullible, American innocence.

[10] See Edmond Taylor, "NATO after Spaak: A Loss and a Warning," *Reporter*, 24 (April 13, 1961), 16–20.

[11] Quoted from Robert Welch, *The Blue Book*, in my "Fantasy on the Right," *New Republic*, 144 (May 1, 1961), 14. For the neoisolationism of Taft, MacArthur, McCarthy, Jenner, and Knowland see Norman A. Graebner, *The New Isolationism: A Study in Politics and Foreign Policy Since 1950* (New York, Ronald Press, 1956).

The American weakness for the posture of outraged innocence was embarrassingly exposed to the world by the Eisenhower Administration's bumbling response, on the eve of a summit conference in May, 1960, to the shooting down over Soviet territory of the U-2 "spy plane." At first denying any responsibility, Administration spokesmen then reversed themselves, but they defended past and even future flights as essential to national security, in effect telling the Soviets that Americans had a right to invade Russian air space. No society, especially not a "closed" one like the Soviet Union, could have accepted such a presumptuous claim. The Kennedy Democrats, for their part, warned of a threatening "missile gap" which they discovered to be a fiction after they had come to power. But if their new estimates of enemy weakness were correct, then the Soviet rearmament program of 1961, stimulated by the loss of military security through exposure of their weapons by U-2 flights, may have been a defensive response to a feared American nuclear superiority, instead of only the blustering aggressiveness of a shoe-pounding dictator, as most Americans righteously pictured it. From the Soviet point of view the massive American nuclear build-up may even have looked like an effort to achieve a "first-strike" and "counterforce" strategy suitable for a surprise attack.[12]

In the nuclear age the devil theory of the enemy can be just as dangerous as the complacent underestimation of him. The alternating excesses of suspicion and condescension which Americans have shown in the past toward Europe should alert them in the present to the need for discriminating judgment upon which the life of civilization may depend. History should flatter no partisans and butter no parsnips, but if it ever can instruct the present for the sake of the future, surely a useful moral can be drawn from

[12] Senator Stuart Symington has said that U.S. estimates of Soviet heavy-bomber strength decreased by 81 percent between August, 1956, and August, 1961, while estimates of Soviet operational ICBM strength decreased by 96.5 percent between December, 1959, and September, 1961. Using these revised estimates, P. M. S. Blackett, a British physicist and military adviser, has pointed out how menacing the American position may look to the Soviets. See his "Steps toward Disarmament," *Scientific American*, 206 (April, 1962), 45–53.

the American past of the dangerous duplicity in the national self-image of injured innocence in an evil world.

No story of the American image of the Old World can be finished while both America and Europe are historically alive. Certainly that relationship, being a living one, has never been static, despite the persistence of static concepts, as archaic as they are tenacious, to describe it. Americans still exaggerate the social and economic mobility of their own society in contrast to Europe, when what properly distinguishes them is their general prosperity and the degree to which each class shares in it.[13] Some of the conventional antitheses could now even be reversed, with more respect for the truth. The average American forgets that he, perhaps more than the average European, is chivalrous, polite, and endlessly anxious about his social place. He forgets that his own society, despite a civil war, is more historically continuous than most European societies, where every layer of society has suffered exile, enslavement, and expropriation. He boasts of American freedom in contrast to Europe, where atheists, socialists, and Communists though far more prevalent produce much less panic than in the American breast. He thinks of himself as "peace-loving," despite his country's record of participation in eight wars since '76, its use of the A-bomb on Japanese cities, and its current worries about the neutralism and pacifism of the formerly condemned "warlike" nations of Europe. He has always scorned the Europeans for their imperialism, and he now finds their empires in dissolution, and his own reputation, because of his far-flung interests in containing Soviet expansion, widely regarded as "imperialistic." He has conventionally mistrusted monarchies as the very symbol of oppression, and he now discovers that modern republics are the most vulnerable to the inroads of the Right and

[13] See Seymour Martin Lipset and Natalie Rogoff, "Class and Opportunity in Europe and the United States," *Commentary*, 18 (December, 1954), 562–568. They find a similar measure of mobility in modern times for both America and Western Europe, despite greater contrasts in styles of life among different classes in Europe. But, as Herbert Luethy points out, the exception is the farm population because American farmers do have more mobility. See "European Traditions and American Sociology: An Exchange," *Commentary*, 20 (December, 1955), 572.

the Left that he deplores.[14] He has thought of his "free enterprise" system as the last bastion of freedom in the world, and he now must face the fact that his own society, ever since the New Deal, is further to the left in providing more social services than France, Italy, or West Germany, while the foreign countries most invulnerable to Communist penetration and most friendly to civil liberties and democratic government are precisely those Western European societies where the tradition of democratic socialism has left its strongest marks—England, Scandinavia, Belgium, the Netherlands.

The American may protest, like Job, that his intentions have always been good and his probity well known, but he will still have to suffer the ultimate affliction of a loss of innocence, even of a reputation for it. Now the European, reversing the roles of the traditional melodrama, accuses the New World of corrupting the Old with the temptations of mass culture: "The Americans make us uneasy because, without wishing us ill, they put things before us for our taking, things which are so ready to hand and so convenient that we accept them, finding perhaps that they satisfy our fundamental temptations."[15] When Cornwallis surrendered at Yorktown, his redcoats played "The World Turned Upside Down." It is a tune American bands should learn to play.

Americans, more than most peoples, believe in their national character as a function of their environment—testimony to the force of the idea of a New World. By their habit of seeing things in polar terms—especially of black and white—they have found in the idea of the Old World a foil for their image of themselves. A large majority of Americans still feel very much more affinity for fellow countrymen of other classes than for Europeans of their own class.[16] This evidence of their democratic feeling also demon-

---

[14] See Erik von Kuehnelt-Leddihn, "America's Myths of Europe," Southwest Review, 40 (Spring, 1955), 170–179.

[15] Jeanne Hersch, in discussion at the International Forum of Geneva, The Old World and the New World: Their Cultural and Moral Relations (UNESCO, 1956), p. 198.

[16] Of nine nations Americans were the firmest believers in the influence of environment on national characteristics, and while 77 percent of the Americans polled felt affinity with their own countrymen of other classes, only

strates the persistent strength of their nationalistic sentiment. But in developed societies "national sovereignty" and "national character" are being reforged in the crucible of modern history faster than men realize, though perhaps not fast enough for man's survival. It has been, however, a major achievement worth celebrating that Americans have made since the Second World War a new appraisal of themselves as powerful partners with Europe in the collaborative venture of Atlantic civilization.

Many Americans, uncertain yet of the scope and duration of their own national responsibilities and interests, are still tempted to be omniscient about what others should do. It is, therefore, an impressive sign of wisdom that in November, 1961, President Kennedy, while affirming American determination to defend Western rights in West Berlin, should counsel his fellow citizens to remember that ". . . the United States is neither omnipotent nor omniscient—that we cannot right every wrong or reverse each adversity—and that therefore there cannot be an American solution for every world problem."[17] In the intellectual community there have been brave efforts on several fronts to disenchant Americans from the old national dream of innocence in a corrupt world. The diplomat George F. Kennan, the theologian Reinhold Niebuhr, the political theorist Louis Hartz, the literary critic Leslie Fiedler, and the historian Daniel J. Boorstin have all pleaded for a more relativized, pluralistic sense of the world.[18] With that sophistication, the American can accept without exaggeration or anxiety the valuable differences between American and European

---

42 percent felt affinity with members of their own class abroad. Only Germany also had this 35-point gap. See William Buchanan and Hadley Cantril, *How Nations See Each Other: A Study in Public Opinion* (Urbana, University of Illinois, 1953), pp. 83–84, 214–215.

[17] Address, University of Washington, November 16, 1961.

[18] See George F. Kennan, *American Diplomacy 1900–1950* (Chicago, University of Chicago Press, 1951); Louis Hartz, *The Liberal Tradition in America* (New York, Harcourt, Brace, 1955); Reinhold Niebuhr, *The Irony of American History* (New York, Scribner's, 1952); Leslie Fiedler, *An End to Innocence: Essays on Culture and Politics* (Boston, Beacon, 1955); Daniel J. Boorstin, "Democracy and its Discontents," *Encounter*, 3 (July, 1954), 15–22. For continuing American-European differences of intellectual style see Francis Golffing, "The American and European Minds Compared," *Commentary*, 28 (December, 1959), 506–514.

styles of life, while both sides of the Atlantic work together for their common goals and the correction of their partial insights by a continuing dialogue.

Europe, divided by the presence of Russian and American power, is still at the center of contemporary history, for its division, tragically symbolized by the Berlin Wall, is a focal point of the Cold War. Europe stirs restlessly in an Atlantic Community spoken for by an American-led military alliance. West Europeans are increasingly unwilling to let their future depend so heavily upon American military decisions. Will the Europeans, if joined by Britain, build political unity and independent deterrent-power out of their growing economic cooperation?

The Cold War has itself ironically tended to reduce the differences between its giant antagonists. Russia has imitated American nuclear technology and economic aid to underdeveloped countries, and America has added to a modest welfare state a massive military-industrial complex. Will an instransigent and bellicose China make Russia and America examine their differences from a new perspective?

History, not the historian, may answer these questions. He can only be sure, as the flickering, familiar image of the Old World blurs into the unresolved image of the new Europe, that Americans must learn to draw new maps. Only then may the Atlantic Community become a partnership of equals.

INDEX

275